TEEN GANGS

Recent Titles in
A World View of Social Issues Series

TEEN GANGS

A GLOBAL VIEW

Edited by
Maureen P. Duffy and
Scott Edward Gillig

A World View of Social Issues
Andrew L. Cherry, Series Adviser

Greenwood Press
Westport, Connecticut • London

Library of Congress Cataloging-in-Publication Data

Teen gangs : a global view / edited by Maureen P. Duffy and Scott Edward Gillig.
    p. cm.—(A world view of social issues, ISSN 1526-9442)
    Includes bibliographical references and index.
    ISBN 0–313–32150–7 (alk. paper)
    1. Gangs—Cross-cultural studies.   2. Juvenile delinquency—Cross-cultural studies.
    I. Duffy, Maureen P.   II. Gillig, Scott Edward.   III. Series.
    HV6437.T44   2004
    364.1'06'60835—dc22   2003060015

British Library Cataloguing in Publication Data is available.

Library of Congress Catalog Card Number: 2003060015
ISBN: 0–313–32150–7
ISSN: 1526–9442

First published in 2004

Greenwood Press, 88 Post Road West, Westport, CT 06881
An imprint of Greenwood Publishing Group, Inc.
www.greenwood.com

Printed in the United States of America

The paper used in this book complies with the
Permanent Paper Standard issued by the National
Information Standards Organization (Z39.48–1984).

10 9 8 7 6 5 4 3 2 1

CONTENTS

SERIES FOREWORD

Why are child abuse in the family and homelessness social conditions to be endured or at least tolerated in some countries while in other countries they are viewed as social problems that must be reduced or eliminated? What social institutions and other factors affect these behaviors? What historical, political, and social forces influence a society's response to a social condition? In many cases, individuals around the world have the same or similar hopes and problems. However, in most cases we deal with the same social conditions in very dissimilar ways.

The volumes in the Greenwood series A World View of Social Issues examine different social issues and problems that are being faced by individuals and societies around the world. These volumes examine problems of poverty and homelessness, drugs and alcohol addiction, HIV/AIDS, teen pregnancy, crime, women's rights, and a myriad of other issues that affect all of us in one way or another.

Each volume is devoted to one social issue or problem. All volumes follow the same general format. Each volume has up to fifteen chapters that describe how people in different countries perceive and try to cope with a given problem or social issue. The countries chosen represent as many world regions as possible, making it possible to explore how each issue has been recognized and what actions have been taken to alleviate it in a variety of settings.

Each chapter begins with a profile of the country being highlighted and an overview of the impact of the social issue or problem there. Basic policies, legislation, and demographic information related to the social issue are covered. A brief history of the problem helps the reader better understand the political and social responses. Political initiatives and policies are also discussed, as well as social views, customs, and practices related to the problem or social issue. Discussions about how the countries plan to deal with these social problems are also included.

These volumes present a comprehensive and engaging approach for the study of international social conditions and problems. The goal is to provide a convenient framework for readers to examine specific social problems, how they are viewed, and what actions are being taken by different countries around the world.

For example, how is a problem like crime and crime control handled in third world countries? How is substance abuse controlled in industrialized countries? How are poverty and homelessness handled in the poorest countries? How does culture influence the definition and response to domestic violence in different countries? What part does economics play in shaping both the issue of and the response to women's rights? How does a national philosophy impact the definition and response to child abuse? These questions and more will be answered by the volumes in this series.

As we learn more about our counterparts in other countries, they become real to us, and our worldview cannot help but change. We will think of others as we think of those we know. They will be people who get up in the morning and go to work. We will see people who are struggling with relationships, attending religious services, being born, and growing old, and dying.

This series will cover issues that will add to your knowledge about contemporary social society. These volumes will help you to better understand social conditions and social issues in a broader sense, giving you a view of what various problems mean to different people and how these perspectives impact a society's response. You will be able to see how specific social problems are managed by governments and individuals confronting the consequences of these social dilemmas. By studying one problem from various angles, you will be better able to grasp the totality of the situation, while at the same time speculating as to how solutions used in one country could be incorporated in another. Finally, this series will allow you to compare and contrast how these social issues impact individuals in different countries and how the effect is dissimilar or similar to your own experiences.

As series adviser, it is my hope that these volumes, which are unique in the history of publishing, will increase your understanding and appreciation of your counterparts around the world.

Andrew L. Cherry
Series Adviser

PREFACE

After three-quarters of a century of thought and research about gangs in the United States, we still have not come up with a satisfactory shared definition of the word *gang*. In the worlds of social science and juvenile justice, gangs are usually described as a social problem. When drugs and crime are a part of gang activities, there is little disagreement about the nature of the problem. Yet what the entity precisely is that we are calling a gang remains unclear. Consequently, putting together this reference book, *Teen Gangs: A Global View,* presented unique challenges. We could not start with a common understanding of the nature of a gang, because none exists. We could not even start with a shared belief that gangs, particularly teen gangs, always represent serious social problems. What we did start with was a recognition that in all of the countries profiled, there is some level of concern among the public or the government about what are described as gangs and some effort to address the issue.

In some of the countries profiled, teen gangs are an emerging issue and little formal documentation about the problem exists. In those cases, the contributors relied on people within the countries who worked directly with teen gangs for current information. These cultural informants provided fascinating "insider" views of the teen gang situation. By their nature gangs are secretive groups, so in the best of cases, obtaining information was difficult. Very few of the countries profiled have the history of research and literature about gangs that the United States has.

All of the contributors to this book provided a description of the teen gang problem or situation. They examined the country's social and political responses to the teen gang problem as well as political initiatives and policies. They looked at how governmental and nongovernmental organizations addressed the issue of marginalized or at-risk youth. The contributors to this book, from diverse backgrounds and cultures, have one thing in common: they care deeply about young people. They are especially concerned about young people who are socially excluded and who cannot, or do not, participate fully in their society.

The contributors represent many perspectives about youth, social inclusion, and the relationship among politics, power, poverty, and gangs within a country. In so doing, they have raised important questions. Are crime and teen gangs always connected? Is there a difference between teen gangs and adult gangs? How has the availability of drugs influenced the gang situation in a particular country? What is the relationship among teen gangs, adult gangs, and organized crime? Is gang formation a legitimate and understandable response to poverty, marginalization, and political oppression? Is gang membership best understood as an individual psychological problem or as a larger social issue? Are teen gangs really a serious problem?

The result is a collage, a multi-layered image of teen gangs from countries in the Caribbean, North and Central America, Europe, the Middle East, Asia, Australia, and the Pacific Islands. It is impossible to talk about teen gangs without assuming some position, either implicitly or explicitly, about power, politics, poverty, and crime. The different perspectives on the subject taken by the contributors provide a broader understanding of teen gangs.

ACKNOWLEDGMENTS

Because we have worked with disaffected and disenfranchised young people, it has been particularly interesting to learn what some countries are doing programmatically to address the needs of such youth and to pull them back into fuller participation in society. Through the work of our contributors, we have been reminded again of the power of culture in shaping all aspects of people's lives, including gang and criminal life. We would like to thank the contributors for their work in putting together this global collage of teen gangs.

We would also like to thank our colleagues in the Counseling Department at Barry University for their continuous support and commitment to youth and families and Wendi Schnaufer at Greenwood Press for her responsiveness and patience. We would especially like to thank Melissa Kolinsky for her trademark care and attention to detail in helping us prepare the manuscript for publication.

INTRODUCTION: A GLOBAL OVERVIEW OF THE ISSUES OF AND RESPONSES TO TEEN GANGS

Maureen Duffy

All of us have a stake in the issues affecting juveniles. In the United States alone, almost 5,000 communities report having juvenile gangs (Moore and Terrett, 1998). These communities document the presence of a total of about 31,000 juvenile gangs with a membership of around 850,000 young people. These numbers reflect the significant impact of juvenile gangs on local communities throughout the United States.

The general public is impacted by youth gangs either through fear of them or by victimization from their crimes. Communities also bear the financial costs of social, legal, and criminal justice services made necessary by young people in gangs. To a greater or lesser extent, young people in gangs in other countries throughout the world are having a similar impact on their societies. Youth gangs raise important questions about the relationship between gang membership and crime. Youth gangs also call attention to the situation of youth who perceive themselves to be excluded from access to societal opportunities and benefits such as jobs and status.

In *Teen Gangs: A Global View*, we have brought together a set of profiles of the youth gang issue in countries throughout the world. The profiles are largely descriptions of the youth gang situation and its relationship to juvenile crime and the larger issues of poverty and politics in the selected countries. Additionally, we have focused special attention on the attempted solutions that government, on the one hand, and private groups such as churches and community-based organizations, on the other hand, have brought to bear on the youth gang problem. Descriptions of the youth gang situation are different from an analysis of the issues raised by the existence of youth gangs. *Teen Gangs: A Global View* provides descriptions of the youth gang situation in countries from the United States to the Caribbean to Central America, from Europe to the Middle East, from Asia to Melanesia and Australia. These descriptions provide a beginning point for both the analysis of the issues raised by the existence of teen gangs and cross-cultural comparisons of the nature of the teen gang problem and attempted solutions.

ISSUES IN DISCUSSION OF TEEN GANGS

Definitions

At this point in time, there is no clear, widely shared definition of what constitutes a youth gang. Neither are there clear criteria for establishing who is a gang member and who is not. In social science research the absence of a consensually shared definition of a youth gang is problematic in developing even basic descriptions of gangs. Social science researchers, theorists, youth workers, government policy-makers, and the public are likely to be operating from different understandings of what constitutes a youth gang. While they all may be using the same word, the meaning of that word for each is likely to vary considerably.

Rob White, in his contribution on youth gangs in Australia (Chapter 1), points out that the media and political leaders may equate youth hanging out on the streets with gang activity. He reminds us that street activity is commonplace among young people and may not necessarily be an indicator of gang activity, although it is often construed as such. Hazlehurst and Hazlehurst (1998) identify "adolescent male membership" (p. 5) as the most basic defining element of a juvenile gang. White (Chapter 1) echoes Howell (1998) and Short (1968) in emphasizing the need to distinguish youth gangs from varieties of other group formations and subcultures, for example, adolescent friendship groups that normally spend a lot of time on the street and other teen subgroups. To further confuse matters, adolescent subgroups, especially in urban areas, may parody gang members in their dress and mannerisms, yet not identify themselves as a gang in the same way as the gang they are parodying.

Illegal activity is the single most important identifier of gang activity (Ball and Curry, 1995), although classic gang theorists such as Thrasher have focused on the sense of solidarity and territoriality of gang members more than on the activities, such as criminal behavior, that gang members may engage in (Thrasher, 1963). Klein (1971) also emphasizes territoriality, along with symbols and, most importantly, the self-identification of the young people as belonging to a gang. Whether a youth gang is defined by where the gang members hang out, how they self-identify, what they look like to others, or whether they act criminally or not, there is still no consensus about what is the most important element in the definition of a youth gang.

The homeless children of the streets of Brazil who engage in crime in order to survive are different from the street gangs of Chicago and Los Angeles. Those American street gangs are not the same as the mixed-age-group gangs linked to organized crime and political patronage that Lorna Black describes in her contribution on the Jamaican posses (Chapter 8). In *Teen Gangs: A Global View*, how gangs are defined and what aspect of gang membership is emphasized will differ somewhat from country to country.

Age and Gender of Youth Gang Members

Indeed, age would seem to be a simple element of a definition of a youth gang, but it is not. There is a trend toward inclusion of both younger and older members in youth gangs, but the most notable increase in membership is among older members (Howell, 1998; Moore, 1990; Spergel, 1995). The age range of the typical youth gang is from 12 to 24 (Howell, 1998); this age range obviously includes young adults.

Mixed-age gangs are not uncommon (Hazlehurst and Hazlehurst, 1998), and some gang theorists, such as Knox (1995), suggest that the very idea of a youth gang makes less and less sense given the increased connections between what are traditionally referred to as youth gangs and organized crime gangs, which include members from a wider range of ages. Bettina Lozzi-Toscano in her contribution on Italian youth gangs (Chapter 7) makes this point very clearly and emphasizes the connections between organized youth gangs and organized crime. However, a modal age for an average youth gang member in the United States is around 17 or 18 (Curry and Decker, 1998). Scott Gillig's article on gang trends in the United States (Chapter 14), notes that females can be gang members, yet it is quite clear that youth gang members across the globe are overwhelmingly male.

Individual Crime, Gang Crime, and Organized Crime

Accepting illegal activity as a central characteristic of gang activity raises significant questions about the relationship between individual crime, gang crime, and organized crime. If an individual who is a gang member commits a crime, when is that crime best understood as an individual crime and when is it best understood as a gang crime? Additionally, if the youth gang has developed a more organized structure and becomes entrepreneurial in nature and linked to organized crime in the community, when is youth gang crime best understood as organized crime? These are very difficult questions to answer, and the distinctions involved are very important ones.

There is a reciprocal relationship between the individual and the gang, with the gang exerting a powerful influence on the individual. At the same time, the individual gang member's needs must be accommodated to a certain extent by the gang. Adolescent gang members commit violent and serious crimes at significantly higher rates than adolescent nongang members (Howell, 1998). Youth gangs demonstrate more serious and more group-based criminal activity, the more formally organized they are (Fagan, 1989). Knox (1995), as noted earlier, raises the question of whether in today's crime environment the idea of a youth gang is even meaningful, given the organized criminal activities, such as drug dealing and money laundering, that gangs as criminal enterprises participate in.

The ability of a youth gang to carry out organized criminal activities is to some extent dependent upon its structure and level of organization. A youth gang composed of young people who hang out together and share similar experiences of demoralization and rejection by society is one view of what a juvenile gang looks like. An alternative view is that of a youth gang as a more formal organization with clear leadership and roles performed by gang members within a framework of rules, expectations, and sanctions for noncompliance. Both forms of youth gangs exist, and the distinction between the two is not necessarily easy to determine from the outside looking in.

More research is needed to understand the relationship between youth gangs and organized crime, in activities such as drug trafficking. Howell (1998) states that "gang involvement appears to increase individual involvement in drug use, drug trafficking, gun carrying, and violence and, perhaps, to prolong involvement in drug sales" (p. 11), while also noting that the relationship between youth gangs and drug trafficking is still unclear. What is clear though is that the more formally structured and organized a youth gang becomes, the more likely it is that it will eventually start participating in organized criminal enterprises, in particular, drug dealing and trafficking.

MARGINALIZATION, EXCLUSION, AND INCLUSION

A theme running through this collection of profiles of youth gangs from around the globe is the concept of marginalization. Marginalization refers to the state of being on the edges or the fringes of society, being left out and not fully included. Alienated or marginalized youth are more likely to join gangs than are young people who fully participate in school and work. Inclusion in society involves some degree of personal ownership of the dominant values of one's culture and community. At the personal level, included members of society feel that they belong, that they are a part of what is going on, and that what they think about things is important and will make a difference. Included members of society feel respected and that they have a voice. Being socially included means having ties to one's community that connect one to other people in meaningful ways. Inclusion means access and opportunity. Included people are insiders; excluded people are outsiders.

Within particular societies, certain groups are often more marginalized than other groups. Young people and minorities are examples of groups that are frequently marginalized. There are a number of social indicators that point to a state of marginalization within a community. These indicators include poverty, unemployment, increased crime, increased school dropout rates, and increased rates of substance abuse and homelessness. People in marginalized communities generally have lower levels of education than those in more socially integrated communities and often lack the job skills necessary to move into a state of fuller social participation. Young people living in poorer communities who have dropped out of school and whose lives are disorganized through substance abuse and lack of job skills are most likely to experience themselves as socially excluded and as outsiders. This combination of social and psychological circumstances makes a young person more at risk for gang membership, and gang leaders recruit in these depressed environments. The term "underclass" is also used to describe people living in these marginalized situations.

A number of theorists about gangs identify the presence of this underclass of excluded members of society as fertile ground for the development and survival of youth gangs (Bursik and Grasmick, 1993; Huff, 1992; Moore, 1991). Individual psychological and family factors can serve as either protective factors or as additional predisposing factors for those in marginalized communities. Adult role models in the family, order and routine within the family, and absence of family violence and addiction are protective. Family disorganization, substance abuse, and parental attitudes negative toward authority and community increase the risk that an already marginalized young person will become a gang member (Esbensen, Huizinga, and Weiher, 1993).

In *Teen Gangs: A Global View*, a number of contributors address the issue of marginalization and emphasize its importance in understanding the cultural context giving rise to youth gang formation. In Chapter 10, Sinclair Dinnen discusses the growth of raskolism in Papua New Guinea against the backdrop of rapid urban growth following independence from colonial rule. The indigenous people of Papua New Guinea, as a result of the country's change in political status and subsequent rapid growth, experienced the disruption of their traditional kinship networks, leaving many alienated and without support. Edil Torres Rivera and Loan Phan clearly implicate a history of colonialism, injury to cultural pride, and associated economic exploitation in the emergence and tenacity of the youth gang problem in Puerto Rico (Chapter 11). Perhaps the most shocking discussion of the relationship between social exclusion and the youth gang problem can be found in Anthony Borrow and Jennifer Walker's contribution on Honduras (Chapter 4). They trace the origins of Honduran youth gangs to deported

Salvadoran gang members from the street gangs of Los Angeles, who upon returning to El Salvador laid the groundwork for the spread of youth gangs to neighboring Central American countries. Borrow and Walker document the claims of groups inside Honduras who believe that government sanctioned extrajudicial murder of youth gang members has been used as a form of social cleansing of a both troubled and troubling segment of society.

Schneider (2002) addressed the issue of marginalization and exclusion of adolescent gang members in post-World War II United States in this way:

Adolescents responded to a labor market that exploited them by quitting or getting fired from jobs, to a school system that did not educate by dropping out, and to families that failed to nurture them by hanging out on street corners. Although the institutions of adolescent socialization encouraged only individual rebellion, adolescents in acts of creativity and imagination established street gangs and forged a gang culture so evocative that its forms were repeatedly commercialized. Gangs were a collective response to the difficulties of adolescent life in poor neighborhoods. (p. 660)

Schneider's position suggests that the very formation of youth gangs was a solution attempt—an attempt on the part of excluded young people to construct a culture of acceptance and participation that the larger institutions of society had failed to provide.

DRUGS AND YOUTH GANGS

The relationship between drugs and youth gangs is graphically portrayed in the chapter on Ireland's youth gang problem (Chapter 5). In this chapter the infamous "needle muggings," in which blood-filled syringes were used as weapons to intimidate victims and extort money and goods from them, are discussed. As with so many issues relating to youth gangs, the relationships among drug use, drug trafficking, and gangs are not clear. About one thing there is not much doubt, however: gang members do use drugs more frequently and at higher levels than do nongang members (Esbensen, Huizinga, and Weiher, 1993; Fagan, 1989).

By its very nature, drug dependency opens the door to increased crime and violence. Addiction requires a steady stream of drugs, and many addicted young gang members increase their criminal activities in order to obtain the drugs needed to support their habits. This is the vicious cycle of drug abuse leading to drug dependency leading to increased crime leading to increased drug use, and on and on.

The sale, distribution, and trafficking of drugs is another matter, and the distinction between organized criminal drug enterprises and youth gangs is less clear. In Ireland (Chapter 5), for example, the emergence of gang violence coincided with the widespread introduction of drugs, especially heroin, into the country in the late 1970s and early 1980s. Jill Duba and Marty Jencius, in their discussion of youth gangs in the Bahamas (Chapter 2), also point to the fact that job opportunities are available in the underworld of drug trafficking for youth gang members and that legitimate jobs are much harder to get. Richard Van Dorn, in his contribution about street gangs in Britain (Chapter 3), makes the point that the drug trade is attractive to adolescent youth gangs whose members are relatively economically disadvantaged and who also suffer from a loss of a sense of identity and place.

Howell and Decker (1999), in their comprehensive review of the primarily U.S.-focused literature related to youth gangs, drugs, and violent crime, document the relationship between the crack cocaine epidemic in the inner cities and increased youth gang violence. They also point out that it can be difficult to distinguish youth gangs from organized crime gangs and that more research and analysis of the relationship between the two is needed. In her discussion of how schools can respond to youth gangs and juvenile crime in Taiwan (Chapter 12), Julia Yang indicates that Taiwanese youth gangs are connected to organized crime, as does Lorna Black in her discussion of gangs in Jamaica (Chapter 8). Black describes Jamaican gangs as having juvenile members, but points out that these members are controlled by the older gang members higher up in the crime gang organization, suggesting a more formal and organized structure.

In many cases, drug use and the sale and distribution of drugs are simply assumed to be a part of youth gang life. As discussed, the research confirms that gang members do more drugs more often. Howell and Decker (1999) emphasize the need for caution in making a direct connection between youth gangs and organized drug crime and counsel against equating the two. The contributors to *Teen Gangs: A Global View*, while not methodologically examining the distinction between youth gangs and organized criminal drug gangs, point suggestively in the direction of youth gang involvement in organized drug crime.

RESPONSES AND FUTURE DIRECTIONS

Responses by government and nongovernmental organizations to the juvenile gang situation can range from minimization and denial of a problem to gross overreaction. Fear of a gang problem's hurting the image of a community or country can lead to understatement and denial. A few particularly vicious or sensational crimes, or frustration with groups of youths hanging out on the streets, can lead to a public perception of a greater problem than actually exists. Both minimizing and exaggerating the nature of a youth gang problem can give rise to inappropriate and counterproductive responses by governmental bodies and nongovernmental organizations. In Chapter 6, Sloane Veshinski discusses youth gangs and juvenile crime in Israel and concludes that the existence of youth gangs in Israel is not widely acknowledged within the country and suggests this could be a function of Israel's larger struggles for its security and survival in a highly turbulent part of the world. Sylvia Fernandez, in her contribution about teen gangs in Malaysia (Chapter 9), notes that behavior that in the past would have been brushed off as the usual school fights or bullying is now described as "teen gangsterism," indicating the significant shift in public perception and tolerance that has occurred.

Responding to a gang problem requires a focus on relationships, both cooperative and adversarial. Gang members have significant relationships with one another, and for a gang to function, there must be some degree of cooperation and coordination among its members. They also have relationships with other gangs, relationships that may be cooperative or adversarial and that alternate between cooperation and conflict, depending upon the time and situation. As discussed, gangs and gang members also have relationships with the larger communities within which they are located. These relationships are often failed ones, marked by a sense of mutual suspicion, anger, and distrust. Gang members' relationships with their communities are characterized by the experiences of rejection, exclusion, futility, and, not uncommonly, overt anger and a demand to be recognized. In turn, communities frequently respond by relating to the gangs with fear, avoidance, and a desire to separate or remove the gangs and gang members from their midst so that they do not have to deal with them.

It makes sense, therefore, that interventions aimed at reducing gang involvement and gang activities, particularly those of a criminal nature, must take into account the complexity of the relationships between the gang and the community and ideally involve collaboration among all stakeholders. The key stakeholders are the gang members, law enforcement, the business and economic community, churches and community organizations, and citizens most impacted by gang related crime.

Responses to gang activity in a community can be to prevent or to intervene or both. Preventive responses are designed to reduce the proliferation of gangs in a community and divert young people from joining them. Interventions are designed to reduce gang activity that already exists, particularly criminal activity, and to provide opportunities for gang members to leave gangs for productive legitimate employment.

Preventive responses are often educational in nature, focusing on antigang and antidrug education. Antidrug education appears to be especially important since research does show an increase in gang involvement among drug-using and drug-selling youth (Esbensen, Huizinga, and Weiher, 1993; Fagan, 1989). Hill, Howell, Hawkins, and Battin (1999) are quite clear in identifying early drug use as a risk factor for gang involvement later. In addition, antigang education programs similar in philosophy to the antidrug education programs such as Drug Abuse Resistance Education (DARE) may also be effective. School-based antigang programs such as GREAT (Gang

Resistance Education and Training), based on the DARE model, focus on helping young people develop gang refusal skills and are being more formally examined (Esbensen and Osgood, 1999). Julia Yang, in her comprehensive research about the youth gang problem and at-risk youth in Taiwan (Chapter 12), describes in detail a host of school-based programs that have been put in place to address these problems. Community policing, a gang intervention that can be both preventive and suppressive, is a gang response strategy that Joanna Headley describes in her contribution on teen gangs in Trinidad and Tobago (Chapter 13).

Interventive responses to youth gangs include: (1) gang suppression through law enforcement activities; (2) community-based programs designed to offer meaningful alternatives to gang membership, primarily by giving gang members access to legitimate jobs; (3) innovative restorative justice programs such as gang and weapons surrenders and victim-offender mediation; and (4) setting of national policy agendas to include resources for addressing youth issues. Gang suppression is usually understood as prosecution and incarceration of gang members and supervision by law enforcement and probation departments.

Community-based gang alternative programs are varied. They focus on providing opportunities to gang members to learn basic job skills. The more effective programs in this category also provide access to legitimate employment through mentoring. Other rehabilitation programs, such as addiction treatment, can be structured to support the goals of community-based gang alternative programs.

In many ways, restorative justice programs seem to offer the most promise for addressing the problems of marginalized youth and teen gangs. Such programs attempt to address the needs of the victim, the offender, and the community by connecting them in a circle of responsibility, amends, and restitution. Ireland's extremely successful Garda Juvenile Diversion Programme (Chapter 5), is an example, as is the gang surrender described in Sinclair Dinnen's contribution on Papua New Guinea (Chapter 10). In promoting a restorative justice focus, Bazemore (1998) states that "a relational approach to rehabilitation cannot be clinical in its focus, but must instead emphasize community socialization networks and naturally occurring processes in its analysis of how most delinquents grow up to be normal, productive adults" (p. 790). As Dinnen notes, however, in his discussion of the gang surrender in Papua New Guinea, the public's enthusiasm for programs like the gang surrender seems to wane in the face of increased crime and threat.

Finally, the policies set by governments at the national level about at-risk youth and juvenile crime are convincing indicators of the direction a country is heading in addressing youth issues. Zero-tolerance and get-tough policies are accompanied by resource allocation to prosecution and incarceration. Resources tend to be allocated toward prevention when risk reduction is the government's policy priority. There is still much unexplored ground in the development of gang alternative and restorative justice programs. The development and refinement of these kinds of programs would be helped considerably by national policies promoting and supporting them.

CONCLUSIONS

Teen Gangs: A Global View provides a window to the world of teen gangs. In each of the cultural descriptions in this volume, the teen gang situation is discussed within the larger framework of associated social and economic conditions. The unique character of the teen gang situation in each country is presented, and important questions are raised by the contributors. These questions address issues related to the nature of teen gangs, the degree of threat posed by teen gangs, their connection to organized crime, and the issues of social exclusion and marginalization of youth. The contributors also invite us to reflect upon the strategies and solutions utilized by various countries across the globe to deal with at-risk youth and teen gangs. Perhaps most important of all, the global view of teen gangs presented in this volume invites us, as thoughtful citizens, to think broadly about at-risk youth and teen gangs and to participate more fully in conversations about how best to respond to them.

REFERENCES

Ball, R. A., and G. D. Curry. "The logic of definition in criminology: Purposes and methods for defining gangs." *Criminology* 33 (1995): 225–245.

Bazemore, G. "Restorative justice and earned redemption: Communities, victims, and offender reintegration." *American Behavioral Scientist* 41 (1998): 768–813.

Bursik, R. J., and H. G. Grasmick. *Neighborhoods and crime: The dimensions of effective community control* (New York: Lexington Books, 1993).

Curry, G. D., and S. H. Decker. *Confronting gangs: Crime and community* (Los Angeles: Roxbury Publishing Co., 1998).

Esbensen, F. A., D. Huizinga, and A. W. Weiher. "Gang and non-gang youth: Differences in explanatory variables." *Journal of Contemporary Criminal Justice* 9 (1993): 94–116.

Esbensen, F., and D. W. Osgood. "Gang resistance education and training (GREAT): Results from the national evaluation." *Journal of Research in Crime and Delinquency* 36 (1999): 194–225.

Fagan, J. "The social organization of drug use and drug dealing among urban gangs." *Criminology* 27 (1989): 633–669.

Hazlehurst, C., and K. M. Hazlehurst. "Gangs in cross-cultural perspective." In *Gangs and youth subcultures: International Explorations*, edited by C. Hazlehurst and K. M. Hazlehurst (New Brunswick, NJ: Transaction Publishers, 1998), pp. 1–34.

Hill, K. G., J. C. Howell, J. D. Hawkins, and S. R. Battin. "Childhood risk factors for adolescent gang membership: Results from the Seattle Social Development Project." *Journal of Research in Crime and Delinquency* 36 (1999): 300–322.

Howell, J. C. *Youth gangs: An overview.* Juvenile Justice Bulletin (Washington, DC: U.S. Department of Justice, Office of Justice Programs, Office of Juvenile Justice and Delinquency Prevention, 1998).

Howell, J. C., and S. H. Decker. *The youth gangs, drugs, and violence connection.* Juvenile Justice Bulletin (Washington, DC: U.S. Department of Justice, Office of Justice Programs, Office of Juvenile Justice and Delinquency Prevention, 1999).

Huff, R. C. "The new youth gangs: Social policy and malignant neglect." In *Juvenile justice and public policy: Towards a national agenda,* edited by I. M. Schwartz (New York: Lexington Books, 1992), pp. 22–44.

Klein, M. W. *Street gangs and street workers* (Englewood Cliffs, NJ: Prentice Hall, 1971).

Knox, G. W. *An introduction to gangs,* rev. ed. (Bristol, IN: Wyndham Hall Press, 1995).

Moore, J. P. "Gangs, drugs, and violence." In *Drugs and violence: Causes, correlates, and consequences,* edited by M. de La Rosa, E. Y. Lambert, and B. Gropper. Research Monograph No. 103 (Rockville, MD: National Institute on Drug Abuse, 1990), pp. 160–176.

———. *Going down to the barrio: Homeboys and homegirls in change* (Philadelphia: Temple University Press, 1991).

Moore, J. P., and C. P. Terrett. *Highlights of the 1996 National youth gang survey. Fact Sheet* (Washington, DC: U.S. Department of Justice, Office of Justice Programs, Office of Juvenile Justice and Delinquency Prevention, 1998).

Schneider, E. "Eric Schneider's response to Andrew Diamond." *Journal of Urban History* 28 (2002): 659–660.

Short, J. F., ed. *Gang delinquency and delinquent subcultures* (New York: Harper and Row, 1968).

Spergel, I. A. *The youth gang problem* (New York: Oxford University Press, 1995).

Thrasher, F. M. *The gang: A study of one thousand three hundred thirteen gangs in Chicago* (Chicago: University of Chicago Press, 1963).

1

AUSTRALIA

Rob White

INTRODUCTION

Research into youth gangs is usually driven by three basic questions: Do gangs exist, are they a problem, and if so, what should be done about them? To address these questions can, however, be a complicated and difficult task. Gang research is fraught with problems, many of them stemming from how we define youth groups and how we interpret the various activities of those who hang around in groups.

Young people in Australia spend a lot of time in the public domains of the street, regardless of social background. However, as construed by the mass media and in the statements of political leaders, youth activity on the streets is in many instances equated with gang behavior. But do gangs as such really exist in Australia? Are they really the threat to society that media portrayals would have us believe?

The notion of a gang can mean different things to different people. Imprecise definitions and perceptions of young people based on stereotypes, however, often feature prominently in media treatments of street-present young people—especially ethnic minority youth. The following discussion examines the nature of Australian youth gangs in greater detail. The aim of the chapter is to clarify the nature of youth gangs in the Australian context and to describe recent work in this area.

PROFILE OF AUSTRALIA

Australia is a large island continent located between the Indian and Pacific Oceans, south of the equator. It is divided into six states and two territories.

Most of its 20 million or so people live in cities on the coast, as roughly two-thirds of the continent is arid or semiarid. Sydney is the largest city, with some 4 million people, followed by Melbourne with about 3 million people. Cities such as Brisbane, Perth, and Adelaide each have more than 1 million residents. Australia, one of the most polyethnic countries in the world, comprises people from over 170 different nationalities and cultural groups, as well as indigenous people (Aborigines and Torres Strait Islanders). The population is thus very diverse in terms of social background, country of origin, cultural and religious practices, languages (although English is the official language), and physical appearance. The official state policy recognizes cultural diversity (or multiculturalism) within a national framework of participation, access and equity, and adherence to Australian law.

GANG FORMATIONS AND GANG-RELATED BEHAVIOR

Periodic media reports about the perceived proliferation and criminal or antisocial activities of youth gangs have long been featured in press stories about young people in many parts of Australia—from Melbourne to Adelaide, from Perth to Sydney (Bessant and Hil, 1997; Collins, Noble, Poynting, and Tabar, 2000; Healey, 1996, for examples). These reports are by no means new. Indeed, the idea of gangs has been associated over a lengthy period of time with various kinds of youth group formations.

From the middle to the end of the nineteenth century, for example, much public concern was directed at the "push larrikins" of Melbourne and Sydney (Murray, 1973). These were groups of young men (the groups were called pushes) who, through their appearance (e.g., the wearing of pointed-toe boots) and behavior (e.g., getting drunk, brawling), became easily identified as threats by the media, the police, and the general public. The streets were the meeting places of the pushes, and they had their origins in the poverty of their members. The push larrikins were born out of a very unsettled state of society and reflected the lack of amusements, recreational outlets, jobs, and overall means of livelihood for these young people. Deviancy was grounded in the form of the gang.

By contrast, public consternation about young people in the mid-twentieth century revolved around the "bodgies and widgies," young men and women who were identifiable by their particular visual styles and leisure concerns (Stratton, 1992). The bodgies and widgies represented a new teenage culture, with an emphasis on fashion (long hair styles for the boys, gabardine skirts for the girls), street presence, dancing, and rock and roll music. From 1950 to 1959 the phenomenon of the bodgies and widgies captured the imagination of the media. They were working-class young people with jobs, who were engaging in the first stirrings of a distinctive teenage consumer-oriented culture. In doing so, they represented a threat to middle-class values and culture, and much of the media condemnation (and distortion) centered on the alcohol use, sexual behavior, and family breakdown associated with the bodgies and widgies. Deviancy was linked to a new youth subculture.

Gangs and Groups

Until recently, there has been relatively little concerted research into the nature and dynamics of contemporary youth gangs in the Australian context (Aumair and Warren, 1994; Collins et al, 2000; Foote, 1993; White, Perrone, Guerra, and Lampugnani, 1999). Much of the knowledge about youth groups, including so-called gangs, has been based on anecdotal information and popular media imagery. Many disputes have taken place over the existence and magnitude of the alleged gang problem. This has mainly been due to problems in defining what a gang actually is. This definitional ambiguity is not unique to Australian conditions—American, Canadian, and European research has increasingly emphasized that gang formation is a social process involving complex forms of membership, transformation, and disintegration (Bjorgo, 1999; Gordon, 2000; Gordon and Foley, 1998; Klein, 1995; Spergel, 1995). Indeed, recent American research challenges popular media images based on traditional stereotypes and demonstrates, for example, that gangs in many cases are not highly organized and that the gangs, drugs, and violence connection applies more to adult gangs than to youth gangs (Howell, 2000).

The specific features of any particular youth group formation will vary greatly (see, for example, Howell, 2000; White et al., 1999). But if the group sees itself as a "gang" and is perceived by others as such, primarily because of its illegal activities, this constitutes the minimum baseline definition of a gang (Maxson and Klein, 1989). Research into youth gangs has to locate these specific kinds of groups within the context of other types of youth group formations (Gordon, 1995, 2000; Gordon and Foley, 1998). That is, it is important that distinctions be made between different sorts of groups—which may include gangs, youth subcultures, friendship networks, school cohorts, sports teams, and so on. As indicated in the discussion of larrikins and bodgies and widgies, a group may be described in the media as deviant, but not necessarily as a gang. Similarly, the reasons for group formation, and the typical focus of activities, can provide insight into differences between groups—for example, when distinguishing between social-centered and criminal-centered activity.

Gang Identity

Major difficulties exist in defining what a gang is. In addition, major problems occur in trying to identify who gang members are and what their precise relationship to a particular youth group formation might be. The question here is not so much the presence of the group, but a particular individual's involvement with that group. Group membership is largely a fluid process, with specific individuals having varying degrees of association over time.

Consider the following: A young person may occasionally associate with a gang, but not be a member. A young person may participate in the activities of a gang once in a while, but not be a member. A young person may desire to be a part of a gang, but not actually become a member. A young person may say he or she is part of the same crowd or gang, but not actually be a member of the relevant core group. A young person may have all the external trappings of a gang member (street-gang culture in the form of dress, posture, talking style) but not be a member of a gang.

Depending on who is defining gang membership, and according to what criteria, there may be dispute over whether a particular individual is, in fact, a gang member. Variables that might be considered include: symbols or symbolic behaviors that tie the person to a particular gang; self-admission of gang membership; association with known gang members; type of criminal behavior; location or residence; police identification as a gang member; other informant identification as a gang member; other institutional identification as a gang member (Howell, 2000). In the end, the issue of individual gang membership can be as contentious as defining particular youth group formations as gangs. In either case, there are major areas of ambiguity and uncertainty. In both cases, as well, things have a tendency to change over time.

The phenomenon of social exclusion appears to be central to the processes of gang identification. Sydney gang research, for example, found that some of the young men who were interviewed presented themselves as a gang to gain a measure of respect (Collins et al., 2000). The symbolic representation of themselves as members of a gang, however, was more at the level of overt performance (i.e., presenting an image of being tough and dangerous) than related to particular kinds of professional criminal activity. The point of claiming gang status was to affirm social presence, to ensure mutual protection, and to compensate for a generally marginalized economic and social position. Significantly, research indicates that where young people themselves claim gang membership, they tend to engage in substantially more antisocial and criminal behavior than those who do not profess to be gang members (Esbensen, Winfree, He, and Taylor, 2001). Who you say you are thus has implications for what you do and with whom. Group identification is thus intertwined with group activity.

Gang-Related Behavior

While American-style gangs, as customarily defined in terms of being highly structured, organized, and criminally motivated (see Perrone and

White, 2000), are less prevalent in Australia and particularly do not appear in teenage group formations, ganglike behavior is a problem requiring further research. For example, a study of ethnic minority youth in Melbourne found that group conflicts, especially street fights, were common across the sample group (White et al., 1999). Whatever the ambiguities of the term *gang* among academics and young people themselves, membership in certain groups or collectivities was nevertheless associated with varying degrees of violence and illegal activity. To outsiders, such street activity could well be interpreted as hallmarks of gang membership and engagement. For insiders, however, group membership was often linked to a form of protection against racism and street violence, rather than a violent outlet. For many, major positive benefits can be derived from group participation with young people from similar class, ethnic, and religious backgrounds.

Youth gang-related behavior can initially be categorized in terms of four types of activities (in another context, some of these activities have been associated with different types of gangs; see United States Bureau of Justice Assistance, 1998, pp. 11–14). The four types of activities are:

1. **Criminal**—in which the main focus of the activity is directed at making money through illegal means, such as property theft or drug selling. This kind of activity may be sporadic and episodic and may not be central to a group's overall activity. Alternatively, it may involve complex relationships, techniques, and skills, in essence a whole culture and highly organized division of labor within which profit making occurs.

2. **Conflict**—in which the main feature is street fighting and where violence is associated with gaining social status and street reputation. This kind of activity is marked by an emphasis on honor, personal integrity, and territoriality (defending one's physical or community boundaries). Issues of self-esteem and identity, constructions of masculinity and self-protection loom large in consideration of why conflicts occur and persist over time.

3. **Retreat**—in which the main activity is heavy drug use and generally a withdrawal from mainstream social interaction. Illegal activity lies mainly in the use of drugs as such, rather than in violence or other forms of antisocial activity. However, because of the drug use, property crimes and crimes of violence may result, often on an impulsive and senseless basis. The presence of drug users may create moral panic or disturb the sensibilities of the public.

4. **Street Culture**—in which the main characteristic is adoption of specific gang-related cultural forms and public presentation of ganglike attributes. The emphasis is on street gang culture, incorporating certain types of music, ways of dressing, hand signals, body ornaments including tattoos, distinctive ways of speaking, graffiti, and so on. It may reflect actual group dynamics and formations or be simply a kind of mimicry based on media stereotypes and youth cultural fads. (White, 2002)

An important feature of these types of activities is that they actually pertain to young people in general rather than to youth gangs specifically; that is, at different times and in different locations young people may engage in one or more of the activities described to a varying extent, depending on social background and other factors. They may do so on their own or with a group, and involvement in particular activities may be for short or long periods of time. In other words, what is described here as gang-related activity need not equate with gang membership. Nor does gang membership necessarily translate into participation in these activities. In addition, it may be the case that individual members of a gang may engage in specific types of illegal activity, such as selling drugs or homicide, but this may not be a function or outcome of the gang as a whole.

Gangs as a Problem

A distinction can be drawn between gangs and gang-related behavior. A further point also needs to be made: that is, not all gang behavior is necessarily criminal, illegal, or "bad." Therefore, one must distinguish between different kinds of gang behavior. More importantly, the question can be asked: When do these gang behaviors become a problem?

Much of the public concern over youth gangs in Australia seems to be driven by images of "color gangs" in the United States. Close examination of the Australian social landscape, however, makes it hard to substantiate the presence of such gangs in this country (Aumair and Warren, 1994; Standing Committee on Social Issues, 1995). Nevertheless, the presence of large groups of young people on the street, or young people dressed in particular ways or with particular group affiliations, appears to have fostered the idea that Australia, too, has a gang problem.

This is especially so in relation to the activities and perceptions of ethnic minority youth. Indeed, in recent years, the hype and sensationalized treatment of youth gangs have tended to have an increasingly racialized character; that is, the media have emphasized the racial background of alleged gang members and thereby fostered the perception that, for instance, "young Lebanese" or "young Vietnamese" equals "gang member" (White, 1996). The extra visibility of ethnic minority youth (relative to the Anglo "norm") feeds the media's moral panic over youth gangs, as well as bolsters a racist stereotyping based on features such as language, clothes, and skin color. In fact, media images and treatments of ethnic minority young people are generally very negative (Maher, Nguyen, and Le, 1999; Pe-Pua, 1996; White et al., 1999). It is frequently the case as well that particular events are seized upon by the media to reinforce the "ethnic" character of deviancy and criminality in ways that stigmatize whole communities.

The image of gangs, a powerful one in terms of public perception, has engendered varying kinds of social reactions. For example, the social status and public perception of young people in groups very much influence the regulation of public space. Many groups of young people—some of which might be labeled gangs—tend to hang out in places such as shopping centers. To a certain extent, much of the concern about gangs is really a misunderstanding of the nature of youth subcultures, of how young people naturally associate with each other in groups, and of the lack of opportunities open to them to circulate and do things in particular places. In most cases, however, the presence of identifiable groups is not the precursor to activity that is going to menace the community as a whole.

NATURE OF AUSTRALIAN YOUTH GANGS

Going beyond media images and sensationalized treatments of the "gang problem" requires grounded analysis of actual groups and their activities. To determine whether there is a gang problem, therefore, it is essential to consider carefully what the research has to say. For instance, a New South Wales inquiry gathered little or no evidence that criminal teenage gangs exist in that state. The report commented that use of the term in a way that implies violence and an organized structure has little relevance to youth activities in Australian communities (Standing Committee on Social Issues, 1995). Certain types of youth gangs do exist; but where this is the case, most such gangs limit their criminal behavior to petty theft, graffiti, and vandalism.

Gang Characteristics

By and large, it can be concluded that most bands of street-present young people in Australia are not "gangs," but groups (Standing Committee on Social Issues, 1995; White, 1996). One study of youth gangs in Melbourne, for example, found that while some characteristics of these groups mirrored the media images (for example, the masculine nature of youth gangs, their preferred hangouts and shared identity markers, such as shoes or clothes), the overall rationale for the groups' formation was simply one of social connection, not crime (Aumair and Warren, 1994).

In their particular study, Aumair and Warren (1994) cite five key characteristics of youth gangs. These include:

1. Overwhelming male involvement that, in turn, reinforced certain "masculine" traits in the group setting (such as fighting prowess, sexual conquest, substance use, and minor criminal acts)
2. High public visibility, given a lack of money and therefore a reliance on free public spaces for recreational purposes
3. An outward display of collective identity, in the form of the wearing of similar styles of clothing, adopting a common name for the group, and so on

4. Organization principally for social reasons and, consequently, low rates of criminal activity, as indicated in the absence of formalized gang rules and a social rationale for gathering together, rather than a criminal objective

5. Differences between public perceptions of the "gang problem" and the real nature of the problem, as illustrated by the fact that most criminal activity seemed to be inwardly focused, involving one-on-one fights and substance abuse.

Much of the criminality exhibited by youth gangs, therefore, is inward looking and linked to self-destructive behavior such as substance abuse, drinking binges, and the like. The popular perception is that gangs seek to violate the personal integrity and private property of the public in general; closer investigation reveals the insular nature of much of their activity (Aumair and Warren, 1994).

Ethnic Youth Gangs

As users of public space, ethnic minority youth are particularly visible owing to ethnic markers such as physical appearance and language and because they often congregate in numbers. Whether these groups of young people constitute gangs as such is a matter of systematic research and careful interpretation. Three recent studies have examined so-called ethnic youth gangs in various Australian cities.

The Adelaide Study. Because of media concerns about street kids and loutish behavior on the part of some young people in the inner city, a study was undertaken in the late 1980s to investigate the potential and actual needs of young Italian-Australians who frequent Adelaide's streets (Foote, 1993). The study found that groups of young men, united around their common Italian heritage, did meet regularly, both in the suburbs and in specific "Italian" areas of the inner city. The groups essentially formed on a social basis, with "hanging around" an activity in its own right shared by group members.

The study found that periodically there were fights between the Italian-Australian young men and other groups. Conflicts tended to be based on ethnic identification and involved the Italians, the Greeks, and the Australians. Sometimes the Italians and Greeks would find solidarity with each other in their common difference with the Anglo-Australians. It was the "wogs" versus the "Aussies."

Fights tended to be caused by taunts and jeers between groups of young people. For the Italian-Australians, this often took the form of racist discourse that attacked their legitimacy as Australian citizens and residents ("They call us wogs and they say go back to Italy"). Group behavior and group protection reinforces the cohesion and identity of the group as a whole.

Rivalry and physical conflicts with other racially based groups reinforce their identity both as Italians and as "macho men." In this context, especially as victors in the fight, they can turn their status as wogs from a point of derision to something of which they can be proud. (Foote, 1993, p. 127)

The themes of social connection, identity formation, collective protection, and active resistance to racist provocation surfaced in other recent studies as well.

The Melbourne Study. A recent Melbourne study of ethnic youth gangs consisted of interviews with young Vietnamese, Somali, Latin American, Pacific Islander, Turkish, and Anglo-Australian people (White et al., 1999). The study found that membership in a defined group tended to revolve around similar interests (such as choice of music, sport, style of dress), similar appearance or ethnic identity (such as language, religion, and culture), and the need for social belonging (such as friendship, support and protection). Group affiliation was perceived as the greatest reason that certain young people were singled out as being members of a gang. This identification process was, in turn, associated with being hassled by authority figures such as the police and private security guards and conflicts between different groups of young people on the street or at school.

To some extent, the media image of youth gangs does have an empirical reference point; that is, many young people do hang out together in groups on the street. And as is the case with most young people, periodic offending and illegal behavior does occur. But this type of activity tended to be a by-product of group interaction rather than a rationale for group formation. Nevertheless, the identification of certain young people as members of this group or that group was also tied to real tensions and problems at the level of intergroup relations among the young people.

For instance, the study found that street fighting and school-based fights were a fairly common occurrence. The specific reasons for the fighting were varied. Racism and treating people with disrespect were crucial elements in the explanation. Likewise, so was the sense of ownership and belonging associated with particular local areas and membership in particular social groups. Social status for these young people is thus something that is both contested and defended and this, in turn, is generally tied to an individual's identification with certain people and places.

The Sydney Study. Another study of ethnic minority youth, particularly in relation to the issue of gang-related behavior, was undertaken in Sydney's western suburbs (Collins et al., 2000). The research involved interviews with Lebanese young people and other community members, as well as media and policy analysts. The research found that a major problem was the "racialized" reporting of crime when the media dealt specifically with "Lebanese" youth. Ethnic identifiers are used in relation to some groups, but not others (such as Anglo-Celtic Australians). Moreover, the "explanations" for such "ethnic crime" tends to pathologize the group, as if there is something intrinsically bad about being Lebanese or, more generally, Middle Eastern.

The study pointed out that the groups that exhibit the highest rates of imprisonment—including, for example, the Lebanese, Vietnamese, and Turkish—also have the highest unemployment rates. Put simply, the issue of social exclusion appears to be central in any explanation of youthful offenses that involve particularly disadvantaged groups. Marginalization was also central to explaining the perception of widespread involvement in youth gangs among Lebanese youth. Even so, the main forms of association among Lebanese young people were first and foremost friendship groups. These groups also functioned as a defense against experiences of racism and exclusion from the cultural mainstream.

The Sydney study found an intersection of masculinity, ethnicity, and class—in such a way as to affirm social presence, to ensure mutual protection, and to compensate for a generally marginalized economic and social position.

This performance of the "gang" functions in several ways: it provides a venue for cultural maintenance, community and identity and at the same time provides the protection of strength in numbers in the face of physical threats by other youth and harassment by police and other adults. . . . Central to their partial negotiation of their experience of racialisation, they affirm a masculine and "ethnic" identity of toughness, danger and respect. (Collins et al., 2000, p. 150)

Assertion of gang membership can thus be interpreted as attempts by the young men to "valorize" their lives and empower themselves in the face of outside hostility, disrespect, and social marginalization.

Gangs and Social Identity

Australian gang studies have largely concluded that the rationale for most youth formations is primarily "fun" (i.e., as part of a social network) rather than "business" (i.e., as part of a criminal network). Nevertheless, while the purpose for a group forming tended to be social rather than criminal, each type of group may, to a lesser or greater extent, engage in illegal activity, fights, or drug use. This, however, is not driven by the agenda of the group as such, nor is it particularly unusual for Australian teenagers and young adults generally. Much of what happens on the street is contingent upon specific circumstances and events. Fighting, for example, is a general feature of (male) street life, but arises due to different causes and involves different individuals and groups, depending on specific conditions.

One of the key findings of recent research is that ethnic background and identity are often equated with gang membership. In the end, however, the issue is less one of gangs per se than one of social identity and the frictions associated with group interactions based on ethnic stereotypes.

RESPONDING TO THE GANG PROBLEM AND SOCIAL DEVELOPMENT STRATEGIES

What is known about street gangs in Australia seems to confirm that their actual, rather than presumed, existence is much less extensive than popularly believed and that their activities are highly circumscribed in terms of violence or criminal activity. Moreover, group actions are seldom directed at members of the general public. Nevertheless, the image of gangs is a powerful one and has engendered varying kinds of social reactions. This has frequently involved the targeting of particular groups by law enforcement officials. Indeed, the problems associated with police–ethnic minority youth relations forms an important part of the image building in relation to ethnic youth gangs.

A New South Wales study, for example, found that ethnic minority young people were more likely than other groups of Australian young people (with the exception of indigenous people) to be stopped by the police, to be questioned, and to be subject to varying forms of mistreatment (Youth Justice Coalition, 1994). Young Vietnamese Australians in Melbourne and Sydney have complained about unfair treatment and racism in their dealings with the police (Doan, 1995; Lyons, 1995). This is confirmed in a recent study of encounters between police and young people of Asian background in Cabramatta [Sydney], which found that the young people were subject to routine harassment, intimidation, ethnic targeting, racism, and offensive treatment (Maher, Dixon, Swift, and Nguyen, 1997).

More generally, a negative interaction between ethnic minority young people and the police breeds mistrust and disrespect. A minority of people in any community are engaged in particularly antisocial behavior and criminal activity. The problem in this case is that the prejudicial stereotyping often leads to the differential policing of the whole population group (White, 1996). Not only does this kind of policing violate the ideals of treating all citizens and residents with the same respect and rights, but it can inadvertently lead to further law-breaking behavior. Clearly, there is a need for concerted efforts to modify existing police practices and to rethink community policing as this applies to ethnic minority young people (Chan, 1997).

Most Australian gang research places great emphasis on proactive and developmental strategies to deal with youth gangs and gang-related behavior (Collins et al., 2000; Foote, 1993; White et al., 1999). Coercive forms of law enforcement are generally seen as appropriate only in certain selective circumstances, rather than as a measure of first resort or the sole means of dealing with gangs (Howell, 2000). Typical recommendations by Australian writers allude to the need for more support services, youth employment programs, greater dialogue between youth and authority figures, and positive strategies that provide young people with constructive ways in which to use their time and energy.

Existing research highlights the importance of dealing with the youth gang phenomenon across a number of dimensions, taking into account the very different social histories and socioeconomic circumstances of the young people. Examples of specific strategies (White et al., 1999) include:

General Educational Strategies. Young people, in general, should be provided with specific education in cross-cultural issues so that the backgrounds, cultures, and patterns of life pertaining to specific ethnic groups would be better understood by all concerned.

Specific Institutional Strategies. Attention should be directed at providing quality educational facilities and services for young people, particularly those based on a multicultural curriculum and atmosphere, where students are provided with adequate individual and group support, and where antiracist strategies and practices are applied across the whole school population.

Police Strategies. Adoption of appropriate community policing practices and establishment of protocols for positive and constructive interaction between ethnic minority youth and police or security guards is essential in restoring social peace and dampening negative relations on the street.

Broad Government Strategies. Strategic action is needed in the area of youth unemployment and in the creation of jobs for particularly disadvantaged groups and communities, especially since there is increasing evidence that certain neighborhoods are likely to become even poorer if sustained intervention on these matters is not undertaken.

Media Strategies. The media need to be strongly encouraged to review program and reporting content, with a view to providing greater information and more well-rounded accounts of specific ethnic minority groups so that the use of gratuitous images and descriptions based on stereotypes are monitored and actively discouraged.

While youth gangs as such are not a major problem in Australian society at present, there is no doubt that without constructive proactive intervention, they could well emerge as an issue of substantive public concern. The preconditions for more serious types of gang formation are beginning to emerge in the Australian context—poverty, high levels of youth unemployment, precarious job markets, and ghettoization in some cities.

CONCLUSION

In Australia most often the gang is simply a group of like-minded young people who enjoy each other's company and who support one another and have life experiences in common. The street will continue to be a key refuge for young people in general, and groups of young people will continue to have fun—and to occasionally "muck around"—as they have done for many decades, indeed centuries. But the precise character of these groups, and the specific activities in which they engage, depend as much as anything on the availability of community resources and the level of social respect accorded to young people, regardless of specific background. Issues of income security, unemployment, and racism as these impact on different groups of young people and their communities are paramount.

REFERENCES

Aumair, M., and I. Warren. "Characteristics of juvenile gangs in Melbourne." *Youth Studies Australia* 132 (1994): 40–44.

Bessant, J., and R. Hil, eds. *Youth, crime and the media* (Hobart, Australia: National Clearinghouse for Youth Studies, 1997).

Bjorgo, T. *How gangs fall apart: Processes of transformation and disintegration of gangs.* Paper presented at the American Society of Criminology Annual Conference, Toronto, Canada, November 1999.

Chan, J. *Changing police culture: Policing in a multicultural society* (Melbourne: Cambridge University Press, 1997).

Collins, J., G. Noble, S. Poynting, and P. Tabar. *Kebabs, kids, cops and crime: Youth, ethnicity and crime* (Sydney: Pluto Press, 2000).

Doan, V. "Indo-Chinese youth: Issues of culture and justice." In *Ethnic minority youth in Australia,* edited by C. Guerra and R. White (Hobart, Australia: National Clearinghouse for Youth Studies, 1995).

Esbensen, F. A., L. Winfree, N. He, and T. Taylor. "Youth gangs and definitional issues: When is a gang a gang and why does it matter?" *Crime and Delinquency* 471 (2001): 105–130.

Foote, P. "Like, I'll tell you what happened from experience . . . Perspectives on Italo-Australian youth gangs in Adelaide." In *Youth subcultures: Theory, history and the Australian experience,* edited by R. White (Hobart, Australia: National Clearinghouse for Youth Studies, 1993).

Gordon, R. "Street gangs in Vancouver." In *Canadian delinquency,* edited by J. Creechan and R. Silverman (Toronto: Prentice-Hall, 1995).

———. "Criminal business organizations, street gangs and wanna-be groups: A Vancouver perspective." *Canadian Journal of Criminology* (January 2000): 39–60.

Gordon, R., and S. Foley. *Criminal business organizations, street gangs and related groups in Vancouver: The report of the greater Vancouver gang study* (Vancouver: Ministry of Attorney-General, 1998).

Healey, K., ed. *Youth gangs* (Sydney: The Spinney Press, 1996).

Howell, J. *Youth gang programs and strategies: Summary* (Washington, DC: U.S. Department of Justice, Office of Justice Programs, Office of Juvenile Justice and Delinquency Prevention, 2000).

Klein, M. W. *The American Street Gang* (New York: Oxford University Press, 1995).

Lyons, E. "New clients, old problems: Vietnamese young people's experiences with police." In *Ethnic minority youth in Australia*, edited by C. Guerra and R. White (Hobart, Australia: National Clearinghouse for Youth Studies, 1995).

Maher, L., D. Dixon, W. Swift, and T. Nguyen. *Anh Hai: Young Asian background people's perceptions and experiences of policing* (Sydney: UNSW Faculty of Law Research Monograph Series, 1997).

Maher, L., T. Nguyen, and Le T. "Wall of silence: Stories of Cabramatta street youth." In *Australian youth subcultures: On the margins and in the main-stream*, edited by R. White (Hobart, Australia: Australian Clearinghouse for Youth Studies, 1999).

Maxson, C. L., and M. W. Klein. "Street gang violence." In *Violent crime, violent criminals*, edited by N. Warner and M. Wolfgang (Newbury Park, CA: Sage Publications, 1989).

Murray, J. *Larrikins: 19th century outrage* (Melbourne: Lansdowne Press, 1973).

Pe-Pua, R. *We're just like other kids! Street-frequenting youth of non-English-speaking background* (Melbourne: Bureau of Immigration, Multicultural and Popula-tion Research, 1996).

Perrone, S., and R. White. "Young People and Gangs." *Trends and Issues in Crime and Criminal Justice* 167 (Canberra: Australian Institute of Criminology, 2000).

Spergel, I. A. *The youth gang problem* (New York: Oxford University Press, 1995).

Standing Committee on Social Issues. *A report into youth violence in New South Wales* (Legislative Council, Parliament of New South Wales, 1995).

Stratton, J. *The young ones: Working-class culture, consumption and the category of youth* (Perth: Black Swan Press, 1992).

———. *Addressing community gang problems: A practical guide* (Washington, DC: Office of Justice Programs, U.S. Department of Justice, 1998).

White, R. "Racism, policing and ethnic youth gangs." *Current Issues in Criminal Justice* 73 (1996): 302–313.

———. "Understanding youth gangs." *Trends and Issues in Crime and Criminal Justice* 237 (Canberra: Australian Institute of Criminology, 2002).

White, R., S. Perrone, C. Guerra, and R. Lampugnani. *Ethnic youth gangs in Aus-tralia: Do they exist?* Seven reports—Vietnamese, Turkish, Pacific Islander, Somalian, Latin American, Anglo-Australian, Summary Report (Melbourne: Australian Multicultural Foundation, 1999).

Youth Justice Coalition, Western Sydney Juvenile Justice Interest Group and Youth Action and Policy Association. "Nobody listens: The experience of contact between young people and the police" (Sydney: Youth Justice Coalition, 1994).

2

THE BAHAMAS

Jill D. Duba and Marty Jencius

INTRODUCTION

Assessing the prevalence and particular cultural aspects of teen gang violence in a country such as the Commonwealth of the Bahamas presents a challenge associated with the gathering of data from limited sources about a fairly new phenomenon. The history of the Bahamas begins before the voyages of Columbus, but throughout most of its modern history, the Bahamas has been one of the numerous colonies of Great Britain. Today, although retaining Queen Elizabeth II as its constitutional head of state, the Bahamas has been an independent commonwealth for over 30 years. Consequently, information sources for this chapter relied primarily on the assistance of cultural informants.

Cultural informants are those individuals who can best represent the culture or the particular area studied (Denzin and Lincoln, 2000). Cultural informants have been used successfully in the past as a strategy for securing information about a culture, especially about aspects of a culture requiring an insider's view to fully understand and appreciate. For this project, cultural informants included police officers, school counselors, youth workers, and ministers. These resources helped paint a picture of the current status of teen gangs in the Bahamas. In addition to a series of personal interviews with cultural informants, the authors sought literature and statistical data to place the problem in a national context, with information on youth crime rates and gang membership.

PROFILE OF THE BAHAMAS

The Commonwealth of the Bahamas consists of more than 700 islands, with only about 30 of the islands inhabited. More-prominent islands include New Providence (home to the capital city, Nassau), Bimini, Grand Bahama Island, Andros, Eleuthera, Abaco, Cat Island, and San Salvador. Spear-headed by the United States's change in political relations with Cuba in the 1950s, and with a growing recognition of the islands' beauty, the Bahamas became a Caribbean tourist center. The British granted the Bahamas self-government in 1964, changed its status to commonwealth in 1969, and in 1973 granted the Bahamas independence within the Commonwealth of Nations.

In 2000 the population of the Bahamas was just over 300,000, with an annual growth rate of 1.7 percent (United States Department of State, 2002). The ethnic breakdown is noted as 85 percent African, 12 percent European, and 3 percent Hispanic. The African population comes from ancestry in the early 1800s, when the islands acted as a staging area for the United States slave trade. Additional African ancestry came from slaves accompanying British loyalists who fled the American colonies during the Revolutionary War.

Attendance at school is compulsory between the ages of 5 and 16. The government and Ministry of Education operate 158 of the 210 primary and secondary schools, with the remaining 52 schools privately operated. There are close to 66,000 children in the Bahamian school system.

Tourism accounts for 60 percent of the gross national product, with banking accounting for 15 percent and agriculture for 3 percent of the GNP (United States Department of State, 2002). Since there are comparatively few tangible products produced in the Bahamas, its economy relies heavily on imports for many of its consumer products. There are no income or sales taxes and government revenues come from tariffs and import taxes.

Socioeconomic Changes as an Independent Nation

The changes associated with independence have led to a people trying to redefine themselves. This period of national identity development, with its attendant changes in economic influences, created a viable breeding ground for teen gangs (Nowak, 2001). Prior English business influence, combined with banking secrecy laws, provided the Bahamas with a rich economic environment. However, following separation from English sovereignty and the tightening of the banking laws in a response to international criticism of a system that easily allows for laundering of drug trafficking money, the Bahamian economy and employment prospects have changed for young people. With the tightening of international banking laws in the Bahamas, the financial incentives available to investors dwindled, and advantages once inherent in the Bahamian banking system disappeared. This changed the economic climate in the Bahamas and forced a dependence on foreign tourism as a primary national resource. Nowak described what is emerging in the Bahamas as the possible "real Bahamian economy," which is removed from its questionable past influences. Today, this economy is driven by service industry jobs based on tourism. Data from the Consultative Committee on National Youth Development (1995) indicated that tourism contributes 60 percent of the gross national product and employs half of the labor force. The current economic dependence on foreign tourism has created a national incentive to reduce delinquent youth gangs.

Bahamians have a saying that describes their symbiotic economic relationship with the United States: "If the U.S. sneezes, the Bahamas catches a cold." This suggests that political and economic changes within the U.S. impact economic issues in the Bahamas, a situation that is clearly exemplified by the reduction in tourism from the U.S. during the Gulf War (Nowak, 2001) and, most recently, after the attack on September 11, 2001. Both of these U.S. incidents reduced travel and tourism to the Bahamas, making a career of service in tourism and hospitality a less attractive source of employment for youths. However, even before these events, the Consultative Committee on National Youth Development (1995) concluded that greater employment opportunities for youth could be found in agriculture, fisheries, and arts and crafts. A change in career direction for young people toward these fields would reduce the economic dependence on foreign capital. These jobs, however, historically have held a stigma with Bahamian youth, who perceive a lack of prestige in such occupations. Any such available positions are therefore shunned by Bahamian youth, only to be filled by newly arriving Haitian refugees (Nowak, 2001). Therefore, despite such possible career alternatives, the pressure to form a personal identity in a nation coming of age in its own right has led many young Bahamians to delinquent alternatives.

With the introduction of drug trafficking in the 1970s, less-legal career paths became available to Bahamian youths. As a result, the country also saw a rise in related crime during those times. Statistics released by the Consultative Committee on National Youth Development (1995) cited that 53 percent of the country's population is younger than 25 and 43 percent of young adults 15 to 24 years of age are unemployed. In 1992, 19 percent of all murders and 13 percent of all robberies were committed by juveniles. Such crime rates were not seen in youth before 1970. In 1993, 27 percent of the total prison admissions fell between the ages of 16 and 25.

THE DEVELOPMENT OF GANGS

The development of gangs in the Bahamas dates back to the 1960s and 1970s, with the formation of groups in New Providence and Grand Bahama

Island. Gangs began as groups of youths gathered in territorial collections of "blocks" associated with regional areas. Craton and Saunders (1998) report that the first blocks associated with rival groups included the Farm Road Boys and the Kemp Road Boys. Burrows and Reid (2002) described the development of gangs in Nassau in regions with ongoing battles between New Providence areas like "The Bottom" and "Harlem," "Kemp Road" and "The Valley." They are described by Craton and Saunders as being "disruptive but not often criminal" in behavior. Nassau's first violent and combative youth gang was the Syndicate, which originally emerged in the East Street area of Nassau as a small group in the late 1970s. Burrows and Reid described the personal motivation for involvement in the Syndicate as being respect, fame, and reputation.

Reactions to the Syndicate, especially by members who had been taken advantage of, led to the formation of the Bahamas' largest gang to date, the Rebellion, which developed as a splinter group in the East Street area and grew beyond the size and range of the Syndicate. Burrows and Reid (2002) describe the early weapons of both the Syndicate and the Rebellion as being "rocks and bottles at first, later cutlasses and flare guns" and eventually, sophisticated guns. Craton and Saunders (1998) describe the Rebellion as a well-structured group whose members would skip school to ride the municipal buses (jitneys), drink alcohol, and commit minor acts of vandalism that included smashing automobile windows, scrawling graffiti, and committing robberies. As the group became better organized, its members wore distinctive clothes (Raiders paraphernalia) and particular colors and carried bats, cutlasses, knives, and eventually, firearms (Burrows and Reid, 2002). They would disrupt parties and attack people at national celebrations such as Junkanoo and the Red Cross Fair.

Initiations for the Rebellion involved getting "jumped in" or being physically beaten by a group of existing members (Burrows and Reid, 2002). Members would form a circle and beat the initiate to the point of injury. This was a test of endurance and courage. It would also eliminate those who wanted to be members but who might back out when trouble came. Initiation for girls would be to have sex with some or all of the gang members. Seeking honor in a gang would include earning one's stripes by doing things that would gain approval of the gang. This often involved violence directed toward rival gangs, robbing, or destruction of property.

Different gangs began to emerge with the splintering of the Syndicate and the Rebellion. A result of the Rebellion splintering was the creation of the Border Boys. Smaller factions of gangs might still retain the identity of the larger gang. Within the Rebellion were several smaller groups, such as the Irish Rebellion and the Gun Dogs. Splintering of the Gun Dogs resulted in the Gun Hawks and the No Mercy Dogs. In addition to the fractioning of larger gangs, groups would also combine into factions that might change alliances. For example, the Gun Hawks linked up with the Border Boys and referred to themselves as the Border Hawks. These new associations might form as a way to fight a common enemy (Burrows and Reid, 2002).

There seems to be a pattern of development of gangs in the Bahamas that differs from island to island. On the more populated and urbanized islands such as Grand Bahama (Freeport) and New Providence (Nassau), the development is typical of what we have described so far. On the more remote Family Islands, teen gangs are at a variety of levels in their development. Finally, the ultimate picture that emerges in the history of gang development in the Bahamas is one of continual dynamic change between and within gangs, with some historic stability across the groups.

Origins of Gangs and Factors That Predispose Persons to Join

Over time, gangs in the Bahamas have developed because of particular factors including social dynamics, immigration, religion, family life, and changes in the moral climate. Social factors include the alienation of youth from the formal institutions of society; a lack of dialogue or communication between youth and the police, government, and civil leaders; a lack of outreach to youth on the part of civic organizations; and an infiltration by organized American gangs (Craton and Saunders, 1998; F. Williams, personal communication, October 1, 2002).

Furthermore, drugs, political corruption, violence on television, and a lack of adult attention to the actions and behaviors of young people have contributed to the development of teen gangs (Burrows and Reid, 2002). Carlos Reid suggests that a "regular diet of negatives," including the influences of cable television, movies, and videos, has contributed to influencing youth regarding the attractiveness of gang affiliation (personal communication, September 24, 2002). Other social reasons cited include an overall lack of respect for others and their property, the absence of national pride, and a general acceptance of criminal activity (Craton and Saunders, 1998).

A factor related to the influence of immigration on the development of gangs is the influx of Haitian refugees and Jamaican residents (C. Reid, personal communication, September 24, 2002). A religious factor influencing gang development is the dissatisfaction of Bahamian youth with traditional religious values and the adoption of what is seen as a more permissive Rastafarian belief. Many family-related influences that have been suggested include single-parent homes where young people are left to supervise themselves and irregular paternal supervision and modeling. Finally, Burrows and Reid (2002) suggest that "seeds of immorality" have influenced the development of teen gangs. These seeds include drug dealing, corruption, sexual promiscuity, and infidelity.

Relevant literature and persons working in the field have suggested particular factors that have predisposed young persons to join gangs. Craton and Saunders (1998) reported that as early as the 1960s and 1970s, gangs began to form because of members' "need to belong." Gangs also provide members with a group with which to identify. In some ways, gangs also provide members with the sense of family that might have been missing at home. In addition, gangs provide a sense of organization, security, loyalty, and individual recognition (F. Williams, personal communication, October 1, 2002). Burrows and Reid (2002) reported that gangs formed because of a need for persons to protect their "territory" or "area." More specifically, teen gangs provide youths with a subculture that the wider society may have failed to provide.

C. Reid (personal communication, September 26, 2002) suggests that teen gangs form in a developmental fashion relying on three stages. These stages are youth groups, delinquent groups, and organized groups. Youth groups are simple aggregations of youths organized around similar interests, locale, or activities. These groups do not necessarily engage in socially deviant or "typical" gang behavior. Quite often, they act as maturational support for the development of a young person's identity. Youth groups tend to risk involvement in antisocial behavior, especially when they recognize that their aggregation holds power and that this power can be wielded for influence. The second stage is described as delinquent groups; included in this stage are youth groups that have advanced to using their power in ways that demonstrate a recognizable separation from mainstream society and acceptable social norms. Organized gangs, the most advanced stage of gangs, include a highly structured and rule-bound system of socialization. This system monitors entry and exit of members, sometimes with harsh and unjust "jumping in" and punishment.

From the clergy's point of view, Bahamian youths get involved in gangs for four reasons:

1. Developing respect from others
2. Forming a sense of love
3. Gaining protection
4. Surviving in their environment. (C. Reid, personal communication, September 26, 2002)

Because of the perceived threat to the public that gang affiliation carries, membership leads to respect in the eyes of most peers. Some would argue that the perceived threat is greater than the actual threat and that public fear of gang activity and danger is greater than the damage that gangs actually perpetrate (F. Williams, personal communication, October 1, 2002). Reid (personal communication, September 26, 2002) claims that there is a lack of love among today's youths and that gang membership serves the function of providing a loving emotional attachment. Gangs also provide immediate protection for members. As youths witness some of the threatening activities of gangs, they feel protection is more assured if they are part of the affiliation. Finally, this protection gives the threatened and disaffiliated youths a better chance of survival on a daily basis. Since gangs are territorial, Reid suggests that youths feel protected by gang membership and that their ability to survive within their locale is strengthened.

Types of Gangs

Accurate data on current gangs in the Bahamas is difficult to assess. Trends in gang development vary across the major islands. However, gangs can be distinguished by their unique habits in dress, symbols, elaborate graffiti, professional sport team affiliations, and particular school affiliations. Data from cultural informants may help the reader to develop a snapshot of current group trends; additional data about current gang activity is provided in Table 2.1.

Reid (personal communication, September 26, 2002) suggests that at this time, roughly 50 gangs are spread throughout the Bahamas. Recent statistics suggest that 54 percent of the Bahamian population are under the age of 25, with approximately 10,000 gang members in the islands and a 10 percent affiliation rate for youths. Reid suggests that youths coming from the Family Islands to Nassau observe the power of gangs and think that they could start the same types of affiliations when they return to their home islands.

Gang Activity: Outcomes or Consequences

Gang activities encompass both primary and secondary impacts. Primary impacts are those behaviors that are a direct result of gang activity. These activities might be reflected in delinquent behavior such as killings, disruptions of schools and public events, drug dealing, robberies, and rapes (Burrows and Reid, 2002). Gangs may also participate in "warring" activities that range from fistfights to drive-by shootings. These behaviors may be employed as a means for gang members to earn stripes to help them build their name, fame, positions, and roles within the group. Less extreme behaviors may include hanging out on the corner, drinking Night Train (an apple-flavored fortified wine popular with street alcoholics and teenagers), smoking herb (marijuana), intimidation, and defending their territory. Gangs also can provide a social outlet for members through less malevolent pastimes, such as parties and boat cruises. Gang meetings can involve discussing gang business or the distribution of contraband (Burrows and Reid, 2002).

Secondary impacts are those influences that stem indirectly from delinquent gang behavior. Children not associated with gangs will avoid walking

Table 2.1
Bahamian Regional Youth Gangs

Name	Headquarters	Estimated Numbers	Colors
Rebellion	Strachan's Corner	2000	L.A. Raiders
Gun Dogs	Bain Town	500	Dog Paraphernalia
Border Cowboys	Hay Street	300	Dallas Cowboys
War Kings	Englerston	200	L.A. Kings
Hoyas	Kemp Road	500	Georgetown Hoyas
Jungles	Ridgeland Park	200	
Hurricanes	Miami Street	150	University of Miami
Sharks	Ida Street	200	San Jose Sharks
Hornets	Yellow Elder	200	Charlotte Hornets
Pirates	Yellow Elder	100	
Demolishers	Bain Town	80	
Hood Rebellion	Centerville	200	L.A. Raiders
Nike	Grove	200	Nike
Monsters	Carmichael Road	100	
Bo Guards	Blue Hill South	100	
No Mercy Dogs	Culmersville	200	
Mason Murderers	Mason Additions	250	
Terminators	Carmichael Road	100	
Gun Hawks	Grants Town	300	
Swamp Dogs	Pinewood	250	
Dukes	Englerston		
Redskins	Washington Street		
Mud Dogs	Abacop		

Note: From *Respect: A Review of Gang Bangin' in the Bahamas,* by D. Burrows and C. Reid, 2002, Nassau, Bahamas: Youth Alive Ministries.

Editor's Note: Membership numbers are difficult to assess and are therefore, imprecise. Some gangs listed above are offshoots from larger gangs; therefore, some membership numbers may be double counted.

to school, attending school activities, or even attending school itself for fear of harassment from gang members (Burrows and Reid, 2002; C. Reid, personal communication, September 26, 2002; F. Williams, personal communication, October 1, 2002). To avoid being mistaken as gang affiliates or members by a rival gang, nongang teens must not wear certain clothes. Nongang youths also often look to gang members as role models and for protection. Gang members can also provide a missing paternal relationship to a youngster.

How the Prevalence of Gangs Is Being Addressed

School counselors suggest gang-reduction workshops for school and youth personnel. These antigang programs can be organized by schools, churches, and civic organizations. School counselors also suggest that the mass media be involved in prevention efforts, as they appear to be influential in spreading the mystique of gang affiliation. Workshops encouraging dialogue between students and teachers to help students develop a sense of personal control and positive identity are recommended, as is increasing the use of classroom guidance to help students learn conflict resolution skills. While he was a school counselor Franklyn Williams (personal communication, October 1, 2002) attempted to put the responsibility for positive action back on the youths he counseled. He encouraged them to take issues less personally, but stated that it was often difficult for youths to make the connection between knowledge of what they should do and developing the ability to act on that knowledge.

Burrows and Reid (2002) suggest that addressing the prevalence of teen gangs should incorporate the following four factors: (1) prevention, (2) rescue, (3) rehabilitation, and (4) information, with "prevention always being the most important aspect" (p. 29). Prevention strategies include youth, sport, church, and police programs. First, Burrows and Reid call for the formation of a youth development fund similar to United Way in the United States. This fund would allocate money for organizations working directly with youths. The second factor, rescue, involves working directly with troubled young gang members to show them that there is a way out. Youth Against Violence (YAV) and Positive Vibes are such rescue organizations. Burrows and Reid believe that churches should appoint persons who will actively intervene on behalf of gang members who want to leave the gang life. The third factor, rehabilitation, addresses the prevalence of drug use and alcoholism among former and current gang members. Programs such as Teen Challenge, The Haven, Bash, and The Dean Granger have attempted to provide rehabilitation services. Finally, the fourth factor, information, addresses the need for the public to be educated about the dangers of gang activity, what individuals, especially children, can safely wear, and which schools are populated with which gangs.

Particular organizations have been developed to address these needs. They include: YAV, Operation Redemption, and Peace on the Street (Burrows and Reid, 2002; C. Reid, personal communication, September 24, 2002). YAV enrolls former gang members in training facilities such as computer or trade schools. To encourage their involvement in constructive activities, former gang members are also aided in finding employment. Operation Redemption, which is cosponsored by YAV and the Ministry of Youth and Sports, assists young men in particular by supporting their exodus from gangs. Employment assistance is provided through employment in such services as lawn care, home maintenance, and carwash duties. Finally, Peace on the Street, a program developed by Reverend Carlos Reid, seeks to reach gang members on an individual level; that is, this program's mission is to break down the sheep mentality of the "man in the mirror" by awakening the talents of members and presenting alternative behaviors. Participants are also encouraged to rediscover their own social and cultural history and the values associated with community in the Bahamas. It is this rediscovery process that Reid hopes will transform behaviors associated with gang participation to behaviors associated with nationalistic pride.

CONCLUSION

Three factors leading to gang involvement that have particular meaning in the Bahamas are the breakdown of the nuclear family, a sense of territoriality, and a means of challenging the national status quo.

The family structure seems to have changed over the years. In the past, working parents used extended-family members to support and monitor youth after school. Over time, the extended family has separated from this role, and youths are left to their own devices. The affiliation with gangs perhaps provides a false means of replacing community and family.

A sense of territoriality is found particularly on islands where towns and townships are separated, as compared with more industrialized islands such as New Providence, where the island is heavily influenced by the city of Nassau. Local pride is shown by defending territory from outsiders. Stories of school buses being vandalized and certain youths being pulled off buses and beaten by rival gangs support the concern about territorial gangs (F. Williams, personal communication, October 1, 2002). With a developing new national identity, young people are finding means to show their uniqueness through associating with groups that are antiestablishment. In addition, as the Bahamas has been designated as a Christian country (per the constitution), youths seeking gang and religious alternatives may look to Rastafarian or Haitian gangs for the sense of a unique identity. In some areas of Grand Bahama Island, Haitian immigrants make up the majority of the community. F. Williams (personal communication, October 1, 2002) indicates that his experience with Haitian students in the school was that their assimilation into Bahamian culture leads to youths either responding by compliance or by acting out in ganglike activities.

ACKNOWLEDGMENTS

Since much of this chapter is derived from cultural informant interviews done over a series of months, the authors would like to acknowledge a few of our primary sources. Thanks go to Reverend Carlos Reid and his wife, Tiffany, directors of Youth Against Violence/Operation Redemption in

Nassau. Franklyn Williams was helpful in providing us with his experience of gang impact in the schools, particularly as it pertained to Grand Bahama Island. Joan Pinto was helpful in giving us some background on gangs and connecting us with other resources in the community.

REFERENCES

Burrows, D., and C. Reid. *Respect: A review of gang bangin' in the Bahamas* (Nassau, Bahamas: Youth Alive Ministries, 2002).

Consultative Committee on National Youth Development. *Consultative report on national youth development* (Nassau, Bahamas: Government Printing Office, 1995).

Craton, M., and G. Saunders. *Islanders in the stream: A history of the Bahamian people from the ending of slavery to the twenty-first century* (Athens, GA: University of Georgia Press, 1998).

Denzin, N. K., and Y. S. Lincoln. *Handbook of qualitative research*, 2d ed. (Thousand Oaks, CA: Sage Publications, 2000).

Nowak, B. J. "Keeping it better in The Bahamas." *Journal of Black Studies* 31(4) (2001): 483–485.

United States Department of State. *Bahama background information*. http://www.state.gov/r/pa/ei/bgn/1857.htm. November 1, 2002.

3

GREAT BRITAIN

Richard A. Van Dorn

We all see the symptoms of gang violence and need to be working on the causes.

Mother whose son was shot and killed in
Manchester, England, in 1999

INTRODUCTION

As recently as 2001, the generally held notion was that street gangs in Manchester, England, were not part of Britain's "civilized" society (Mares, 2001, p. 153). This view might partially explain why there is little research into British gang culture. From what research is available, it appears that gang behaviors and criminal activity have become more focused and violent, with children joining gangs at earlier ages. News media reports are documenting a picture of British gangs more closely resembling structured and cohesive units, with members focused on the use and distribution of drugs, the commission of violence, the use of weapons, and the protection of fellow gang members (O'Brien, 2002; Thompson, Harris, and Blenford, 2002). While these images may not resonate with British society as a whole, evidence reviewed throughout this chapter indicates that this is indeed the case in certain areas.

Despite the escalation in gangs and gang behaviors in Britain over the past decade and in Europe as a whole, there is still a persistent denial that street gangs are a problem (Klein, 2001). Klein has labeled this denial the "Eurogang Paradox," referring to the notion that since European gangs, in both dress and behavior, are not entirely similar to American gangs, then there must not be a gang problem. Part of the difficulty in recognizing the presence of gangs stems from the fact that American gangs are often used as the reference point (Mares, 2000); however, American gangs frequently do not resemble media stereotypes. Interestingly, as researchers were organizing the Eurogang workshop that was held in 1998, England's Home Office stated that there was not a gang problem and therefore declined to participate in the workshop (Weitekamp, 2001). What can be gleaned from the available research, however, appears to indicate a strong, and continually developing, gang presence in certain parts of Europe (Klein, 2001), leading to the conclusion that more research is needed into the nature and types of gangs present in Europe, including Britain.

PROFILE OF GREAT BRITAIN

Britain is located in western Europe and has a total population of approximately 58 million people, the majority of whom live in the southern and the eastern parts of the country. London is Britain's capital and home to approximately 7 million people. The country is somewhat diverse with regard to ethnicity (English, 81.5 percent; Scottish, 9.6 percent; Irish, 2.4 percent; Welsh, 1.9 percent; Ulster, 1.8 percent; West Indian, Indian, Pakistani, and other, 2.8 percent) and religious affiliation (Anglican, 27 million; Roman Catholic, 9 million; Muslim, 1 million; Presbyterian, 800,000; Methodist, 760,000; Sikh, 400,000; Hindu, 350,000; Jewish, 300,000); however, the level of diversity varies greatly from region to region. In recent decades Britain has experienced an increase in single-parent families. Currently, a single parent heads approximately 22 percent of families with dependent children; more specifically, females head approximately nine of ten single parent families.

Demographics: The Current Situation

No amount of statistical manipulation can conceal what everyone on the estates in our inner cities already knows—that it is the gangs and drug dealers rather than the forces of law and order that are in charge.

Oliver Lewton, Shadow Home Secretary
July 2002

Prior to examining the current gang picture in Britain, it will be advantageous to briefly review definitions of gangs as these definitions provide context and have implications for prevention and intervention strategies. However, as can be seen from the varied definitions presented next, while there may be agreement that gangs exist, there is little consensus as to how

to define them. According to Williams and Van Dorn (1999), four definitions of gangs can be identified from the literature (p. 200–201):

1. A gang is an organized social system that is both quasi-private and quasi-secretive
   and one whose size and goals have necessitated that social interaction be governed
   by a leadership structure that has defined roles; where the authority associated
   with these roles has been legitimized to the extent that social codes are operational
   to regulate behavior of both leadership and rank and file; that plans and provides
   not only for the social and economic services of its members, but also for its own
   maintenance as an organization; that pursues such goals irrespective of whether
   the action is legal or not; and that lacks a bureaucracy (Jankowski, 1991, p. 29).

2. A gang is a group of individuals who have symbols of membership, permanence,
   and criminal involvement. A gang member is a person who acknowledges membership in the gang and is regarded as a gang member by other members (Decker
   and Curry, 1999, p. 247).

3. A gang has the following characteristics: a denotable group comprised primarily
   of males who are committed to delinquent (including criminal) behavior or values
   and who call forth a consistent negative response from the community such that
   the community comes to see them as qualitatively different from other groups
   (Klein, 1995).

4. A gang is a well-defined group of youths between 10 and 22 years old. Most
   research on youth gangs has concluded that the typical age range is 14 to 24,
   although researchers have identified gang members as young as 10 and in some
   areas have identified generational gang members from the same family (Huff,
   1998).

These four definitions of gangs may appear to emphasize different aspects
of what each author feels represents the most salient aspects of gangs and
gang culture; however, there are commonalities. Specifically, social codes
and symbols of membership represent constraints upon external, or public,
behaviors and appearance; criminal involvement and values often undergird
the foundation of gang behaviors and beliefs. Finally, there are varying degrees of acknowledgment; gang members themselves acknowledging membership, other members of the gang acknowledging that that person is a
member, or community members acknowledging that the group is different
from other groups or that the group consistently elicits a negative response
from the community.

Klein (2001) further delineates gangs and gang structures by identifying
five typologies of gangs:

1. The *traditional gang* is large (one to several hundred members) and long-
   standing, often lasting more than 20 years, has distinct subgroups, a wide age
   range, and is territorial.

2. The *neotraditional gang* on the other hand is newer than the traditional gang

(usually ten years old or less) and often has between 50 and 100 members. The neotraditional gang is also strongly territorial, with distinct subgroups.

3. The *compressed gang* usually has up to 50 members and is newer and smaller than previously discussed gangs. The compressed gang is still in a state of developmental flux—it is unclear if it will develop into one of the more complex gangs with a broader age range and distinct subgroups.

4. The *collective gang* is very similar to the compressed gang except that it is older and has a broader range of ages for members. However, the collective gang has yet to develop subgroups and does not have a strong sense of territoriality.

5. The *specialty gang* is different from the other gangs in that its focus is on specific crimes as opposed to a wide variety of offenses. In its criminal specialization, the specialty gang is usually territorial, small—fewer than 50 members—and relatively new—less than 10 years old. (pp. 14–17)

These definitions and typologies demonstrate the multiple complexities that gangs and gang culture present, from simple identification and classification to eventual prevention and intervention strategies. However, as will become evident later, they also demonstrate that much work needs to be done regarding the defining and classification of British gangs, which will help with the implementation of eventual intervention strategies.

The minimization or downplay regarding the current gang problem in Britain makes obtaining a clear and accurate picture of gangs and gang behavior very difficult. However, recent surveys provide insight into how some residents view the current gang situation. The Manchester Crime Survey (MCS) asked residents of Manchester their thoughts on multiple types of crime. When asked about problems in the local area, 44 percent of respondents said that gangs of youths were a "big problem." This level of concern regarding gangs was higher than concern about vandalism, drug and alcohol use, and drug dealing in Manchester (Manchester City Council Crime and Disorder Team, 2001). Another survey, the Crimestoppers Youth Crime Survey, was administered to a nationally representative sample of 10 to 15 year olds. When asked who or what they feared the most, 46 percent of respondents answered "teenage gangs." Again, this level of concern relating to gangs was higher than concern about any other problem including "people on drugs," "drunks," "bullies at school," and "racists" (Crime Reduction College Information Team, 2002).

The Edinburgh Study of Youth Transitions and Crime (ESYTC) is a longitudinal survey of approximately 4,300 youths that explores possible gang membership, in addition to other criminal and delinquent behaviors and attitudes. Specifically, just over 26 percent of 12- to 13-year-old youths surveyed said that they hung around with at least three others and that they described their group as a gang (Smith et al., 2001). Further, boys were statistically no more likely than girls to report that they belonged to a "gang"; however, boys were more likely than girls to say that their "gang" had a name and used special signs or sayings (Smith et al., 2001). While the respondents' use of the term *gang* may not be the same as researchers', the fact that respondents endorsed special signs and sayings for their group lends credibility to some sort of gang behavior or culture for some respondents. The ESYTC also found strong correlations between friends' delinquent involvement and police contact and their own delinquent involvement and own police contact. While much debate exists regarding the causal ordering of friends' or gangs' delinquent behavior and one's own delinquent behavior, the relationship is strong (Battin, Hill, Abbott, Catalano, and Hawkins, 1998).

Two of the largest surveys in Britain, the British Crime Survey (BCS) and the Youth Lifestyles Survey (YLS), do not ask specifically about gang involvement or gang crime. However, each of the surveys provides information that can be seen to be related to gangs and gang behavior. First, the BCS, a nationally representative annual survey of between 10,000 and 40,000 respondents per year, queries individuals about their fear of crime and recent experiences with victimization (Kershaw, Chivite-Matthews, Thomas, and Aust, 2001). Examining four crimes that have traditionally been linked to gangs, 24 percent of those surveyed thought it was either very or fairly likely that they would be burgled in the next year; 11 percent thought it very or fairly likely that they would be robbed or mugged within the next year; and finally, 31 percent and 33 percent of respondents thought it was very or fairly likely that their car would be stolen or they would have something stolen from their car within the next year, respectively. However, the rates of those who worry about crimes associated with gangs were higher. Specifically, 52 percent, 41 percent, 40 percent, and 16 percent of respondents indicated that they were very or fairly worried about being the victim of a burglary, mugging, physical attack, or racially motivated assault, respectively (Kershaw et al., 2001).

The YLS comprises a representative sample of 4,848 twelve to thirty year olds wherein respondents were asked about their own and their friends' levels of criminal involvement. Males with friends who had committed criminal offenses or who had been in trouble with the police were over three times as likely to be involved in criminal offending themselves (Flood-Page, Campbell, Harrington, and Miller, 2000). The relationship between females' offending and that of their friends was even more striking, with a sixfold increase in the likelihood of own offending (Flood-Page et al., 2000). Again, this research does not allow for the causal ordering of the relationship between respondents' offending and their friends' offending.

While some of the research findings reviewed above do not have direct implications for the current gang situation, they can, with caution, be used to indirectly provide information about some aspects of the current gang culture in Britain. Specifically, these data provide insights into the peer and own offending relationship that has empirically been tied to gang membership (Battin et al., 1998), as well as to the perceived significance of crimes routinely associated with gangs.

While there have been few large scale empirical examinations of gangs in Britain, there have been smaller ethnographic case studies restricted to specific locations. It is from these studies that one can glean a significant amount of information regarding the current state of gangs in specific areas of Britain. However, as these are ethnographic case studies restricted to specific locales, their generalizability to Britain as a whole is limited.

Mares reports on various gangs in three different locations of Britain. First, Mares reports on two gangs, the Gooch and Doddington, in Moss Side, near Manchester's city center, exemplifying what appears to be an ever-developing gang situation in certain parts of Britain. Newly formed gangs in the larger metropolitan areas including London, Liverpool, Birmingham, and Manchester appear to have been formed around ethnicity and, more notably, the sale of drugs (Mares, 2001). This focus on the sale of drugs would initially lead one to believe that these gangs would fit well into Klein's typology of specialty gangs. However, a closer look shows that this is not the case (Mares, 2001).

Mares (2001) indicates that the Gooch and Doddington have been in existence since at least the 1980s, when their strong involvement in dealing drugs began. Concomitant with their involvement in drug dealing was an increase in the levels of violence in Moss Side. Specifically, Mares indicates that in the last six months of 1992, police received reports of at least 100 shooting incidents. In the past three years 13 people have been killed, and in the first five months of 2002 there were 20 reported shootings; further, it is believed that most of these violent incidents were related to gangs and the sale of drugs (Joseph, 2002).

With respect to the development of neotraditional gang structures, Mares (2001) indicates that there are upwards of 90 members in each gang, including those who are incarcerated. He also observes a wide age range, between 10 and 30 years old, with subgroups based on age and friendship. Finally, Mares found that gang members in Moss Side were involved in numerous other criminal activities not limited to car thefts, protection rackets, and robberies.

Taken in its totality, it appears that the gangs that Mares (2001) observed in Moss Side have, in spite of their initial focused involvement in the sales of drugs, developed neotraditional status. If this is indeed the case, prevention and intervention efforts are more difficult, as the gang culture is more deeply rooted (Klein, 2001); in some cases, the problem may seem intractable. While Mares's description of gangs in Moss Side is not meant to be representative of the gang situation in Britain, it does provide a picture of difficulties that one area is experiencing.

Mares (2000) also focused on Salford. Besides the geographic difference between Salford and Moss Side and the different racial and ethnic makeup of the gangs, the gangs in these two districts are mostly similar. The gang members in Salford are predominantly white; whereas the majority of gang members in Moss Side are of Afro-Caribbean descent. Regardless, the levels of violence, age range, and size of the gangs are all comparable, with Salford having a slightly smaller number of members in each gang (Mares, 2000).

One other notable difference between gangs in Salford and Moss Side is the link between organized crime and adolescent gangs. As younger gang members "age out" of adolescent gangs, they often ingratiate themselves with an organized crime structure. However, this demarcation between organized crime and adolescent gangs is not distinct; rather, organized crime in Salford is believed to influence adolescent gangs from an "early stage" (Mares, 2000, p. 158).

In contrast to gangs in Moss Side and Salford, which are seen as having a neotraditional structure, the gangs in Wythenshawe, which is located in south Manchester have a more compressed structure (Mares, 2000). The gang members in Wythenshawe are mostly white, with about 25 members ranging in age between 14 and 18, though there are also members outside this age range. Though the criminal patterns of the gangs in Wythenshawe vary, the use of "extreme forms of violence" and the sale of drugs are minimal. These gangs mostly commit smaller, nonviolent crimes, and though there is a strong sense of territoriality that does lead to gang fights, rarely are weapons involved (Mares, 2000). Finally, and perhaps most importantly for compressed gangs, they are often seen as being at a critical stage in development, or in developmental flux (Klein, 2001). Without effective intervention at this point, there is an increased likelihood that these gangs could develop a neotraditional structure with a broader diversity of crimes, more members, and eventually a more violent culture. As is evident from the review above, the types of gangs present in parts of Manchester and their consequent behaviors vary, not only by gang but by geographic location as well.

Thompson (1995), who is a journalist, documents the behaviors of other gangs that he has observed, including but not limited to Jamaican gangs (Yardies) and Asian gangs. In his book *Gangland Britain*, Thompson provides a detailed account of gang culture in London. Again, as with the review of Mares's work above, the same caveats regarding specific locations and generalizability apply here as well.

Thompson paints a very violent and far-reaching picture of gangs in London, especially when discussing the Yardies and Asian gangs. Thompson reports that the Yardies' organization is currently based, and focused, on the sale and distribution of crack cocaine; however, their introduction into the British drug culture started with the sale and distribution of marijuana (Thompson et al., 2002). In support of this point, Thompson indicates that between 1974 and 1978, the amount of marijuana seized in Britain averaged 5,500 pounds (2,500 kilos) per year. In 1979 that amount had more than doubled to 14,200 pounds (6,445 kilos), and in 1980 the amount had increased threefold to over 40,500 pounds (18,400 kilos) (Thompson et al., 2002). However, as the sale of crack is more profitable than the sale of marijuana, Thompson indicates that the Yardies soon shifted their focus. Accordingly, the average cocaine seizures in Britain between 1983 and 1986 were about 175 pounds (80 kilos) per year. However, in 1987 there were 880 pounds (400 kilos) seized (Thompson et al., 2002). Thompson attributes the spikes in the availability of both marijuana and crack cocaine during the 1980s to the Yardies, along with corresponding increases in gun violence and murder. While other structural factors have undoubtedly influenced the increases in the availability of drugs and the incidences of gun violence and murder, Thompson posits that the gang culture is largely responsible.

There are those who believe, as reported in the publication the *New West Indian* (2001), that the Yardies and their violent behaviors, however, are "more myth than reality" and that the police will not formally acknowledge the existence of Yardie gangs. Though the existence and violent culture of Yardie gangs in Britain may be contested, Thompson's position is well supported by in-depth interviews with gang members in addition to reports of special police investigations and task forces designed to reduce the impact of gangs and gang behavior.

Asian gangs in Britain, according to Thompson (1995), were formed out of a need for protection. In the late 1960s and throughout the 1970s, racial tension in Britain increased as a result of perceived job losses to recently immigrated Pakistanis. Consequently, many white youths, mainly skinheads associated with the National Front, began assaulting immigrants, blaming them for their loss of jobs, giving rise to the term *Paki-bashing* (Brake, 1980; Burke and Sunley, 1998). To protect themselves from further attacks, third-generation Asians formed gangs and fought back (Thompson, 1995). Originally, support within the Asian communities for these new "protection" gangs was high; however, that soon changed. According to Thompson (1995), these Asian gangs soon began victimizing members of their own community if they did not pay specified amounts of protection money. Additionally, Asian gangs began importing and selling large quantities of heroin, with current reports indicating that they are trying to diversify their drug sales to include crack cocaine (Thompson, 1995).

Thompson represents Asian gangs in Britain as highly structured, going so far as to describe a multilevel configuration of these gangs as well as their duties and responsibilities. While this level of organization is different from that ascribed to the Yardies, who are seen as operating from a more individualistic perspective (Thompson, 1995), both of these gangs are depicted as highly violent, territorial, and strongly involved in the sale and distribution of drugs.

Thompson's portrayal of Asian gangs as well structured is different from Mares's experiences with the Gooch and Doddington in Moss Side and Salford, which he reports are more individualistic, with delineation between gang activities and the sales of drugs and other criminal activities (Mares, 2001). This portrayal of the Gooch, Doddington, and Salford gangs is more similar to Thompson's picture of Yardie gangs. The different depictions and organizational structures presented above for the Gooch, Doddington, Salford, and Wythenshawe gangs, and Yardie and Asian gangs, reinforce the position that more research into British gang culture is needed.

Regardless of differences in their specific findings, Thompson and Mares both identify gangs as a problem for specific locations in Britain. While gangs in Britain may not resemble American gangs or may not be consistently present or developed throughout the country, it does appear that in certain communities there is a gang presence. Moreover, this gang presence is often linked, either empirically via ethnographic studies or in the popular press, to the sale and distribution of drugs or other criminal activities including protection rackets, car thefts, and robberies. However, much more research is needed, not only to describe the current situation but also to develop and implement interventions.

Finally, it is important to briefly discuss risk and protective factor research and its implications for gangs and gang members (cf., Williams and Van Dorn, 1999). While not specifically designed to study gang behavior or gang involvement, the Cambridge Study in Delinquent Development provides invaluable insights into criminal offending and its consequences. The Cambridge Study, similar to other longitudinal studies in the United States— including the Seattle Social Development Project (Hawkins and Catalano, 1987), the Pittsburgh Youth Study (Loeber, Van Kammen, Farrington, and Stouthamer-Loeber, 1998), the Rochester Youth Development Study (Thornberry, 1987), and the Denver Youth Development Survey (Esbensen and Huizinga, 1993)—attempts to identify the causes and consequences of serious criminal behavior (Farrington, 1995). Accordingly, as seriously delinquent and violent youths are at an increased risk of gang membership, findings from this and other longitudinal studies can also aid in predicting and, more importantly, preventing future gang involvement (Hill, Howell, Hawkins, and Battin-Pearson, 1999). Specific to the Cambridge Study, risk for future delinquency was identified in six different areas (Farrington, 1995):

1. Disruptive childhood behavior
2. Family history of criminal behavior
3. Low intelligence or school failure
4. Parental difficulties in child rearing (e.g., lack of supervision, inconsistent discipline)
5. Impulsivity (e.g., increased risk taking)
6. Economic deprivation.

While not based in Britain, the Seattle Social Development Project (SSDP), which is similar to the Cambridge Study in many respects, has identified various risk factors for gang involvement. In the family domain, characteristics predicting gang involvement include parental attitudes favoring violence, low bonding with parents, low parental income, sibling antisocial behavior, and poor family management practices. Predictive factors in the school domain include having a learning disability, low academic achievement, low school attachment, low school commitment, and low academic aspirations. At the neighborhood level, predictive factors include a high proportion of delinquent youths, the availability of marijuana, and low neighborhood attachment. Individual factors include early marijuana use and early drinking, early violence, antisocial beliefs, externalizing behaviors, and poor refusal skills. Finally, associating with delinquent peers was also linked to future gang involvement (Battin et al., 1998; Hill et al., 1999). These findings from the SSDP, again, while not drawn from a British sample, do provide another avenue for future investigations and cross-national studies of British gangs and gang behavior.

HISTORY OF GANGS IN BRITAIN

Because they had not the mental stamina to be individuals they had to huddle together in gangs. . . . It is the desire to do evil, not lack of comprehension which forces them into crime.

Article from the *Evening News* written by
a physician describing Teddy Boys
December 1954

There is little debate that Britain has a long and varied history of "gangs" of youths (Humphries, 1995; Thompson, 1995; Wallace, 1962). Some, however, find it easier or more appropriate to label Britain's historical gang context as that of multiple "subcultures" (Burke and Sunley, 1998), as opposed to gangs or, more specifically, specialized gangs (Klein, 2001). This review will briefly focus on four types of historical gangs, or youth subcultures, present in Britain from the 1950s forward: Teddy Boys, Mods, Rockers, and Skinheads. For a comprehensive review of gangs during the time period between 1889 and 1939, see Stephen Humphries's book, *Hooligans or Rebels*.

Teddy Boys, or Teds, have been described as youths that congregated in an attempt to "defend, symbolically, a constantly threatened space and a declining status" (Jefferson, 1976, p. 81). This level of "defense" was in response to growing structural inequalities of postwar Britain that resulted in the loss of space, specifically land, which consequently led to the erosion of extended kinship networks (Burke and Sunley, 1998; Jefferson, 1976).

The subsequent development of "group-mindedness" was an attempt to reaffirm traditional slum-working-class values and a strong sense of territory (Jefferson, 1976).

In an attempt to reclaim what they perceived was being taken from them (for example, land, identity), Teddy Boys developed a unique style of dress that had been historically identified with aristocratic or well-to-do segments of the population, originally in an attempt to buy status; however, with later modifications, the Teds used their style of dress to differentiate themselves from other groups (Jefferson, 1976). This style of dress, which was often seen as effeminate (Brake, 1980), can also be seen as a partial catalyst for the Teds' extreme touchiness to insults, which often led to highly publicized fights or violence. Jefferson's and Brake's hypotheses about the Teds' propensity to fight with other youths or with other groups of Teddy Boys were linked to the Teds' perceived lack of status. All the Teds believed they had was self and the cultural expression of self through dress and appearance (Jefferson, 1976), and when they were insulted or viewed as feminine, the Teds' first response was to fight back or become violent (Brake, 1980).

While the Teds' unique style of dress was one basis for fighting and violence, their worsening social position was another. In the 1950s the Teds perceived the influx of Cypriot people as causal to, instead of coincidental to, their worsening social conditions. Consequently, Teds were involved in many highly publicized attacks on Cypriot people and their businesses. This eventually culminated in the 1958 race riots in Nottingham and Notting Hill (Jefferson, 1976).

Teddy Boys are also remembered for their attacks on youth clubs and bus conductors. Jefferson posits that the attacks on clubs were simply revenge tactics, the result of Teddy Boys being banned from many clubs, sometimes on reputation alone. The attacks on bus drivers were often fueled by alcohol and ease of escape, as they often took place late at night (Jefferson, 1976).

Emerging subsequent to the Teddy Boys were the Mods. The main pursuit of the Mod life was simple: leisure and living solely for the night in an attempt to compensate for their lowly daytime status (Hebdige, 1976). The Mods developed their unique style, including dress, in response to—or maybe, more appropriately, in opposition to—conservative working-class values; the Mods strived for, and lived, the "practice of cool" (Hebdige, 1976, p. 74). Whether it was the art-school high-camp Mods wearing makeup and carrying handbags, the mainstream Mods dressed in suits and pointed shoes, or the scooter boys with their decadent chromed scooters (Brake, 1980), the relevance of style to the Mods cannot be overstated, as it was all about style (Hebdige, 1976).

The Mods were highly influenced by the "indigenous British gangster style" (Hebdige, 1976, p. 89). Well-known protection gangs from South and East London began recruiting working-class teenagers into a surreptitious lifestyle rife with intergang warfare that ideally suited the Mod lifestyle

(Hebdige, 1976). In order to maintain this lifestyle, which was focused on nightlife, Mods quickly became intimate with, and dependent upon, the use of amphetamines (Burke and Sunley, 1998; Hebdige, 1976).

At the same time the Mods were about, another group of youths known as Rockers were also present and often clashing—albeit sometimes greatly exaggerated by the media—with the Mods (Brake, 1980; Hebdige, 1976). Pete Townshend's rock opera *Quadrophenia*, based on the Mod experience (released as a film in 1979), also featured aspects of the often tumultuous relationship between the Mods and the Rockers. The Rockers, while often viewed in a historical context as inseparable from the Mods, were their exact cultural opposite (Brake, 1980). As opposed to the Mods' highly stylized appearance and cool demeanor, the Rockers were aggressive and seen as very masculine (Brake, 1980; Burke & Sunley, 1998).

The Rockers were entrenched in unskilled manual labor, trapped in the working-class culture. Ironically, the Rockers fought to reject this connection to working-class culture (Burke and Sunley, 1998), often subscribing to a nomadic romanticism that was sometimes violent, with loyalties only to each other. The Mods were highly antiauthority and antidomestic (Brake, 1980)—they believed themselves to be "real men" (Burke and Sunley, 1998).

Brake describes two types of Rockers: the Bikers and the Greasers. The Bikers, synonymous with Marlon Brando's classic role in the *Wild Ones*, were dressed in black leather and studs. They viewed the motorcycle not only as transportation, but as an object of intimidation and mastery that reaffirmed to them, and projected to others, their sense of masculinity (Brake, 1980). The Greasers, on the other hand, were not tied to the motorcycle. However, in every other way they were similar to the Bikers—from their "studied scruffiness" (Brake, 1980, p. 77) and aggressive masculinity to their palpable contempt for the Mods (Brake, 1980; Burke and Sunley, 1998).

Finally, Skinheads emerged in the late 1960s as an offshoot of the hard Mods (Brake, 1980; Burke and Sunley, 1998). Their differentiation from other groups also came in their dress and style; however, the skinheads' expression of their attitudes was something entirely different from others. Skinheads wore a distinctive uniform of boots; close-cropped hair; short, wide jeans; and braces over button-down shirts (Burke and Sunley, 1998, p. 45). This style of dress, much like the Rockers', communicated a sense of being hard and macho, masculine, conservative, and territorial (Brake, 1980; Burke and Sunley, 1998). More memorable than their dress, style, and territoriality, however, were their racist values and attitudes. It is their racist behavior that has garnered much infamy for skinheads. As stated previously, skinheads were involved in what came to be known as Paki-bashing, or assaulting Asian immigrants. However, skinhead violence was not limited to Asian immigrants, or even race. Skinheads also attacked hippies, students, and homosexuals (Brake, 1980).

The high degree of open hostility expressed toward other groups by skin-heads has been viewed as an effort to reestablish traditional working class values and recover territory that was seen as being threatened by the influx of immigrants (Brake, 1980). However, as Pearce and Brake have previously argued, the racist attitudes expressed by skinheads can be equally seen as a function of traditionally held values toward homosexuals and immigrants by mainstream Britons (Brake, 1980; Pearce, 1973). Skinheads, however, became a convenient media target and were labeled as deviant, thus allowing for the dismissal or minimization of British "immigration and race relations legislation" and populist attitudes (Brake, 1980, p. 78).

One of the more interesting issues of resonance between the current and historical gang or youth subcultural contexts in Britain is the belief that they are the result of youths' position of relative disadvantage due to deindustrialization, which led to increased status frustration (Mares, 2000). American scholars have advanced similar positions, most notably William Julius Wilson (1991). Wilson (1987, 1996) argued that between the 1970s and the 1990s, when macrostructural changes related to the deindustrialization of central cities occurred, the majority of residents in central cities were low-income minorities. These macrostructural changes included a shift from goods-producing to service-producing industries and a relocation of manufacturing jobs from central cities, thereby polarizing the labor market into high- and low-wage opportunities (Sampson, 2001). With this polarization, there was a subsequent out-migration of middle- and upper-income families, especially African American families, from central cities. This out-migration removed a potential social buffer that could have deflected some of the effects of prolonged joblessness and industrial transformation (Sampson, 2001; Wilson, 1987). A similar argument is being made for Britain's historical development and current state of gangs and youth subcultures.

GANGS TODAY: POLITICAL VIEWS AND PUBLIC POLICIES

It is all very well for him to come here and shed crocodile tears, but the authorities never do anything.

Resident of Longsite commenting on
the Lord Mayor of Manchester's speech
and the perceived political inaction
regarding the gang problem,
June 2002

As has been discussed previously in this chapter, there appears to have been a general denial that gangs are broadly present in Britain, or that they represent much of a problem (Weitekamp, 2001). It is not surprising then that there has been little specific public policy directed toward gang prevention or intervention.

One exception is the city of Manchester, which is taking an aggressive approach to minimizing gang behavior (Crime and Disorder Team, 2001). Manchester's willingness to address gang-related issues might have been motivated by the results of the Manchester Crime and Disorder Audit previously discussed (Manchester City Council Crime and Disorder Team, 2001). Specifically, the residents of Manchester have made it clear that one priority is the reduction of gang and gang behavior, which the majority of these residents feel has increased in the past two years (Manchester City Council Crime and Disorder Team, 2001). Key findings from this audit led the Manchester City Council, in collaboration with other agencies, to develop ten key priorities for the reduction of gang and other violent behavior.

Of Manchester's ten priorities, priority one—the reduction of street violence—is the most closely tied to gang culture and therefore has interventions specifically targeted at the reduction of gangs and gang behavior. Specifically, the recently created Manchester Multi Agency Gang Strategy (MMAGS), composed of resources from the Greater Manchester Police, the National Probation Service of the Greater Manchester Area, and the Manchester City Council, was developed to address the causes of gang membership and provides "opportunities and support for alternative and more positive life choices" (Greater Manchester Police, 2002, p. 1).

To accomplish these goals of prevention, deterrence, and consequences, the MMAGS has identified six action steps (Crime and Disorder Team, 2001):

1. Enforce the law through multiagency targeted crackdowns
2. Deter young people from entering into a gang/gun culture and divert them toward alternatives
3. Provide support to young people and families who are most vulnerable
4. Secure the conviction and/or rehabilitation of gang-involved offenders
5. Reduce the wider impact of gangs on the community
6. Create an environment for commercial investment.

In addition to these action steps, the MMAGS aims to improve the quality of information available to the members of the partnership. This includes collection and analysis of data on a monthly basis and distribution of information on trends and characteristics of street violence to participating agencies.

Other priority areas identified by the Manchester Crime and Disorder Team (2001) include the reduction of robbery, residential burglary, vehicle crime, youth nuisance, antisocial behavior, racist incidents, and drug-related crime. For each of the priorities identified, the Manchester Crime and Disorder Team has also delineated goals, action steps, and related interventions.

THE FUTURE OF BRITISH GANGS

It is all about people coming together and agreeing on one subject and saying that enough is enough.

Organizer of the Gangstop March that
took place in Manchester in 2002

The ability to predict the course of British gangs is difficult, as so little empirical work has been done on the subject, especially when compared to the surfeit of research regarding gangs in the U.S. For instance, the following questions regarding gangs in Britain remain unanswered. How many gangs and gang members are there? What is the racial and ethnic background and ages of these gang members? In what types of behaviors are these gangs and gang members involved? What types of weapons are at their disposal? These questions and their relevance can be seen in the various gangs that have been reviewed in this chapter. All of the gangs, whether in Moss Side, Wythenshawe, or London, were focused on different activities, were differentially organized, and had different levels of access to and usage of weapons.

Prior efforts by law enforcement agencies to intervene by grouping together delinquent peers have resulted in iatrogenic effects (Dishion, McCord, and Poulin, 1999), as has been the case with gang members (Klein, 1969). Specifically, the bringing together of gang members, or youths with highly antisocial behaviors, attitudes, and value structures often results in the reinforcement and strengthening of these values, not the intended opposite (Henggeler, Melton, and Smith, 1992).

Second, future research and interventions ought to be grounded in a risk and protective factor framework. Adhering to this perspective allows for the identification of multiple leverage points. As exemplified in Farrington's (1995) findings from the Cambridge Study, identifying risk and protective factors allows for targeted interventions gleaned from prospective longitudinal research designs. By answering questions such as those mentioned above, interventions and policies based on empirically validated typologies of gangs can be implemented.

CONCLUSION

It is clear that the historical or theatrical view of Ace Face and his fellow Mods doing battle with the Rockers in Brighton does not approximate the current situation. Instead, gangs in certain parts of Britain more closely consist of groups of youths organized around race and ethnicity (Mares, 2000), the sale of drugs and other delinquent activities, and loss of identity or place in society (Jefferson, 1976; Mares, 2000), who sometimes exhibit extreme violence facilitated by access to weapons (Mares, 2000, 2001; Thompson, 1995).

Further, the gangs reviewed in this chapter cannot be pigeonholed into a single typology. Each gang serves different functions, is organized around different principles, and can be expected to have a different life span. Therefore, when intervening, one must treat each gang according to its own unique characteristics. However, even prior to intervention there must be a clear picture of the current gang situation, not just in certain cities or enclaves but also throughout the country.

Specifically, if it is discovered that urban areas are no longer the sole domain of gangs, as appears is the case in Wythenshawe, a suburb of Manchester, attention must also be focused on suburban areas. Indeed, as research from the United States has shown, once the population of an area reaches 50,000 individuals, there is little to no difference in how many adolescents report a presence of gangs in their school, and even at lower population thresholds, the likelihood of students' acknowledging a gang presence is still high (Howell and Lynch, 2000). More to the point, gangs in America are no longer an urban phenomenon; instead, they have moved into, or developed in, suburban and rural areas. It must be determined whether this is the case in parts of Britain. Further, newly developed gangs in all locations, if not addressed, have the potential to move from specialty or compressed gangs to neotraditional gangs to traditional gangs. To decrease the likelihood of this progression occurring, targeted interventions and policies are best implemented early.

Britain, like the rest of the countries reviewed in this book, still has much work to do in describing and minimizing the impact of adolescent gangs. However, Manchester has had success with the implementation and evaluation of its Crime and Disorder Reduction Strategy based on priorities shaped by community input and research. Part of the process for the rest of Britain begins with asking the right questions and the recognition of a gang problem in certain parts of Britain. Many residents of Britain are calling for a decisive and effective action in remedying the current state of gangs in their country.

REFERENCES

Battin, S., K. G. Hill, R. Abbott, R. F. Catalano, and J. D. Hawkins. "The contribution of gang membership to delinquency beyond delinquent friends." *Criminology* 36(1) (1998): 93–115.

Brake, M. *The sociology of youth culture and youth subcultures: Sex and drugs and rock 'n' roll?* (London: Routledge & Kegan Paul, 1980).

Burke, R., and R. Sunley. "Post-modernism and youth subcultures in Britain in the 1990s." In *Gangs and youth subcultures: International explorations*, edited by K. Hazlehurst and C. Hazlehurst (London: Transaction Publishers, 1998), pp. 35–66.

Crime and Disorder Team. *Manchester crime and disorder reduction strategy 2002–2005: Making Manchester safe* (Manchester: Manchester City Council, 2001).

Crime Reduction College Information Team. *Crimestoppers youth crime survey.* Crimereduction.gov.uk, October 2002.

Decker, S. H., and G. D. Curry. "Gang prevention and intervention with African American males." In *Working with African American males: A guide to practice*, edited by L. E. Davis (Thousand Oaks, CA: Sage Publications, 1999), pp. 247–258.

Dishion, T. J., J. McCord, and F. Poulin. "When interventions harm: Peer groups and problem behavior." *American Psychologist* 54(9) (1999): 755–764.

Esbensen, F., and D. Huizinga. "Gangs, drugs, and delinquency in a survey of urban youth." *Criminology* 31(4) (1993): 565–589.

Farrington, D. P. "The development of offending and antisocial behaviour from childhood: Key findings from the Cambridge Study in Delinquent Development." *Journal of Child Psychology and Psychiatry* 36 (1995): 929–964.

Flood-Page, C., S. Campbell, V. Harrington, and J. Miller. *Youth crime: Findings from the 1998/99 Youth Lifestyles Survey* (London: Home Office, 2000).

Greater Manchester Police. *Gang violence being targeted by partners* (press release) (Manchester: Greater Manchester Police, 2002).

Hawkins, J. D., and R. F. Catalano. *The Seattle Social Development Project: Progress report on a longitudinal study* (Washington, DC: National Institute on Drug Abuse, 1987).

Hebdige, D. "The meaning of Mod." In *Resistance through rituals: Youth subcultures in post-war Britain*, edited by S. Hall and T. Jefferson (London: Hutchinson, 1976), pp. 87–98.

Henggeler, S. W., G. B. Melton, and L. A. Smith. "Family preservation using multisystemic therapy: An effective alternative to incarcerating serious juvenile offenders." *Journal of Consulting and Clinical Psychology* 60 (1992): 953–961.

Hill, K. G., J. C. Howell, J. D. Hawkins, and S. R. Battin-Pearson. "Childhood risk factors for adolescent gang membership: Results from the Seattle Social Development Project." *Journal of Research in Crime and Delinquency* 36(3) (1999): 300–322.

Howell, J. C., and J. P. Lynch. *Youth gangs in schools* (NCJ 183015) (Washington, DC: U.S. Department of Justice, Office of Justice Programs, Office of Juvenile Justice and Delinquency Prevention, 2000).

Huff, C. R. *Comparing the criminal behavior of youth gangs and at-risk youths* (Washington, DC: U.S. Department of Justice, Office of Justice Programs, 1998).

Humphries, S. *Hooligans or rebels? An oral history of working-class childhood and youth 1889–1939* (Cambridge, MA: Blackwell Publishers, 1995).

Jankowski, M. *Islands in the street: Gangs and American urban society* (Berkeley, CA: University of California Press, 1991).

Jefferson, T. "Cultural responses of the Teds." In *Resistance through rituals: Youth subcultures in post-war Britain*, edited by S. Hall and T. Jefferson (London: Hutchinson, 1976), pp. 81–86.

Joseph, C. Residents march against guns. *BBC News* [Television broadcast], June 1, 2002.

Kershaw, C., N. Chivite-Matthews, C. Thomas, and R. Aust. *The 2001 British Crime Survey* (London: Home Office, 2001).

Klein, M. "Gang cohesiveness, delinquency and a street work program." *Journal of Research in Crime and Delinquency* 6(1) (1969): 135–166.

———. *The American street gang: Its prevalence and control* (New York: Oxford University Press, 1995).

———. "Resolving the Eurogang paradox." In *The Eurogang paradox: Street gangs and youth groups in the U.S. and Europe*, edited by M. W. Klein, H. J. Kerner, C. L. Maxson, and E.G.M. Weitekamp (Dordrecht, The Netherlands: Kluwer Academic Publishers, 2001), pp. 7–20.

Loeber, R., W. B. Van Kammen, D. P. Farrington, and M. Stouthamer-Loeber. *Antisocial behavior and mental health problems: Explanatory factors in childhood and adolescence* (Mahwah, NJ: Lawrence Erlbaum Associates, 1998).

Manchester City Council Crime and Disorder Team. *Manchester Crime and Disorder Audit 1998–2001* (Manchester, UK: Manchester City Council, 2001).

Mares, D. "Globalization and gangs: The Manchester case." *Focaal* 35 (2000): 1000–1019.

———. "Gangstas or lager louts? Working class street gangs in Manchester." In *The Eurogang paradox: Street gangs and youth groups in the U.S. and Europe*, edited by M. W. Klein, H. J. Kerner, C. L. Maxson, and E.G.M. Weitekamp (Dordrecht, The Netherlands: Kluwer Academic Publishers, 2001), pp. 153–164.

Maxson, C. L. "A proposal for multi-site study of European gangs and youth groups." In *The Eurogang paradox: Street gangs and youth groups in the U.S. and Europe*, edited by M. W. Klein, H. J. Kerner, C. L. Maxson, and E.G.M. Weitekamp (Dordrecht, The Netherlands: Kluwer Academic Publishers, 2001), pp. 299–307.

The New West Indian. "Who are the Yardies?" *The New West Indian* 10 (2001).

O'Brien, J. "Gangs raising specter of fear." *London Free Press* (13 July 2002).

Pearce, F. "How to be immoral, pathetic, dangerous, and sick all at the same time." In *Mass media and social problems*, edited by J. Young and S. Cohen (London: Constable, 1973).

Sampson, R. J. "How do communities undergird or undermine human development? Relevant contexts and social mechanisms." In *Does it take a village? Community effects on children, adolescents, and families*, edited by A. Booth and A. C. Crouter (Mahwah, NJ: Lawrence Erlbaum Associates, 2001), pp. 3–30.

Smith, D. J., S. McVie, R. Woodward, J. Shute, J. Flint, and L. McAra. *The Edinburgh Study of Youth Transitions and Crime: Key findings at ages 12 and 13* (Edinburgh, UK: University of Edinburgh Centre for Law and Society, 2001).

Thompson, T. *Gangland Britain: Inside Britain's most dangerous gangs* (London: Hodder and Stoughton, 1995).

Thompson, T., P. Harris, and A. Blenford. "They're lethal, unfeeling—and no one can touch them." *The Observer* (28 April 2002).

Thornberry, T. P. "Toward an interactional theory of delinquency." *Criminology* 25 (1987): 863–891.

Wallace, E. *When the gangs came to London* (London: Arrow Books, 1962).

Weitekamp, E.G.M. "Gangs in Europe: Assessments at the millennium." In *The Eurogang paradox: Street gangs and youth groups in the U.S. and Europe*, edited by M. W. Klein, H. J. Kerner, C. L. Maxson, and E.G.M. Weitekamp (Dordrecht, The Netherlands: Kluwer Academic Publishers, 2001), pp. 309–322.

Williams, J. H., and R. A. Van Dorn. "Delinquency, gangs, and youth violence." In *Youth violence: Current research and recent practice innovations*, edited by J. M. Jenson and M. O. Howard (Washington, DC: NASW Press, 1999), pp. 199–225.

Wilson, W. J. *The truly disadvantaged: The inner city, the underclass, and public policy* (Chicago: University of Chicago Press, 1987).

———. "Studying inner-city social dislocations: The challenge of public agenda research." *American Sociological Review* 56(1) (1991):1–14.

———. *When work disappears: The world of the new urban poor* (New York: Knopf, 1996).

4

HONDURAS

Anthony Borrow and Jennifer Walker

INTRODUCTION

The phenomenon of delinquent teen street gangs in Honduras is epidemic, with a dramatic increase in the number of self-identifying gang members and gangs in both urban and rural parts of the country. However, this is not simply a Honduran phenomenon and, in fact, is very much related to factors in the United States. In many ways U.S. economic policies, U.S. immigration laws, and U.S. street gangs have influenced the proliferation of gangs not only in Honduras but throughout Central America.

The formation of self-identifying teen street gangs has created much fear, confusion, and anger in Honduran communities. It is difficult to travel to parts of Honduras and not see walls painted with graffiti that indicate which gang claims that turf. It is commonplace to be assaulted by gang members, and residents in the poorer barrios are well accustomed to being robbed and do not trust the police or their ability to effectively intervene. As an example of police inefficiency, only 5 percent of the perpetrators of violent death were captured (Girón, 2002). Delinquency has gradually escalated in Honduras to such an extreme that it seems as if nobody is safe, not even in one's own home (Girón, 2002). The Honduran government's response to these gangs has resulted in a zero-tolerance policy, which, in turn, has led to accusations of human rights violations that include social cleansing and death squads to eliminate the problem of these teen gangs. Such attempts to eradicate current gang members are shortsighted and doomed to failure, as there are many more young persons ready to take their place. To form

an adequate response to the phenomenon of teen street gangs, it is important to understand the various individual, social, and global factors that have
influenced and supported their formation. A little background information
about Honduras may help set the stage for understanding its gang phenomenon.

PROFILE OF HONDURAS

The Republic of Honduras, located in Central America, is bordered to
the northwest by Guatemala, to the west by El Salvador, and to the south
by Nicaragua. The Caribbean Sea rims most of the northern part of Honduras. There are approximately 6.4 million people living in Honduras's estimated area of 43,300 square miles (112,090 square kilometers). The
country is divided into 18 departments for administrative purposes. The
most populous towns are the capital city of Tegucigalpa (1,127,600), San
Pedro Sula (486,800), La Ceiba (112,700), and El Progreso (111,300).
Approximately 53 percent of the total population are 19 years of age or
younger (U.S. Census Bureau, 2000). Statistical analysis of demographic
information reveals a significantly higher propensity to commit crime for
young persons in Latin America than in other countries (Leyva, 2001).

Economically, Honduras is one of the poorest countries in the Western
Hemisphere. Unemployment is high (23 percent) and more than half the
population lives below the poverty line. As a result, there is intense competition for work, and wages are maintained at a low level. The typical wage
is generally inadequate to provide for the basic necessities of daily living
(food, clothing, and shelter). As a result, many families are separated, as one
or both parents venture north to the United States in search of work. Further complicating the situation is the general inadequacy of the educational
system. In 2001 it was estimated that 27.3 percent of the population over
the age of 15 were unable to read and write. Statistically, Honduras tied
with Nicaragua for the lowest literacy level in Latin America, with an average
of 4.74 years of schooling for 25-year-olds (Immigration and Naturalization
Services, 1999). Inadequate skills and training produce an ever-increasing
number of unskilled laborers.

After several decades of military control, a democratic civilian government
was elected in 1982. The current president of Honduras, Ricardo Maduro,
has declared war on common and organized crime. This war targets delinquency and, in particular, members of teen street gangs. Corruption has
been a theme that Cardinal Oscar Andres Rodriguez has spoken against
("Cardenal," April 14, 2001). There are several instances of members of the
police force being involved in the sale and distribution of drugs. Laws are
poorly enforced, and many homicides are not adequately investigated. There
is a general sense of mistrust between the citizens and the police ("Gautama
acusa a la Policía," May 31, 2002).

In summary, a number of factors work against Honduran youths, including: demographics, poverty, poor education, drug abuse, disintegration of the family, violence, reduced employment opportunities, and corruption. These factors have resulted in profound desperation and hopelessness that predispose youths to violence and prepare them for gang membership (Equipo de Reflexión, Investigación, y Comunicación [ERIC, IDESO, IDIES, IUDOP], 2001, p. 266).

BASIC POLICIES, LEGISLATION, AND DEMOGRAPHIC INFORMATION RELEVANT TO TEEN GANGS

It is estimated that there are about 100,000 gang members in Honduras (Torres, 2002); however, this number is greatly disputed. President Maduro estimates the number to be about 6,000 (*Maduro impulsa*, 2002). The huge discrepancy is largely because of the difficulty in defining and identifying gang members. There are many gang sympathizers—young children often support gang members even if they do not agree with or understand some of the delinquent behavior and violence associated with the gangs.

Delinquency and violence have generated significant interest since 1990, when statistical information relating to crime and delinquency rates increasingly began to emerge. A recent report analyzes crime and delinquency during the period between 1996 and 2000; however, only 13 of the 18 departments were able to submit data for this period (Leyva, 2001). Nevertheless, it is important to recognize that little or no reliable information was previously available to analyze criminality in Honduras. Currently, there are four main sources for information: the police, the DGIC (Department of Criminal Investigation), the forensic examiner, and medical records.

Utilizing numbers from the police department, Table 4.1 shows crimes reported in Honduras from 1994 to 2002. However, it should be noted that police records tend to produce lower results than those from the DGIC. Further, it should be understood that the tabulated data is incomplete, as it represents only 218 of the 298 municipalities; 80 of the municipalities have not implemented procedures for gathering such data (Girón, 2002).

Legislative Codes

Two major legislative codes promulgated by the National Congress of Honduras relate to gangs. The first is the *Código de la Niñez y de la Adolescencia*. The second code, *Ley de Policia y de Convivencia Social*, was instituted in March of 2002 and deals with law enforcement and the community.

In 1990 the National Congress of Honduras published the *Código de la Niñez y de la Adolescencia* to formally recognize the rights of children and adolescents and to serve as a guide to the principles that should be taken into consideration when creating national economic, social, and cultural pol-

Table 4.1
Recorded Deaths and Punishable Crimes in Honduras 1994–2002

Year	1994	1995	1996	1997	1998	1999	2000	2001	2002	Total
Violent Deaths	2076	2148	2418	2520	2505	2337	2176	2342	755	19277
Death by Car Accident	734	643	695	501	413	642	625	740	140	5133
Deaths (Other causes)	969	941	582	472	0	551	215	219	85	4034
Total Deaths	3779	3732	3695	3493	2918	3530	3016	3301	980	28444
Injured	4257	2285	3469	2430	2556	1939	2221	2521	852	22530
Lesions (Knife or machete wounds)	3170	1642	1532	1437	1192	1614	1785	2050	670	15092
Car Accident	12041	2449	1796	2254	2737	4979	5833	4715	1745	38549
Assault	683	283	672	526	55	73	119	103	28	2542
Theft	2633	1000	341	412	851	1018	3687	3803	1184	14929
Car Theft	1296	1668	1881	1708	1530	1398	1930	1850	750	14011
Rape	91	15	18	13	26	15	69	230	70	547
Kidnappings	4	13	31	17	19	24	13	37	12	170

Note: Figures from "27 mil hondureños han muerto violentamente desde 1994" [27 thousand
Hondurans have died violently since 1994], by C.E. Girón, 2002, *La Prensa*.

icies. Since many gang members are minors, it is important to understand the existing legislation regarding the rights of children and adolescents.

According to the *Código*, children have the right to life, health, social security, dignity, freedom of expression, education, sports and recreation, the environment, and a family. The protection of these rights is the responsibility of society as a whole, even though the direct care is the responsibility of the parents.

Article 24 protects the dignity of the child from inhumane, violent, atrocious, humiliating, or destructive treatment, even if such treatment is intended as a form of discipline or correction. Yet teen gang members are subject to inhumane and violent treatment on a daily basis. Although children have the right to seek refuge, help, and direction when they are the victims of abuse, in practice, those rights do not apply to teen gang members. Articles 93 and 94 state that the government is responsible for taking preventive and disciplinary measures against the threats to, or violations of, children's rights; however, such measures are not applied when the same government is involved in violating the child's rights.

The *Código de la Niñez y de la Adolescencia* outlines the basic legislation in place to protect teens from various dangers that may negatively influence their psychological, social, and moral development. It also states what rights children have, and calls for the creation of programs to support the healthy development of children and adolescents. Finally, it outlines how children who are at "social risk" and who have come into conflict with the law are to be treated. These laws represent the ideal, but the reality of how children and adolescents are treated is quite different. Although programs for reporting child abuse or children with drug abuse problems exist in name, these programs are either not utilized by the public because of their ineffectiveness or are simply facades with no real programs in place.

HISTORY OF HONDURAN GANGS

Around 1992, due to a change in U.S. immigration laws, there was a mass deportation of Salvadoran youth from the Los Angeles area. While many of the parents worked, these Latino youths had been thrust into an unknown culture where they had to struggle to differentiate themselves. Eventually, Latino street gangs were formed in Los Angeles, the two most prominent being the 13th Street and 18th Street gangs. When the Salvadoran members of these gangs were deported back to El Salvador, they brought with them what they had learned in the streets of Los Angeles, along with a lot of anger. Thus, the gang phenomenon as it exists today in Honduras was introduced to Central America and began to spread. Similarly, Honduran youth who spent time in the U.S. and were subsequently deported brought back experiences that were often violent and filled with hardship. By 1993 the gang problem seemed to be spreading from the larger cities to the more rural areas of Honduras (Equipo de Reflexión, Investigación, y Comunicación [ERIC, IDESO, IDIES, IUDOP], 2001).

By 1996 reports of gang-related violence were increasingly more common, with the majority of the attacks taking place in schools (Equipo de Reflexión, Investigación, y Comunicación [ERIC, IDESO, IDIES, IUDOP], 2001). In 1997 it became commonplace to read about gang members killed or wounded, and the words *maras* (gangs) and *chimbas* (handmade pipe guns) had come into common usage. It is estimated that by 1997, there were about 200 gangs with about 35,000 members in San Pedro Sula, the second most populous city. However, these numbers were somewhat exaggerated, as they did not distinguish between gang sympathizers and the more permanent hard-core members (Equipo de Reflexión, Investigación, y Comunicación [ERIC, IDESO, IDIES, IUDOP], 2001). The more conservative estimates in 1998 indicated that there were approximately 6,000 gang members in the San Pedro Sula area. Nevertheless, by 1998, the newspapers claimed that there were "more than 60,000 young persons in gangs in all of Honduras," and more than 151 gangs in the capital city of Tegucigalpa, with approximately 14,848 youths involved (11,987 males and 2,861 females). The article also claimed that about 22,000 more youths were gang sympathizers and were ready to join the gangs. In 2001 various human rights groups estimated that there were approximately 100,000 gang members in Tegucigalpa (Agence France Presse, 2001).

In Honduras, the two major gang cliques are the 18th Street and 13th Street cliques, each of which contains several gangs. The *Mara Salvatrucha*, a gang originally from El Salvador, and the *Vatos Locos* are predominantly associated with the 13th Street clique. Members of a 13th Street clique are generally the enemies of those associated with the 18th Street cliques. There is a general sense of partnership among members of the different gangs that belong to the 13th Street clique. Most of this partnership comes from shared experiences in detention facilities, where 13th Street and 18th Street groups are segregated from one another for security reasons. Gang members arriving at a detention facility will seek out protection from members of their clique, thus solidifying the bonds between different gangs of the same clique (Equipo de Reflexión, Investigación, y Comunicación [ERIC, IDESO, IDIES, IUDOP], 2001).

Political and Social Responses

In October 1998, in an effort to combat increasing occurences of street crimes, the military was sent into the major cities of Honduras to support the police forces. However, these measures did not prove successful and public frustration grew, leading to strong support of vigilante justice (Immigration and Naturalization Services, 1999). In a 1996 study, 41.6 percent of the respondents identified delinquency over poverty (10.39 percent), unemployment (12.69 percent), and the cost of living (17.38 percent) (Leyva, 2001) as the major problem affecting Honduras.

Current political efforts are aimed at improving the general sense of security. President Maduro has initiated a zero-tolerance policy on delinquency that targets two major groups: teen gang members and those involved in kidnappings. However, such policies have not erased the people's general mistrust of the police force, which has been accused of corruption for several years. Gang members claimed that they had received names, weapons, and money from police officers to kill rival gang members, so that the police would not have to enter gang-infested neighborhoods (personal communication, sources within Honduras, July 2002). Other police personnel have been accused of receiving money and organizing the sale and distribution of drugs. All of this has produced a general public mistrust of the police to the extent that the public is often uncooperative with police investigations. In part, the silence is supported by a fear of retribution. If people give information to police that leads to the arrest of a gang member, they have good reason to believe that they, too, may become victims of gang violence. The police seem to be unable to provide a sense of protection, and the current political climate has led to the creation of community watch groups (*comités de vigilancia*). These watch groups, however, have much more authority than neighborhood watch groups in the United States. As an example, one community watch group charges 50 *lempiras* (approximately $3) per month per household. These funds are used to buy weapons and ammunition for the watch group. The members of the watch group have the power to question, detain, remove, beat, or shoot, at their discretion, anyone who seems to be providing a nuisance to the community or who seems to be involved in gang-related activity. The watch groups have been created in the 123 municipalities that have the highest level of insecurity and violent crime, at a cost of 25 million *lempiras* (approximately $1.5 million).

A curfew has been established, and any minor found in the streets after 10:00 P.M. can be taken to the police station. The curfew attempts to restore a sense of safety and control to the evening streets and, for the most part, is respected.

Political Initiatives and Policies to Address the Teen Gang Problem

Despite the growing problem of teen gangs, for many years there was no legislation dealing directly with this phenomenon. On March 7, 2002, the National Congress published the *Ley de Policía y de Convivencia Social* (The Law of the Police and Social Life). This document is the first to define what the government considers to be gang members and particular activities that they must avoid. It also specifies penalties should the law be violated. The *Ley de Policía y de Convivencia Social* is a good first step in addressing the phenomenon of teen gangs; however, it is so broadly focused—covering activities as diverse as prostitution, public gatherings, animal control, theater, dogfighting, and bull runs—that it is unable to give the needed in-depth attention that this subject deserves.

The ninth chapter of the law deals directly with vagrancy and gangs. Article 90 defines a pernicious gang as a group of adolescents (ages 12 to 18) who gather and act together to assault others (or provoke violence among themselves), damage public or private goods, or act in such a way as to disturb the public. Article 91 states that adolescents who are part of a teen gang, carry any type of weapon, bother others in a threatening way, use flammable materials or explosives, or consume alcohol or drugs in public will be immediately detained and placed before a judge so that they can receive the appropriate social education.

In theory, the emphasis is not on punishing the teen gang members but rather on recognizing the importance of giving the adolescent sufficient opportunities and education to become a contributing member of society. In practice, many have become frustrated with the lack of punishment and have turned to taking matters into their own hands. Although the law allows for the treatment of minors who are involved in gangs or who have chemical dependency issues, enforcement and rehabilitation programs are virtually nonexistent. As can be seen, laws are in place to counter typical gang behavior. There are laws against the use of alcohol and drugs, graffiti, public disturbances, and violence. However, the enforcement of these laws is often all too lax.

Social Views, Customs, and Practices

Gang members experience a general sense of isolation. In a culture that highly values community, gang members are excluded from community life in several ways, the most obvious being from the workforce. Tattooed teen gang members are generally not eligible for employment. Some tattoo removal programs have been helpful in allowing gang members to reintegrate into the workforce, but much more than tattoo removal is needed. It is estimated that 80 percent of the gang members have not enrolled in high school, indicating that they have also been excluded from the educational system (Torres, 2002). With such exclusions, teen gang members have no legitimate place or voice in the community. The sense of exclusion and isolation increases the need for these youths to bond together for protection and for moral, emotional, and physical support (Equipo de Reflexión, Investigación, y Comunicación [ERIC, IDESO, IDIES, IUDOP], 2001, pp. 298–300). Not finding a legitimate source of meaning and power, teen gang members frequently turn to illegitimate sources.

Assaults, killings, and drug trafficking are commonplace and have left many Hondurans frightened for their safety. It is generally considered unsafe to go outside after dark—and certainly not alone. Honduran citizens frequently read about gang violence and the series of deaths that are the results of that violence. Gang members are seen as a public nuisance, and there is a general sense of lack of caring when they are killed; however, there is also a voice that recognizes that something is inherently wrong with declaring war on one's own children (Calderón, 2002).

WHY HONDURAN KIDS JOIN GANGS

In El Progreso, Honduras, a church gang-intervention program called EXISTIR, which means "to exist," was founded after several gang members were allegedly assassinated extrajudicially. The founding belief of the program was that every child has the right to exist, even gang members. The program attempted to provide skills-training classes for gang members so that they could find work. The program also tried to provide gang members with spiritual, personal, and educational formation. Many of the young men were enrolled in a local high school; however, it became apparent to administration and faculty that these young men had a difficult time fitting in. The way the gang members spoke, dressed, and related to one another drew attention from the other students, and they were often excluded from daily activities. It became apparent that it was necessary not only to teach the gang members how to behave in more socially acceptable ways but also to speak to the student body about gang members and why they join gangs.

What most kids who are in gangs are looking for is a sense of companionship, identity, and protection. Almost all of the gang members in Honduras came from families where one or both parents had left the home. Typically, the reasons for the parents' leaving were financial, as they sought employment in the United States. As a result, the children often experienced a sense of not being worthy of their parents' love and attention. Frequently, the kids would move in with a grandparent or aunt; however, they would, in various ways, be deprived of the love, attention, and discipline that they craved from their own parents. Ultimately, the kids were convinced that they were not valued within their families, and so they began to seek to meet their physical and emotional needs on their own.

Teen gangs provide a strong sense of companionship and camaraderie. As the kids develop reputations, gang nicknames are usually given. These nicknames help to provide a sense of identity for the young people. In addition, because the young people generally become sources of frustration not only for their families but also for the community, they become targets and are frequently threatened with violence to conform to societal norms. It becomes necessary for the kids to band together and form gangs so that they can protect one another. Whenever a member of the gang is attacked or insulted, the entire gang is attacked. Hence, there is safety in numbers. Interestingly enough, gang members do not primarily seek drugs, violence, and pain but rather the same things that any other adolescent desires: to be loved, accepted, understood, valued, and safe. Another advantage of gang membership is that, because of the strong communal nature of the group, many of the basic necessities of life can be provided to youngsters who are not able to get them at home. The gang will provide food, clothing, and shelter for its members in need. Thus, there are often very practical reasons for kids in Honduras to join gangs.

Gang initiation in Honduras typically involves some type of "beating-in," whereby new members to be initiated are required to defend themselves from other members of the gang for a specified period of time. The purpose of the beating-in is to prove their commitment to the gang and to show that they will be able to help in the defense of the barrio (neighborhood). Someone who runs away from a fight proves to be a dangerous and unreliable companion. For safety reasons, it is important that members prove they are willing and able to endure the blows that become part of gang life in Honduras. Alternatively, new gang members may be sent on a mission into enemy territory to prove their bravery and ability to get out of dangerous situations.

Gang Activities

The gangs in Honduras are known for hanging out in the streets. Since these young men do not have jobs, they frequently stand on the corners and are great observers of what happens on the streets. They know who enters and leaves their neighborhoods (*barrios*), who uses and deals drugs, who is abusive in the home, who is faithful to his wife, and who is not. As a result of their constant hanging around, they gain a reputation for being lazy. As they call attention to various injustices within the barrio, they receive threats and are insulted and mistreated.

Not having a job, frustrated with not being able to get one, and aware of the various forms of violence surrounding them, many of the members turn to drugs to help deal with the pain that is the reality of their lives. However, to pay for the drugs, they need money. The gangs in Honduras tend to operate as a family; everyone contributes what they can for the maintenance of the gang. The funds are then used to provide for everyone. Unlike the larger society from which they are excluded, no one is barred from enjoying the resources of the gang. Since most gang members do not work, they rely on charging a "transportation tax" to those who pass through the barrio. Generally, the tax is one or two *lempiras* (approximately 15 cents). Those from the barrio are exempt from paying the tax, but taxi drivers and others are expected to pay. Should one choose not to pay, the gang members will often use force. Although some may see this as a type of theft, to the gang members it is simply the way things are.

The taxes collected often do not provide enough funds for the drugs and weapons the gang members need. As a result, funds are obtained through impromptu assaults on those passing through the barrio. Usually, these assaults are for the purpose of obtaining a nice pair of shoes, a watch, relatively small amounts of cash, and so forth. They usually involve the use of some type of knife, a machete, or a *chimba* (homemade pipe gun) to instill fear in the victim. One of the primary missions of the gang is the defense or protection of the barrio from invasion by rival gangs who might try to come in and rob from the inhabitants. In a very real way, the gang members provide protection to women, children, and the elderly, who might otherwise be easy targets.

Gang members in Honduras also mark their territory with graffiti to indicate the area that they control and protect. The graffiti serves as a history of the gang's members and its activities. Most of the graffiti simply lists the names of the gang members or the gang symbols (for example MS, 13, 18, or some other gang name). Occasionally, members of one gang will infringe on the territory of another in an attempt to gain control and show their dominance over an area. These missions frequently result in injuries and occasional fatalities of both gang members and innocent civilians who get caught in the crossfire. Typically, these turf wars take place in the evening hours. As a result of the constant threat of an impending attack, some Honduran gangs have rules forbidding the use of certain drugs such as Resistol (glue) or other inhalants because they make the user less capable of defending the barrio.

Another way of recording gang history is through tattoos. The tattoo is seen as a way of proudly showing association with a gang. Not all gang members in Honduras tattoo themselves; however, many do, recording the names of friends who have been killed or the number of enemies they have killed. These tattoos make it easy to identify gang members and often make it difficult for them to find work—employers discriminate against gang members owing to the perceived (and sometimes real) risk that hiring may entail. Because gang members are the targets of violent attacks, many business owners prefer not to have them working for their companies, since that might bring an increased likelihood of an attack by rival gang members at the place of business. The EXISTIR program encouraged gang members to remove their tattoos and helped to provide tattoo removal services. The removal can be seen as a sign of betrayal to the gang, so it carries with it the risk of punishment by the gang, most often in the form of some type of beating, possibly even death ("12,000 jovenes," 2003).

Despite the frequent violence, drug use, and other delinquent activity of the gang, there is also a strong sense of loyalty that members feel toward the group. In many ways gang members serve as an alternate family. Most of their time together is spent discussing the daily events of their barrio and sharing with each other the trials and tribulations of that day. These conversations can be quite lively and enjoyable as members poke fun at one another, joke, and laugh at the craziness of their lives.

In summary, gang members see themselves as responsible for controlling and protecting their turf. In contrast to gangs in the United States, the street gangs in Honduras are not based on showing ethnic pride, since the Honduran culture is, for the most part, not ethnically diverse. However, gang members in Honduras engage in many of the same behaviors that U.S. gang members do. They spray paint graffiti on walls, use and sell drugs, are involved in assaults, and occasionally go on missions to try to claim more territory.

Social Cleansing and Extrajudicial Killings

Several human rights organizations have studied and documented the various human rights violations against Honduran teen gang members. The April–August 2001 Executive Report of the Committee of Relatives of the Missing Detained in Honduras (*Comité de Familiares de Detenidos Desaparecidos en Honduras* [COFADEH]) on the situation of human rights in Honduras includes several references to the systematic killing of suspected teen gang members. Even more disturbing is that some of these deaths are directly linked to Honduran security forces and are often left unresolved and underinvestigated. Between 1998 and 2001 a list of 606 assassinations revealed that 60 percent of those killed were minors. The COFADEH believes this represents culpable negligence on the part of Honduran authorities. In the year 2000, 320 young persons between the ages of 13 and 27 were violently killed without an adequate attempt to discover who the perpetrators of these deaths were—despite the fact that many of the killings had similar characteristics. As one report stated, "this situation is extremely troubling, because the State seems to be tolerant in the face of such serious acts, especially those committed by its own security agents" (Comité de Familiares de Detenidos Desaparecidos en Honduras [COFADEH], 2001, p. 6).

Public insecurity has allowed for the systematic assassination of young persons presumed to be delinquents (that is, teen gang members). In 2001 it was estimated that police-supported death squads killed an estimated 1,000 teen gang members (Agence France Presse, 2001).

"Also, in the last ten years, execution against suspected delinquents has been utilized as a type of social cleansing, generally tolerated by the institutions in charge of administering and enforcing the law" (COFADEH, 2001, p. 10).

Andres Pavón, president of the Committee for the Defense of Human Rights in Honduras (CODEH), said his group had evidence that death squads were operating along the Atlantic coast and in central Honduras, and that they were being financed by businessmen "obsessed with eliminating alleged criminals" (Mejia, 2000). Commenting on current policy, Pavón has cautioned that what is even more dangerous is that in the war against delinquency, the "enemy" is unknown, in the sense that the enemy has not been adequately identified ("Juristas Inician el Lunes," 2002).

Business owners and their families are frequently targets for kidnapping for ransom ("Empresarios Toman Liderazgo," 2002). Although these kidnappings are not usually perpetrated by gang members, the "war against delinquency" often lumps the two together. In the last several years there has been an alarming increase in the number of kidnappings. In 1996 there were five reported kidnappings. By 2001, only five years later, the number of kidnappings was up to 45 ("Juristas Inician el Lunes," 2002). Although a separate battle, the fight against kidnappings shows an increased proclivity toward the use of force in Honduran society in response to frustration.

Hope House (Casa Alianza) in Tegucigalpa has also documented the systematic killing of teen gang members and street kids as a form of social cleansing. In a controversial report released in 2001, it estimated that police or agents of the state were to blame for at least 7 percent of the killings of young adults under 23 years of age (Elton, 2001). Other analysts have expressed similar fears. They claim that the current policy of zero tolerance is very much like that of the 1980s, when those who sympathized with revolutionaries were killed by the armed forces. The only difference is that now they are killing gang members, while the drug dealers and the corrupt continue to live freely (Torres, 2002).

ATTEMPTS AT REHABILITATION

There are various attempts at rehabilitation of gang members. A Catholic church, as part of the EXISTIR program team, has attempted to offer social, vocational, and spiritual formation to a group of adolescents, many of whom were semiactive gang members. The program provided them with educational scholarships to a local parochial school; however, the negative impact that these youths appeared to have on the other students prompted the school's administration to not allow these students to return for a second year. The response of the school is similar to that of society at large—the problem seems too big to be overcome. Despite the best efforts of the program, the support offered seemed to create an unhealthy dependence and, ultimately, did not empower the teens to face the harsh realities of life in the barrios.

State programs have also struggled to provide adequate forms of rehabilitation. The state-run facility in San Pedro Sula, referred to as El Carmen, was designed to house 150 youths. However, in 1998 the facility housed more than 400 teens. As a result, the quality of the rehabilitative efforts suffered. For most of the teens, their experiences at El Carmen reaffirmed their gang identity rather than offering a positive alternative, because they would bond together there with other gang members of their clique for protection and emotional support (Equipo de Reflexión, Investigación, y Comunicación [ERIC, IDESO, IDIES, IUDOP], 2001). Privately funded rehabilitations, although rare, generally seem to be spoken of positively by those who participate in them. Such programs are often more professional and have a more holistic focus (technical, academic, and religious) (Equipo de Reflexión, Investigación, y Comunicación [ERIC, IDESO, IDIES, IUDOP], 2001).

As part of an in-depth study of the gang phenomenon in Honduras, the Equipo de Reflexión, Investigación, y Comunicación (ERIC) is in the process of studying the various agencies involved in rehabilitating gang members. These centers are principally located near the major cities of Tegucigalpa and San Pedro Sula. In the former, four programs are currently involved in working toward the rehabilitation of gang members (HATILLO, HATEVA, Casa Alianza, and XIBBALBA). In Rivera Hernandez, a community near San Pedro Sula, there is a program by the name of CONREMA. In Tela, there is the Centro San Juan Bosco, which provides a work program in which boxes are produced. The government agency responsible for protecting the rights of minors has abandoned its early attempts at rehabilitating gang members through incarceration and, instead, has opted to try community service, home visits, or placing the teen gang member with another family (Equipo de Reflexión, Investigación, y Comunicación [ERIC, IDESO, IDIES, IUDOP], 2001).

HONDURAS'S PLANS TO ADDRESS THE TEEN GANG PROBLEM

The previous president, Carlos Roberto Flores, was accused of being involved in the hiring and organization of death squads to kill gang members. President Maduro has stated from the beginning of his presidency that his primary mission is to fight delinquency and, shortly after taking office, he declared a "war against delinquency" (Calderón, 2002). As part of his fight, he has initiated a zero-tolerance policy. The current approach to teen gangs is one of brute force. At the beginning of the operation, some 7,300 police and an unspecified number of the National Guard were sent to various communities to retake control of these neighborhoods. In addition, a fund was set up to provide for the family members of those fallen officers who are injured or killed during this war. It is hoped that such efforts will restore the public trust that, through years of corruption and ineffectiveness, has withered, keeping many Hondurans living in a perpetual state of fear. In the Cabañas Barrio an average of two buses per day are assaulted by gang members, and the police have been unable to control the situation ("Dos Buses de la Ruta," July 17, 2002). The war on delinquency is meant to show that gangs are not an unbeatable foe, even if the war is to be long, painful, and expensive.

There is also talk about considering the death penalty and lowering the age for which a teen can be punished as an adult for more serious offenses. These measures show that Maduro wants to present a "tough-on-crime" image ("Maduro," 2003). However, UNICEF has advised against lowering the age at which minors can be tried as adults ("UNICEF Advierte," 2003). Financing for this war is coming partially from the government, and partially from private funds donated by business owners. Maduro is also pushing for increased neighborhood watches and the participation of the citizens to help in the fight. He is unwilling to have 5,000 to 6,000 delinquents assaulting and controlling 6 million citizens. The president pledges that, along with the rest of the Honduran citizens, he is willing to risk his life in this battle against delinquency. There are personal reasons for Maduro's tough stance against delinquency; in 1997 his son Ricardo was kidnapped and killed. Maduro admits that his zero-tolerance policy is fueled by the death of his son, but he denies that his motives are vengeful. He claims that the policy is modeled on a program against crime and corruption implemented in New York City ("Muerte di mi Hija," 2001). Maduro states that his priorities for his term in office are public safety, health, and education ("Presidente Maduro," 2002).

Bruce Harris, executive director of Casa Alianza (Hope House) in Latin America, stated

There is no hope here, no jobs and no social programs. When there are no social programs, you have to steal to eat and that's when society labels these kids as delinquents. . . . Because there is no alternative or rehabilitation program for kids in conflict with the law, society takes into their own hands what they consider to be justice. And they are killing kids. (Elton, 2001)

Some have criticized Maduro's war against delinquency as a ploy to boost his presidential image while failing to address the root of the problem, most especially the grave poverty that affects at least 64.5 percent of Hondurans who are unable to meet their most basic needs (Calderón, 2002).

CONCLUSION

The seeds of the current Honduran teen gang problem originate in the United States, especially in Los Angeles, and continue to be nourished by a series of social and economic factors that have resulted in the disintegration of the family structure in many of the poor barrios of Honduras. A general sense of frustration and hopelessness has overtaken many Honduran youths, who see little future in their home country. Confronted with the harsh realities of extreme poverty and frustrated with the lack of attention given to their needs, many youths have turned to teen gangs as substitute families. Due to corruption and other factors, the police force has not been able to adequately respond to the crimes that these youths commit. Out of frustration, vigilante groups have formed to target teen gang members. The cycle of violence is self-perpetuating, and the president's current war against delinquency seems to encourage further violence in an attempt to eliminate these youths from society rather than address the more difficult root causes of the violence. Government programs are either nonexistent or inadequate to provide for the educational, psychological, and spiritual needs of teen gang members. Many believe that rather than exiling these youths, it seems more appropriate to take steps to integrate them into society and listen to their legitimate cries against the injustices that keep them and their families enslaved in harsh poverty with no foreseeable exodus. Whereas many refer to teen gang members as antisocial, others prefer to see these teens as reacting to the unsocial and often violent treatment they have received (Leyva, 2001). It is a challenge to see that these youths are demanding to be recognized and respected as they call attention to the various socioeconomic injustices that surround them. Some see the solution to the teen gang problem as having less to do with changing the teens and more to do with changing the realities of the communities in which they find themselves immersed.

REFERENCES

Agence France Presse. (2001). Juvenile gang members executed by police hit-men in Honduras. Retrieved August 1, 2002, from http://www.asylumlaw.org/docs/honduras/HON_1/SEC%20I/Juvenile%20gang%20members.pdf.

Calderón, M. T. (2002). "Los riesgos de la 'guerra contra la delincuencia' " [The risks of "war against delinquency"]. *La Insignia*. Retrieved August 1, 2002, from http://www.lainsignia.org/2002/febrero/ibe_108.htm.

"Cardenal: 'Gobernantes han crucificado al pueblo en la cruz del hambre' " [Cardenal: "Governors have crucified the people in the cross of hunger"]. *La Prensa*. Retrieved April 14, 2001, from http://www.laprensahn.com/natarc/0104.

Comité de Familiares de Detenidos Desaparecidos en Honduras [COFADEH]. (2001). Situación de los derechos humanos en Honduras: Resumen Ejecutivo Abril–Augosto 2001 [Situation of human rights in Honduras: Executive report April–August 2001]. Retrieved August 1, 2002, from http://www.cofadeh.org/resumen/resumen_ejecutivo_2001_08.rtf.

"Dos buses de la ruta 5 atacan a diario en el barrio Cabañas" [Two buses from route 5 are attacked everyday in the neighborhood of Cabañas]. *La Prensa* (July 17, 2002): 28A.

Elton, C. (2001). "Youth killings in Honduras are escalating; Gangs, police being blamed." *The Houston Chronicle* [Electronic version]. Retrieved August 1, 2002, from http://www.asylumlaw.org/docs/honduras/HON_1/SEC%20I/Youth%20killings.pdf.

"Empresarios toman liderazgo en la lucha contra el crimen" [Entrepreneurs take leadership in the fight against crime]. *La Prensa*. [Electronic version]. Retrieved May 29, 2002, from http://www.laprensahn.com/natarc/0205/n29001.htm.

Equipo de Reflexión, Investigación, y Comunicación (ERIC—Reflection, Research and Communication Team); Instituto de Encuestas y Sondeo de Opinión (IDESO—Institute of Interviews and Public Opinion); Instituto de Investigaciones Económicas y Sociales (IDIES—Institute of Economic and Social Research); Instituto de Universitario de Opinión Pública (IUDOP—University Institute of Public Opinion). *Maras y Pandillas en Centroamérica Volumen I* (San Salvador: Central American University, 2001).

"Gautama acusa a la Policía de estar infiltrada por el crimen organizado" [Gautama accuses the police of being infiltrated by organized crime]. (May 31, 2002). *La Prensa* [Electronic version]. Retrieved August 1, 2002, from http://www.laprensahn.com/natarc/0205/n31002.htm.

———. (2000). Perspective series: Honduras update on human rights conditions. Retrieved August 1, 2002, from http://www.ins.gov/graphics/services/asylum/ric/documentation/pshnd00.pdf.

Girón, C. E. (2002). "27 mil hondureños han muerto violentamente desde 1994" [27 thousand Hondurans have died violently since 1994]. *La Prensa*. Retrieved August 1, 2002, from http://www.laprensahn.com/natarc/0207/n08004.htm.

"Juristas inician el Lunes debates para reformar las leyes contra el crimen" [Jurists initiate debates on Monday to reform the laws on crime]. *La Prensa* [Electronic version]. Retrieved June 8, 2002, from http://www.laprensahn.com/natarc/0206/n08005.htm.

Leyva, H. M. (2001). Delincuencia y criminalidad en las estadísticas de Honduras, 1996–2000 [Delinquency and criminality in the statistics of Honduras, 1996–2000]. Retrieved August 1, 2002, from http://www.hondurasinfo.hn/esp/pub/estudios/DELINCUENCIA_Y_CRIMINALIDAD.PDF.

"Maduro impulsa proyecto 'vecino vigilante' " [Maduro promotes project "watchful neighbor"]. *La Prensa* (July 17, 2002): 12A.

"Maduro: 'Luchare por bajar la edad punible' " [Maduro: "I will fight to lower the punishable age"]. *La Prensa* [Electronic version]. Retrieved January 25, 2003, from http://www.laprensahn.com / nacionales.php?id=816 & tabla=January_2003&fechah=20030125.

Mejia, T. (2000). Rights-Honduras: Government accused of financing death squads. Retrieved August 1, 2002, from http://www.asylumlaw.org/docs/honduras/HON_1/SEC%20I/Government%20accused.pdf.

"Muerte de mi hijo tiene mucho que ver con la lucha contra la delincuencia: Maduro" [The death of my son has much to do with the fight against delinquency: Maduro]. (December 4, 2001). *La Prensa* [Electronic version]. Retrieved August 1, 2002, from http://www.laprensahn.com/natarc/0112/n04007.htm.

"Presidente Maduro: 'Mi lucha no es en el fútbol' " [President Maduro: "My fight is not in soccer"]. *El Tiempo* (July 17, 2002).

Torres, J. C. (2002). "Madura ante el reto de las 'maras' " [Madura faces the challenge from the "maras"]. *Hoy Centroamérica* [Electronic version]. Retrieved May 7, 2002, from http://www.hoy.islagrande.cu/HonduMaduro.htm.

"12,000 jovenes se han borrado tatuajes" [12 thousand young men and women have removed their tattoos]. *La Prensa* [Electronic version]. Retrieved January 20, 2003, from http://www.laprensahn.comlpoliciales.php/?id=613&tabla=January_2003&fecha=20030120.

"UNICEF advierte que no se debe bajar la edad punible" [UNICEF advises that the punishable age should not be lowered]. *El Tiempo* [Electronic version]. Retrieved January 29, 2003, from http://www.tiempo.hn/NACION~1/nacio03.htm.

U.S. Census Bureau. (2000). *Population summary for Honduras.* Retrieved August 1, 2002, from http://www.census.gov/cgi-bin/ipc/idbsum?cty=ho.

5

IRELAND

Maureen Duffy

INTRODUCTION

Crime—in particular, juvenile crime—has only come to the consciousness of the Irish in the last decade or so. Awareness of crime in Ireland came crashing into focus with the murder, in Dublin, of Irish journalist Veronica Guerin in July of 1996. She was an investigative reporter for Ireland's *Sunday Independent* and had done extensive research about the drug and criminal gangs in Dublin, many of which are connected to serious organized crime and include young people. She wrote about gang leaders with names such as The General, The Coach, and The Penguin—people who, were they not so violent and ruthless, would sound like characters from second-rate movies.

Guerin was at a traffic light in Dublin, in her red sports car, when a gun-wielding motorcyclist opened fire on her and killed her. The people of Ireland responded with horror and fear to Guerin's murder. If someone could be killed by gang members for just doing her job, was everyone now at risk? Guerin's life and work are the subject of a book by Emily O'Reilly (1998) and are also the subject of a recent movie, starring Cate Blanchett as Veronica Guerin, called *Veronica Guerin*. Whether Guerin's murder crystallized a rampant drug and crime problem in Ireland or was the catalyst for exaggerations about the nature of the Irish crime problem is the subject of ongoing debate.

PROFILE OF IRELAND

Ireland is a geographically and politically divided country consisting of a total of 32 counties. Twenty-six counties make up the Republic of Ireland, an independent constitutional republic that has its own democratically elected government and its own parliament, the Oireachtas. The Irish Parliament consists of the president, the Dáil, and the Seanad, all of which are located in Dublin, the capital city of Ireland. The leader of the political party with the most members elected to parliament is named as the *taoiseach*, or prime minister, the leader of the government. The president of Ireland is a separately elected position. The president assumes a more ceremonial and symbolic role and is not the political leader of the country.

Northern Ireland comprises six northern counties. Northern Ireland is a part of Great Britain, and members elected to government in Northern Ireland sit in the British House of Parliament in London, known as Westminster. Northern Ireland has been the site of what is referred to as "the troubles." "The troubles" is the name given to the most recent period in Northern Irish history dating from the late 1960s, during which there has been ongoing sectarian violence between the Irish Protestants and the Irish Catholics. The divisiveness and violence is both religious and economic, with the Catholics historically the more economically disadvantaged of the two groups in Northern Ireland. In 1998 the famous Good Friday Agreement, known as the Belfast Accord, established the Northern Ireland Assembly and a power-sharing executive department. This agreement was supported by the governments of Great Britain and of the Republic of Ireland as well as by most political parties in Northern Ireland. The principles of the agreement supported the right of the people of Northern Ireland to determine their own political future, whether that would mean remaining a part of Great Britain, joining with the Republic of Ireland, or becoming independent of either.

Population of Young People

The total population in the Republic of Ireland, as of the preliminary report from the 2002 census, is 3.92 million people, with about 25 percent of those between the ages of 10 and 24. About 38 percent of the Irish population is under 25 (Central Statistics Office, 2002), making Ireland a country with one of the youngest populations in the western world. A quarter of the current Irish population is in the age group most vulnerable to gang affiliation and involvement in teen and young adult crime.

Teen gangs in Ireland, especially in the capital city of Dublin, are most associated with what are called housing estates in the inner cities. Housing estates are typically high-density areas of government-owned or -subsidized dwellings, usually small, and centered in areas that are economically disadvantaged. It is in these depressed areas that marginalized youth are vulnerable to the attractions of gang activities. In Dublin, gangs of youth have been identified in housing estates in Ballyfermot, Crumlin, Tallaght, Ronanstown, and Finglas, to name a few.

SOCIALLY EXCLUDED OR AT-RISK YOUTH

In Ireland, as in most western countries, youth are identified as "at-risk" if they or their families have certain characteristics. These characteristics include drug abuse or dependency in the family; a family member with a criminal record; truancy; quitting school early (dropping out); absentee, impaired, or mentally ill parents; poverty; and/or previous contact with the Juvenile Liaison Scheme (juvenile justice system). The designation "at-risk" is not precise but usually includes the presence of one or more of the factors just mentioned.

In Ireland, those involved in setting policy for at-risk youth use the terms *inclusion* and *exclusion* to highlight important social ideas. *Exclusion* refers to "a state of being out of the mainstream of the community or culture." *Excluded* youth consist of young people who are inadequately educated, unemployed or underemployed, living in poverty, involved with the criminal justice system, drug-involved, and generally not participating in the responsibilities and benefits of membership in Irish society. "Included" youth consist of those who are fully participating in the responsibilities and benefits of Irish society and those who were formerly excluded but who are being reintegrated into society through participation in various governmental or nongovernmental programs aimed at helping them.

In 1987 the Irish Youth Foundation commissioned a large national survey of young people between ages 16 and 24. They found that Irish youth feared unemployment more than anything else, that their confidence about their future was low, and that unemployed youth felt particularly alienated from the political system of their country (Irish Marketing Surveys, 1987). These findings suggest that many young Irish people feel excluded from the benefits their society has to offer. They see those benefits as accruing to others but not to themselves.

The use of the terms "inclusion" and "exclusion" to describe the conditions of young people are interesting in a number of ways. These terms call attention to social conditions and factors at the social level, such as poverty, unemployment, and problems of addiction and mental illness. Terms like "juvenile delinquents" and "gang members" call attention to the status of a person at the individual level and do not take into account the social conditions within which that person is living. While there is a public perception in Ireland that much crime is related to juvenile offenders and an understandable outcry against the violence perpetrated by these offenders, there is also an appreciation among policy makers of the social conditions leading to youth crime.

In 1992 the *Urban Crime and Disorder Report* by Ireland's Department of Justice presented a profile of the young Irish person in trouble with the law. This young person felt chronically uncared about; experienced domestic violence, alcoholism, or drug addiction in the family; or was himself or herself a victim of child abuse. For the young person in trouble with the law, school was too difficult and too demanding, and was perceived as irrelevant. As a result of chronic unemployment in his or her family, the young person saw the Irish welfare system, and not employment, as a means of support and survival. Entertainment and excitement came from hanging out with equally disenfranchised peers, who did drugs, went joyriding, and defied authority. This profile is the picture of excluded youth who are at risk for criminal activity and gang involvement.

The social concept of inclusion also has practical and ethical implications at the program level. Where inclusion is a stated goal, young people cannot be kicked out of, or expelled from, a program. The practice of inclusion counters the more typical experience of marginalized youth who either fail to meet the minimal standards for continuation in school, for example, and are exited or drop out or whose noncompliant and/or antisocial behaviors result in expulsion from sports or training programs. Inclusion-focused programs designed for at-risk youth make it extremely difficult for the young person to be kicked out. Inclusion counters the traditional cycle of failure and social isolation that is common among at-risk youth.

It is difficult to know exactly what percentage of the population of young people in Ireland are considered at risk. However, at the 1996 European Youth Forum, 19 percent of young people between ages 15 and 24 in Ireland were defined as socially excluded, or "at risk" (European Youth Forum, 1996). Crime statistics and juvenile justice statistics provide another indicator of a society's at-risk or socially excluded young people. Thirty-nine percent of people in custody (jails, prisons, houses of remand) are under the age of 25 (Central Statistics Office, 2002, p. 128) "Thirty-eight percent of all crime is committed by juveniles aged 14 to 17 years of age, up from 16 percent of the total in 1984" (Harvey, 1993, p. 17).

GANGS IN IRELAND

Drugs and Gangs

The International Youth Foundation's Ireland report stated: "Drugs became a serious problem in Ireland in the late 1970's, substantial quantities of heroin coming into the country in the early 1980's. Heroin is considered the most serious threat to young people, being distributed in inner-city estates by drug gangs" (Harvey, 1993, p. 18). The actual correlation between drug use in the inner-city housing estates of Dublin and other large Irish cities such as Cork, Limerick, and Galway and teen gang membership has not been formally researched or documented. What is documented is that the social conditions supporting both drug use and gang membership are similar. Harvey (1993) also stated "the average abuser of heroin and other serious opiates is an unemployed man, living in the parental home, who started injecting drugs at 19. Many are early school leavers, coming from areas associated with poor housing, vandalism, unemployment and crime" (p. 18).

Commenting on the connection between social marginalization, drug abuse, and teen gangs, Myers (1997) stated that "Dublin is now full of these gangs of youths who are embarking upon lives of utter futility, violence, alcohol and drugs" (para. 9). In a newspaper report in *The Irish Times*, several parents of adolescent boys were interviewed and reported that their own sons had been set upon by gangs of youths and threatened or beaten, and these parents had resorted to not allowing their own teenagers to go into the city center as they had done in the past ("When Boy Meets Boy," 1998). In this article, Andrew Conway, a senior child psychologist, is quoted as saying, "It's a phenomenon affecting 14- to 17-year-old boys, in particular. It used to be that teenage gangs fought on their own patch and would attack other gangs in their area. The difference now is that they'll fight in any area, and more at random" (para. 9).

The Garda Síochána is the police force in the Republic of Ireland. In its *2001 Annual Report*, Garda Síochána (2002) reported that the number of offenses attributable to juveniles increased significantly over the year 2000. That being said, the number is still small relative to other Western countries. No juveniles were charged with murder in 2001, and there were 468 reported incidents of assault attributable to young offenders. There were 95 sexual assaults, including attempted rape, attributable to juveniles in 2001. Forty-three percent of drug offenses prosecuted in 2001 were committed by person 21 years of age and under, the overwhelming majority being male (An Garda Síochána, 2002, p. 122).

The presence of organized serious criminal drug gangs in Ireland has also been documented. These gangs exist both in the Republic of Ireland and in Northern Ireland, and there is some coordination of activities between the gangs on both sides of the border. Veronica Guerin was killed by drug gang members because of the nature of her journalistic investigations into their criminal enterprises, in particular, drugs and money laundering.

While heroin remains a serious problem in Ireland, especially for young people, drug seizures in 2001 primarily involved marijuana, or cannabis. By category of drug seized in Ireland in 2001, cannabis accounted for 68 percent of the seizures, ecstasy for 16 percent, heroin for 9 percent, and cocaine for 3 percent of all drug seizures. The majority (80 percent) of drug-related offenses prosecuted were for possession (An Garda Síochána, 2002).

After the death of Veronica Guerin, a host of anticrime legislation was introduced in Ireland, accompanied by intense law enforcement activity, effectively putting many of the criminal gang enterprises of that time out of business. In a report in *The Irish Times*, Ireland's leading daily newspaper, detectives working in Dublin stated that after the cleanup following Guerin's death, what was left was a group of minor criminals, all in their early 20s or younger, competing for the turf left when major gang figures associated with her death and with criminal drug activity were arrested ("Young Criminals Step Up the Violence," 2000). These up-and-coming gang leaders were part of gangs tied to inner-city housing estates, controlling turf in the Dublin drug trade. There is an apparent trend toward the involvement of younger males in both gang and drug abuse activities in Dublin.

More research is needed in Dublin and in Ireland, in general, to determine how drug dependency and gang activity are connected. The evidence in Ireland certainly does not support the conclusion that all drug-dependent youth are gang members. The evidence does support the presence of teenagers and young adult males in organized or quasi-organized gangs that control certain parts of the cities, particularly inner-city housing estates, and that generate revenue from the drug trade. These gang members commit violent acts from murder to assault, robbery, and purse-snatching. Gang members in Dublin, and addicted youth who may or may not be gang members, have become notorious for "needle muggings," in which victims are threatened with syringes filled with blood. The use of blood-filled syringes as a weapon became popular in the early 1990s. In fact, the official crime statistics of Ireland show a category for robberies and burglaries with a needle (An Garda Síochána, 2002, p. 97).

In Northern Ireland, a recent report stated that there were approximately 80 criminal gangs operating in Northern Ireland, with over 400 members (Northern Ireland Organized Crime Task Force, 2001). A little over half of the gangs had ties to republican or loyalist paramilitary organizations. These are serious criminal gangs that generate millions of dollars of illegal revenue annually through illegal activities such as drug running, racketeering, and smuggling goods. The gangs connected to loyalist and republican paramilitary organizations channel some of their ill-gotten money to these paramilitary organizations, which then use the money to finance violence and continued sectarian strife. Disaffected, at-risk young people in depressed parts of Northern Ireland, attracted to the rhetoric of intolerance and hate, begin to associate with these more serious gang members and eventually make gang membership a way of life. In Northern Ireland gang membership is associated with over half of the gangs with loyalty to paramilitary organizations supporting violence between the Catholics and Protestants.

The basic problem with discussion of teen gangs begins with the definition of what is a gang (Esbensen, Winfree, He, and Taylor, 2001). The Irish situation bears this out. Is there a commonality between the gangs of young adolescents who hang out together in inner-city housing estates and who profess a sense of common group identity and the violent, organized drug gangs responsible for the murder of Veronica Guerin? If there is something in common between Irish teen gangs and the more serious organized crime gangs, how can we best understand what it is? The organized criminal gangs prey on the disaffected, socially excluded youth described in this article and seduce them into low level participation initially. It seems that gang membership in Ireland today is more a continuous variable rather than a categorical one, meaning that there are gradations of involvement that defy the traditional categories of "wannabees," active gang members, and former gang members.

Irish policy-makers and intervention programs to date have focused more on the issues of exclusion and at-risk youth and have targeted interventions at that level rather than at the level of gang involvement. It remains to be seen whether more gang-specific programming will be required in Ireland or whether the focus on moving youth from social exclusion to social inclusion will cast the net wide enough to reel in those young people either flirting with, or actively involved in, gangs.

POLITICAL INITIATIVES AND POLICIES RELATED TO EXCLUDED OR AT-RISK YOUTH

The Irish police force (Garda Síochána) established a very successful diversion program for juveniles in 1963. The purpose of the program is to provide intervention at an early stage for juveniles meeting certain criteria, who would then be cautioned rather than prosecuted for an offense. The upper age limit for participation in the program has been raised from 17 to 18 in recent years. The official name of the program is the Garda Juvenile Diversion Programme, formerly known as the Juvenile Liaison Scheme. The Garda Juvenile Diversion Programme is a family- and community-based intervention program. Eligible youths who have committed crimes are given either a formal or informal caution in lieu of criminal prosecution.

The informal caution is used when the crime committed is a minor offense. The caution is delivered by the Juvenile Liaison Garda, usually in the young person's home, with his parents or guardians present. A formal caution is used when the offense is more serious and is delivered by the Garda District Superintendent at the Garda station in the presence of the youth's parents or guardians. Juveniles who are cautioned through this program may also be required to have supervision by the Garda who is acting as the Juvenile Liaison Officer. This supervision is conducted in a variety of places, from the street in the youth's neighborhood to the sports field to the youth's school and home. The program encourages the forging of relationships of respect and trust between the youth and the Garda, who represents authority and requires the youth to participate in society by carrying out certain responsibilities that have been placed upon him or her. In 2001 there was an increase of 5 percent in utilization of the program over the year 2000, with 8,832 juveniles participating in 2001 (An Garda Síochána, 2002). Since 1963 a total of 127,582 youthful offenders have participated in the Garda Juvenile Diversion Programme, 78 percent of whom were male and 22 percent female (An Garda Síochána, p. 105). The programme has been nothing short of spectacularly successful. As of 1996, 89 percent of the youth who were diverted into the programme reached their eighteenth birthdays without reprosecution (Bresnihan, 1999).

It is worth reflecting upon the success of the Irish Garda Juvenile Diversion Programme. The programme seems to zero in on a number of elements deemed essential in effective intervention programs. In this program the juvenile is managed within the context of his family and the community. By dealing with the juvenile within his or her family and community context, the central relationships in the youth's life are acknowledged and preserved. The youth is held accountable for misdeeds and crimes but is simultaneously helped to redirect toward fuller and more meaningful participation in society. The accountability that is required of juveniles in the Garda Programme forces them into greater societal participation within their own communities, not apart from them, as would be the case in a more centralized and bureaucratic type of intervention program. Families are involved in the process and are witnesses to the administrations of the cautions, which is the "holding accountable" aspect of the program. Families are fully aware of the conditions of the program and consequences for unsatisfactory completion. Families also become witnesses then to the success or failure of the juvenile in the diversion program. The Garda Programme locates the juvenile within his or her network of existing societal relationships and works within that network to help turn the juvenile toward prosocial behaviors. The Irish Garda Juvenile Diversion Programme is an intervention model with a sound basis in family and community psychology that could be adopted by other countries and communities, including the United States.

The New Irish "Children Act"

Up until 2001 the juvenile justice system in Ireland was governed by the 1908 UK Children Act. In 2001 the government of Ireland finally enacted into law the new Children Act, which provides for a variety of different approaches to youthful offenders depending upon what stage the juvenile is at within the justice system. For example, early intervention and prevention approaches would be used for at-risk youth or youth who have been informally cautioned; whereas other approaches, including confinement or incarceration, would be used for youth convicted of more serious crimes who were not diverted through the Garda Juvenile Diversion Programme.

Restorative Justice as an Irish Social Ideal

The philosophy and assumptions underlying the Garda Juvenile Diversion Programme are consistent with Irish cultural values and beliefs. Prior to the 1980s, adolescent boys who misbehaved or who committed minor offenses in groups with others were not thought of as a gang or as threatening. Authorities within the community, whether they were the local Garda, teachers, neighbors, or parents, would handle the situation of a wayward boy themselves. In Ireland "the lads" has long been a common expression describing groups of young males who hang out together and go out drinking at local pubs or dances. Minor offenses were regarded more as expected mischief that needed to be handled straightforwardly by appropriate adults within the community. "The lads" were seen as needing to sow their wild oats.

Psychological labeling of misbehavior as "acting out" or "oppositional" or "conduct disordered" was not nearly as common in Ireland prior to the 1980s as it is now. The introduction of drugs into Ireland in the late 1970s and early 1980s brought the beginnings of increased crime, gangs, and violence. Public perceptions began to shift as people became understandably impatient with petty crime and fearful of more violent crime against persons. Juvenile offenses no longer were viewed as mischief or as an adolescent rite of passage. With the so-called needle crimes and the death of Veronica Guerin, public perception became less tolerant, and there was an increased demand for swift apprehension and punishment of juvenile offenders. Sectors of the Irish public began to adopt a zero-tolerance position about juvenile crime.

Yet at its heart, the Irish culture is a communal one, rooted in community, even though the community of today is often an urban, sophisticated one, rather than a rural one of an earlier era anchored by the parish Catholic Church. For most Irish people the image of the local Garda marching offending youths down the main street of the town to be given a stiff lecture at the Garda station and then released to parents is still a desirable image. Intervention at the local level, whether by the Garda or by neighbors, is part of the communal nature of the Irish culture. Additionally, given the overwhelmingly Catholic identity of the Republic of Ireland, the notion of forgiveness and transformation is also a part of the cultural value system. The importance of community in Ireland and the role of forgiveness and transformation as cultural values make Ireland a country where programs based on the idea of restorative justice are likely to be both acceptable and workable. Innovative programs for juvenile offenders, based on this idea of restorative justice, are being developed and implemented.

Philosophy of Restorative Justice

The core values of restorative justice are acknowledgment of wrongdoing, repentance and restitution in some form, and reconciliation. For the juvenile offender restorative justice involves acknowledging a wrong or hurt done, making amends for that wrongdoing, and beginning the process of reconciling with the victim and reintegrating into the wider community. In the context of restorative justice wrongdoing is seen not only as harm to the individual but also as harm to the community, and all stakeholders therefore must be involved in healing (Bazemore, 1998; Etzioni, 1998; Van Ness and Heetderks, 1997; Zehr, 1990). The burden of responsibility for addressing and solving crime within the framework of restorative justice is conceptually shifted from the criminal justice system to the community at large. Since the community has been hurt by crime, the community must take responsibility for addressing crime in its midst and creating meaningful systems for victim, offender, and community healing. Such systems of healing include supporting victims of crime, insisting on offenders' assuming responsibility for their crimes, and developing programs for restitution and reintegration of the offender. The core values in restorative justice programs are not ostracism or retribution but repentance and reconciliation. In Ireland, Bresnihan (1999) describes restorative justice as congruent with Irish cultural values and with the philosophy of the Irish Penal Reform Trust. Restorative justice programs, especially for offending youth, are alternatives to the traditional retributive, or punishment-based, approach and seek to repair social bonds that have been ruptured by crime and other wrongdoing. Such programs are increasingly being adopted by the international community for youthful offenders, in particular for those socially marginalized youth most likely to be lured by gang life (Goren, 2001). Restorative justice programs that are well integrated into a community offer real alternatives to membership in a gang.

RESTORATIVE JUSTICE AND JUVENILE OFFENDERS IN IRELAND

Family Conferencing

The Garda Juvenile Diversion Programme also includes a restorative justice component called family conferencing. In family conferencing all stakeholders—namely, the juvenile, his or her family, the victim, juvenile liaison officers, and others who represent the community—meet together to develop a comprehensive plan. The prongs of the plan include proactive support of the victim and ways for the offender to make meaningful restitution to the victim and community. The offender, during family conferencing meetings, comes face-to-face with the harm that has been done to the victim and has the opportunity to directly witness the consequences of his or her offending behavior. The offender is held accountable and must assume responsibility for making restitution to the victim. A concrete plan for doing this is worked out. Likewise, the community becomes a key stakeholder by holding the offender accountable for developing life skills that will enable him to be a productive, included member of society. In turn, the community is held accountable for providing concrete support and resources to the offender in order to facilitate the offender's transition to a participatory, productive, nonoffending lifestyle. Mentoring, employment opportunities, life skills training, vocational training, and family- and community-based counseling are all examples of concrete support strategies that the community can provide to the offender through restorative justice programs.

Youth Diversion Projects

The Department of Justice, Equality, and Law Reform, through the Garda Síochána, has allocated over 20 million eurodollars (€1 = $1 approximately) for the development of a wide range of projects to help offending and at-risk youth in youth diversion programs avoid future antisocial and criminal behavior (European Youth Forum, 1996). These projects include sports activities, service activities, and training and educational programs.

Youth Affairs Section of the Department of Education and Science

The National Action Plan Against Poverty and Social Exclusion 2001–2003 promotes and funds programs aimed at helping at-risk youth deal with issues of addiction, poverty, lack of adequate job skills, juvenile crime, social disaffection, and related problems. The Action Plan gives support at the national policy level for the development of programs designed to help socially excluded youth, including gang members, address problems that are keeping them out of constructive participation in society.

Streetwise

Streetwise is a coalition of Irish organizations interested in the situation of Irish homeless youth, and children and adolescents in the care of the state. Coalition members work together to develop accurate information about homeless youth and at-risk youth in residential care of the state through national surveys (Streetwise, 1991). Members also advocate for at-risk youth by monitoring the social services the youth receive.

Barnardo's

Barnardo's is an independent, nongovernmental organization with multiple project sites in Dublin providing a full range of prevention and intervention services to at-risk families and young people in economically depressed areas of the city. Many of the Barnardo's project sites are located in postal districts with the highest gang membership rates.

STEPS (Irish Society for the Prevention of Cruelty to Children)

STEPS is a drop-in service for youth in several larger cities in Ireland, namely, Dublin, Cork, Wexford, Waterford, and Limerick. This program allows young people to drop in at the program office and receive counseling, from informal to formal, based on their individual needs. It is another effort in Ireland to provide at-risk young people with the resources they will need to shift from an excluded to an included status.

CONCLUSION

Ireland is confronting the dilemma of what to do with offending youth and a public perception of increased crime and increased gang membership brought about by increased drug use among young people since the 1980s. How serious the teen gang problem is in Ireland and whether teen gangs are conduits for induction into more serious organized drug and crime gangs cannot be fully understood without focused research and documentation of the teen gang problem. In the meantime, the country does have some very innovative programming for at-risk youth, designed to bring youth into full participation or inclusion in society.

There is a question of how real the teen gang problem is in Ireland. Ireland has been in a period of unprecedented economic growth and prosperity, characterized by the name Celtic Tiger, used to describe Ireland's booming economy in recent years. A consequence of increasing affluence can be decreasing tolerance for disaffected youth on the fringes of society who make themselves known by their apparent antisocial habits of dress and behavior. Combine the presence of such young people with an increased crime rate, and the stage is set for a public reaction of fear and disgust and a cry to rein in such teens by whatever means necessary.

Yet in the policies and programs of both governmental and nongovernmental organizations, as described above, there is clearly a strong belief that social exclusion and further marginalization of young people serves no one— not the teens, their families, or the wider community. The core values of the Irish people, their essentially social and communal culture, and their adherence to Judeo-Christian beliefs of forgiveness and redemption provide

a solid basis for further development of prevention and intervention programs for disaffected, at-risk youth. Ireland can be a very hopeful place for
troubled youth, but the seeds of intolerance for economically disadvantaged
and marginalized young people are clearly there. The principles of restorative justice provide a real hope for bringing together the different perspectives of the different stakeholders—the community worried and hurt by
crime, the victim personally harmed by crime, and the young offender who
must be held accountable and also supported into social participation. Phil-
osophically, in Ireland crime is the community's responsibility, not the juvenile justice system's alone.

REFERENCES

An Garda Síochána. *Annual Report 2001* (Dublin, Ireland: The Stationery Office,
    2002).
Bazemore, G. "Restorative justice and earned redemption: Communities, victims,
    and offender reintegration." *American Behavioral Scientist* 41 (1998): 768–
    813.
Bresnihan, V. "Restorative justice in Ireland." In Scottish Executive Central Research
    Unit, *Children, young people and crime in Britain and Ireland: From exclusion
    to inclusion—1998* (Edinburgh, Scotland: The Stationery Office, 1999).
Central Statistics Office. *Statistical yearbook of Ireland 2002* (Dublin, Ireland: The
    Stationery Office, 2002).
Department of Justice (Ireland). *Urban crime and disorder: Report of the interde-
    partmental group* (Dublin, Ireland: The Stationery Office, 1992).
Esbensen, F. A., L. T. Winfree, N. He, and T. J. Taylor. "Youth gangs and defini-
    tional issues: When is a gang a gang, and why does it matter?" *Crime &
    Delinquency* 36 (2001): 194–225.
Etzioni, A. "Civic repentance." *American Behavioral Scientist* 41 (1998): 764–767.
European Youth Forum. (1996). *Ireland*. Retrieved from http://www.youthinclude.
    org/Country%20Profiles/Ireland.doc.
Goren, S. "Healing the victim, the young offender, and the community via restorative
    justice: An international perspective." *Issues in Mental Health Nursing* 22
    (2001): 137–149.
Harvey, B. *Policies, programs and philanthropy for children and youth in Ireland* (Bal-
    timore, MD: International Youth Foundation, 1993).
Irish Marketing Surveys. *Young Ireland survey* (Dublin, Ireland: Irish Marketing Sur-
    veys/Irish Youth Foundation, 1987).
Myers, K. (1997, April 4). "An Irishman's diary." *The Irish Times*. Retrieved Septem-
    ber 25, 2002, from http://www.ireland.com/newspaper/opinion/1997/
    0404/archive.97040400098.html.
Northern Ireland Organized Crime Task Force. *Confronting the threat to Northern Ire-
    land society from serious and organized crime: Strategy 2001–2* (Belfast, UK:
    Northern Ireland Office, 2001).
O'Reilly, E. *Veronica Guerin: The life and death of a crime reporter* (London: Random
    House UK Ltd., 1998).

Streetwise. *At what cost? A research study on residential care for children and adolescents in Ireland* (Dublin, Ireland: Streetwise, 1991).

Van Ness, D., and K. Heetderks. *Restoring justice*, 2d ed. (Cincinnati, OH: Anderson Publishing Company, 1997).

"When boy meets boy." (1998, November 24). *The Irish Times.* Retrieved August 15, 2002, from http://www.ireland.com/newspaper/education/1998/1124/archive.98112400181.html.

"Young criminals step up the violence." (2000, March 13). *The Irish Times.* Retrieved August 1, 2002, from http://www.ireland.com/newspaper/ireland/2000/0313/archive.00031300028.html.

Zehr, H. *Changing lenses: A new focus for crime and punishment* (Scottsdale, PA: Herald Press, 1990).

6

ISRAEL

Sloane Veshinski

INTRODUCTION

A 15-year-old is killed by a group of his friends over ice cream; a 14-year-old is stabbed outside of his classroom by a 17-year-old classmate. These are examples of teen violence in Israel. In 2001 the *Jerusalem Post* reported that Israel was number one among ten industrialized countries in the level of violence among 12- and 13-year-old children. While the Israeli government does not report the relationship between youth crime and gang activity, there are indications that teen gang activity does exist. Israel is a country that has dealt with war since its establishment almost 60 years ago, but it is also dealing with violence among its youth. It has been suggested that the issue of teen gangs has been overshadowed by the ongoing Arab-Israeli conflict. The following chapter will introduce you to Israel—its laws, its people, and the issue of teen gang activity. The teen gang problem seems to be an emerging one, and as a result, there is little formal research or academic literature about it. Therefore, information related to the teen crime problem in Israel was obtained through cultural contacts and information cited by police, law enforcement, and the media.

PROFILE OF ISRAEL

Israel is located at the intersection of three continents, Europe, Asia, and Africa, although geographically it is located on the continent of Asia, in a portion of land called the Middle East. Bordering Israel are Lebanon, Syria,

Jordan, and Egypt, along the coastline of the Mediterranean Sea. Israel is a country that is 290 miles (467 kilometers) long and 85 miles (129 kilometers) wide. Comparing Israel to a state in the United States, it would be slightly smaller in size than New Jersey. Israel is divided into settlements that are similar to small communities or neighborhoods in the United States. There are 231 Israeli settlements and civilian land-use sites in the West Bank (near the Gaza Strip), 42 in the Israeli-occupied Golan Heights (in the north tip of Israel), 25 in the Gaza Strip (to the west) and 29 in East Jerusalem (located in the central part of Israel) (Central Intelligence Agency, 2000). The capital of Israel, and its largest city, is Jerusalem. Israel's other large cities include Tel Aviv, Haifa, and Be'er Sheva.

Israel has been plagued by war and violence since its establishment as the State of Israel on May 14, 1948. As a result of ongoing turmoil, the issue of violent behavior exhibited by some adolescents has been overlooked, underestimated, and unaddressed until the last five years, according to media reports. The focus for most Israelis has been, and continues to be, the overall safety of the Israeli people and the continuation of Israel as a state.

In order to clearly understand the nature of the problem of teen violence in Israel, it is first important to get a sense of the country, its people, and how its political system and system of justice operate, as well as how the Israeli system views teens and teen gangs.

Population

According to the Israel Ministry of Foreign Affairs (1999b), the population of Israel has grown sevenfold since its inception in 1948. The ministry puts the current population at 6.3 million people. This includes the ethnic groups of Jews and non-Jewish citizens such as Arabs, Ethiopians, and immigrants from the former Soviet Union. European- and American-born Jews comprise 32 percent of the population; Israeli-born Jews, 21 percent; African-born Jews, 15 percent; Asian-born Jews, 13 percent; and non-Jews, primarily Arabs, 20 percent of the total population of Israel. There is a large youth population in Israel, with 35 percent of Israeli Jews under the age of 25 and 11 percent of Israeli Arabs under the age of 25. In Israel, 80 percent of the population is Jewish, 15 percent is Muslim (mostly Sunni Muslim), and 2 percent is Christian (Central Bureau of Statistics, 2001).

The official language of Israel is Hebrew, although Arabic is used predominantly by the Arab minority. English is the most common foreign language spoken (Central Intelligence Agency, 2000).

Education

Education is mandatory for all Israeli citizens aged 5 through 18. Education is provided free of charge through government-subsidized preschool programs and public elementary, middle, and high schools. In the year 2000 there were an estimated 1,953,936 students in the Israeli public school system (Central Bureau of Statistics, 2001). Israel's university system is comprised of seven major universities. These universities offer a wide range of subjects in the areas of sciences and humanities and serve as research institutions with worldwide reputations. Also, Israeli universities offer a diversity of curriculum in academic courses and vocational training. Israel has a reputation as being a leader in scientific research and development, which offsets its lack of natural resources and provides a marketable product for the country. According to the Central Bureau of Statistics (2001), there were a total of 113,010 students in the Israeli university system. These students had courses of study predominantly in the areas of social sciences, humanities, science and mathematics, and engineering, with only a small percentage studying law and medicine.

Government and Public Order

The government of Israel is a parliamentary democracy, with legislative, judicial, and executive branches. The head of the State of Israel is the president. The president of Israel does not hold the same power as the president of the United States. In Israel, the presidential position is one that is largely ceremonial and formal in nature, and serves as a symbol of Israel as a unified country. The president is elected by the *Knesset*, or congress, the legislative arm of the government. The *Knesset* is a 120-member unicameral (having one legislative chamber) parliament that operates with full sessions and through its 14 currently standing committees. *Knesset* members are elected to four-year terms through countrywide elections. The Cabinet of Ministers administers all national and foreign affairs. The government is led by the prime minister, who is elected by popular vote to a term, and is responsible to the *Knesset*. The judicial branch is formed by three levels of courts: magistrate's court, district courts, and the Supreme Court.

Israel has no formal constitution, "although some functions of a constitution are filled by the Declaration of Establishment (1948), which formalized Israel as an independent state, the Basic Laws of the parliament (*Knesset*), and the Israeli citizenship law" (Central intelligence Agency, 2000, p. 4). A "mixture of English common law, British mandate regulations, and in personal matters, Jewish, Christian, and Muslim legal systems" compose the Israeli legal system (Central Intelligence Agency, 2000, p. 4). In the Israeli legal system, there is no jury and all decisions are made by the presiding judge.

In Israel's criminal justice divisions, crimes fall into one of three classifications: felonies, misdemeanors, and contraventions. A felony is defined as a crime with a minimum punishment of imprisonment of more than three years; a misdemeanor is defined as a crime with a minimum punishment of imprisonment of more than three months and up to three years; and a contravention is defined as a crime with a maximum punishment of up to three months or a fine of up to 7,000 New Israeli Shekels (approximately $2,300) (Weisman, 1990).

TEEN CRIME

The age of legal responsibility for criminal acts in the State of Israel is 12 years. The Youth Probation Service (YPS) is under the auspices of the minister of Labor and Social Affairs. The YPS oversees the "laws and regulations that define the functions of the probation officers," the most important of which is the Youth Law (Trial, Punishment, and Care) 5731–1971 (Israel Ministry of Foreign Affairs, 1999a, p. 11). All minors accused of any crime are referred to the YPS prior to the onset of any legal proceeding so that diagnostic services, recommendations, and sentencing policies can be reviewed and completed. The YPS also has the authority to close a file if it believes that adjudicating the case is not in the public interest (Israel Ministry of Foreign Affairs, 1999a). There is now a debate going on through the Youth Probation Service to address the lack of formal criteria for the opening and closing of a juvenile file (filing or not filing of charges). Formal criteria would provide more direction to juvenile probation officers. Previously, decisions were made about opening or closing a juvenile file on a case-by-case basis by the probation officers. Currently, there is no law or rule indicating whether or not a juvenile should be charged with a crime based on the severity of the crime.

With regard to incarceration, Israel has a system of 11 prisons and 3 detention centers. There are 5 maximum security prisons, 2 minimum security prisons, 1 juvenile facility, 1 female facility, and the rest are mixed prison populations. These facilities are maintained by the Israel Prison System (IPS). The Youth Protection Authority, under the jurisdiction of the minister of Labor and Social Affairs, provides residential placement for youths aged 10 to 20 who have been referred by the court and who have been removed from their homes by Juvenile Court order. This branch of the YPS serves 650 youth per year in 10 residential care centers and 16 youth hostels (Israel Ministry of Foreign Affairs, 1999a). Offenses by juvenile offenders are categorized as (1) crimes against the security of the state and public order, (2) bodily harm, (3) crimes against property, and (4) other offenses (Central Bureau of Statistics, 2001).

TEEN GANGS

Up until 2002 there was no notation or mention of specific teen gangs in the Israeli popular press or in research done on teen violence in Israel. While there has been a documented history of increasing rates of teen violence, the term *teen gang* has not been utilized. Israel charges teens (or

Juvenile Files Opened by the Israel Police Juvenile Department

Year	Juvenile Files Opened
1994	21,385
1995	23,545
1996	25,727
1997	28,600
1998	29,308

Note: Table created using figures found in "Police: Help Needed to Fight Juvenile Crime," by H. J. Gleit, June 14, 1999, *The Jerusalem Post*.

marginal youth, as they are termed) with the specific crime(s) allegedly committed and does not mention gang membership.

The Central Bureau of Statistics (2001) has reported that in 1965 the total number of reported juvenile offenders was 5,330, or 46 percent of the total population of juveniles. In 1999 the percentage of juvenile offenders was 2,788, or 32.1 percent of the juvenile population. The 1999 statistics were based on juveniles aged 12 to 19 years. While it appears that the total number of crimes committed by juveniles has decreased, the Center for Social Policy Studies in Israel (2001), in their *Social-Economic Review*, indicated that in 1980, 12 percent of teens in the 15- to 17-year age group were termed marginal youth. An adolescent who is neither in school nor holding a job is defined as a "marginal youth." In 2000 approximately 7.75 percent of juveniles were classified as marginal. These statistics would indicate that there has been a decrease in juvenile crime since the start of record-keeping. This is an issue of great debate, as it appears that the numbers are not truly representative of the experiences of the schools and the Israel Police Juvenile Department.

According to research done in 1998 by the Bar-Ilan University in conjunction with the World Health Organization, boys aged 11 to 16 in Israel ranked second among 28 countries as being most likely to have carried a knife, club, or handgun at least once in a 30-day period of time. This research included 8,394 Israeli students of mixed ethnic heritage (Lazaroff, 2002). To further address this issue, Deputy Commander Suzy Ben-Baruch, head of the Israel Police Juvenile Department, as cited by the *Jerusalem Post*, stated that "juvenile crime has risen sharply over the last decade" (Gleit, 1999, para. 1). The number of juvenile files opened between 1994 and 1998 reflects this increase.

Although Deputy Commander Ben-Baruch did not include population growth statistics for teens, it would appear that this increase in teen crimes is not proportional to the increase in population. Teen crime files between 1994 and 1998 increased approximately 37 percent. She also indicated that the number of violent crimes and drug-related crimes for juveniles has increased dramatically from 310 drug-related offenses in 1993 to 2,137 in 1998 and from 4,533 violent offenses in 1993 to 11,060 in 1998 (Gleit, 1999). The Israeli Central Bureau of Statistics (2002) has indicated that there has been a 28 percent increase in the overall population of Israel from 1990 to 1999.

An example of this trend of increased violence is the story of Yevgeny Yakobovitch, a 15-year-old male from the neighborhood of Har Yona ("Dove Mountain"). As reported by the *Jerusalem Post*, Yevgeny was attacked by "a group of six teenage boys . . . pounding him with brass knuckles, slitting his throat with kitchen knives and then, as he tried to crawl for help, bashed in his skull with an aluminum bat. Several members of this murderous group were his schoolmates" (Arnold, 1999, para. 1). The reported reason for the attack was that he had denied a friend a bit of ice cream and referred to him as "a fat cheapskate." The police later indicated that the youths involved with the crime had been using a specific substance that was a popular pastime at the school.

Interestingly, at no time was this group referred to as a gang, although Tom Gumpel, Hebrew University education professor, indicated in the article by Arnold that a possible explanation for the murder could have been the psychology of gangs. This position of gang psychology is being disputed by Israel Superintendent Moshe Berkovitz, who "denied that gangs or racism were a factor in the murder—several of Yevgeny's attackers were also Russian immigrants—Gumpel said the gang dynamic was clear" (Arnold, 1999, para. 61). This tragedy, if nothing else, clearly showed the differences in perception about the presence or absence of organized teen gangs in Israel.

Only 11 days prior to the report of Yevgeny's death, the *Jerusalem Post* had reported that according to one study, "the prevalence of bullying in Israel's schools is eighth among 28 Western countries" ("Setting a Better Example," 1999). The overarching concern of this study was not so much the number of weapons carried or beatings that took place but the increasing belief that the violence "will increase in both quantity and seriousness" ("Setting a Better Example," 1999, para. 2). Parents cited in this article indicated that the only way for their children to remain safe in school was to "join a gang." Again, this was yet another reference to gang activity, but no movement toward specifically identifying groups of violent offending youth as a "gang" has occurred, in spite of the parents' belief that safety for their children, in school, was obtained through gang membership.

March 2001 brought to Israel its first case of murder on school grounds. On March 12, 2001, Lior Attias, aged 14, was stabbed just outside of his classroom by a 17-year-old schoolmate. The only explanation was that the murder was the result of a school-yard brawl. The 17-year-old faces charges of manslaughter and illegal possession of a weapon (Fisher-Ilan, 2001). This incident, as well as a survey reported by the *Yediot Aharonot* daily as cited in the *Jerusalem Post* article by Lefkovits (2001), indicated that Israel was the world leader in youth violence. Lefkovits indicated that Israel was ranked number one among 10 industrialized countries in the level of violence among 12- and 13-year-old children. "The survey cites 24 percent of Israeli pupils aged 12–13 reported being subject to physical violence in 1999, compared with 10 percent of American kids their age" (Lefkovits, 2001, para 6). The figures are buttressed by police statistics, which point to a nearly 13 percent increase in the number of juvenile files police have opened in 2001 compared with 2000 (Lefkovits, 2001, para. 6).

Benbenishty, Zeira, and Astor (1999) have indicated in their research that Israel ranked eighth for exposure to bullying and eleventh for involvement in bullying. Yitzhak Kadman is the executive director of the National Council for the Child, which has been indicating that there would be a "severe increase" in juvenile violence for five years. Harari (2001) further reported that in the first half of 2001, "there was a 15 percent increase in the number of drug charges: 330 compared to 283 the previous year, and a further 16.5 percent increase in those in possession of drugs not for personal use (43 compared with 36 in 2000)" (para. 6).

TEEN GANGS AND ETHNICITY

A historical search of the *Jerusalem Post*, the leading daily newspaper in Israel, resulted in no specific references to teen gangs until the year 2002. It was then that teen crime activity was first characterized as "gang" or "teen terror cell" behavior. In both of these instances, the youths identified as being part of the teen gang, or terror cells, were of Arab descent and were not Israeli Jews. Research completed by the National Council for the Child as part of the first Beersheba Conference for Child Welfare indicated that since 1993 the number of teen immigrants suspected of crimes as compared with all teens has tripled. Overall, crimes committed by immigrant teens as compared with all crime suspects more than doubled in 2000. The research also showed that children aged 12 to 15 committed 1,296 more crimes than the 16- to 17-year-olds during the same period. With regard to drug-related crimes, there was an increase of 58 percent, with 546 criminal incidents in 2000 as compared with 316 in 1998 ("Sharp Rise in Teen Immigrant Crimes," 2002, para. 4).

This research calls attention to ethnic minority status, racial and ethnic tension, and socioeconomic factors when considering crime in general, and juvenile crime in particular, in Israel. This position is further supported by a study of Israeli students' exposure to school violence, completed in April 2002 by Benbenishty and others of the Hebrew University of Jerusalem, which looked at 21,577 pupils in fourth through eleventh grade in 410 schools across Israel. In their study they found that boys are more in danger of being involved in school violence than girls, and Israeli-Arab students, particularly the Bedouin, are more at risk. Further, the research indicated that the higher level of violence in Arab schools is environmental as opposed to cultural (Benbenishty, Zeira, and Astor, 1999). Their research also suggested that factors leading to violence, such as poverty and stress, are more present in the Israeli-Arab community (Benbenishty et al., 1999). This research also indicated that violence by teens had dropped slightly, as compared with a recent similar study. The Education Ministry director, General Ronit Tirosh, and Yitzhak Kadman of the National Council for the Child indicated that the drop was the result of additional counselors and the implementation of prevention programs aimed at decreasing teen violence.

This new group of statistics brought on a wave of articles in the press and internal discussion among those who work with juvenile crime about the need to address and implement programs to begin the process of decreasing crime in and out of the schools. As stated by U.S. Senator Patrick Moynihan and cited by the *Jerusalem Post*, "An atmosphere of resignation or a process of 'defining deviancy down' . . . will ensure that violence will increase" ("Setting a Better Example," 1999). As far as teen gangs are concerned, the term *gang* is beginning to be mentioned in the press in relation to juvenile crime, and the dramatic incidents described above are suggestive of gang activity in Israel, although there is debate about whether it is a real problem.

PROGRAMS AND POLICIES

Since approximately 1996 there has been a concerted effort on the part of the government of the State of Israel to address policies that speak to the issue of teen violence. There has been a focus on prevention programs for "marginal youths" and intervention programs for young offenders. This effort has proven to be a three-pronged approach involving the police, the schools, and outside researchers. The following section will introduce some of the programs currently being implemented as well as future plans for program implementation.

Police Intervention

ASA. In the State of Israel, with its current laws, if a teen is in trouble and the police are aware, they are not permitted to inform the teen's school. Privacy laws prevent the police from communicating with the school, so it may be that both the police and the school are assisting the same child. In a program being developed for implementation in 2003 called Asa (a Hebrew acronym for violence, drugs, and alcohol), police, schools, municipal workers, and youth workers will collaborate in an effort to decrease teen crime and drug and alcohol use. A confidentiality clause will allow committee members to share information so that they can better track teens and the services provided to them. As a result of the change in confidentiality rules, there is a hope that teen crime will decrease as a result of increased organized communication.

The primary function of Asa will be prevention. This program will be located in nine different cities in Israel, including Beersheba and Tel Aviv. The main goal of the Asa program will be to place youth officers in each school involved in the pilot program. There are approximately 300 schools in Israel that have already implemented the youth officer program in their school. Further, Asa will assist in the creation of after-school programs to increase their ability to track teens in and out of school. This program will be funded in part by the Israel police and by the Education Ministry, which have contributed significant financial resources that will be matched by each participating municipality. The slogan for this program is, It takes a community to raise a child (Lazaroff, 2002, para. 3). This model of team or community collaboration often involves religious or faith-based community organizations and has been successful in some areas of the United States.

Community Policing

Since 1996 the Israeli police have had an effort under way to increase the numbers of police on the street focusing on teen crime, as well as supervising teens with whom they have ongoing contact. This program has been researched and evaluated by the Jerusalem-based JDC-Brookdale Institute (Habib, Ben-Rabi, and Argov, 2000a). The findings of this research were reported by the institute in 2000. Of the current activities evaluated—namely, youth supervision and policing activities, information dissemination activities, and special work methods—the JDC-Brookdale Institute made the following recommendations to improve services and, secondarily, to decrease teen crime activity:

- *Reinforcing and increasing the professionalism of police activity.* This involves increasing the number of police units working with youth. Research findings indicate the effectiveness of crime prevention activities by police, including professionalism in the areas of investigation, supervision, and prevention (specifically information dissemination and school contact). This is being accomplished by hiring two staff officers whose sole responsibility will be to work with teens.
- *Promoting joint activities with community agencies.* This is in line with world trends and research that supports creating partnerships within the community to prevent youth crime. This has been shown to be effective in the Safe School program and the Window on the Police program.

On a different level, police involvement is perceived (primarily in the "Safe School" model) as contributing to, and advancing, local initiatives that improve the school atmosphere. The investment in manpower and funds received through the model's implementation, and the feeling that "something great is happening," can serve as an impetus for an activity that is essentially educational. (p. 4)

This is also in line with statistics showing that there is an increasing rate of school truancy that can further be addressed through this model.

A more recent study by the JDC-Brookdale Institute further addressed the recommendations voiced in its previous report. These new recommendations include more accountability with regard to the services being provided, specifically the introduction of a method of goal setting and development of measures for planning and evaluating outcomes (Habib, Ben-Rabi, and Argov, 2000c). Other areas include work with minors and new immigrant minors, rights of minors, crimes in which victims and perpetrators are minors, and police decisions to open files and seek indictments, as well as the implications of those decisions. These recommendations emphasize the need for increased manpower, more crime units, and greater involvement of police in youth activities. The recommendations also underline the importance of keeping better records on those youths for whom files were not opened and charges were not filed, and of police specifically trained to work with the new young immigrant population—specifically Russian and Ethiopian (Habib, Ben-Rabi, and Argov, 2000b).

School-Based Crime Prevention

The Vilna'i Report. As a result of the increased numbers of violent crimes being committed in the schools, the minister of Science, Culture, and Sports, Matan Vilna'i, presented the minister of Education, Yossi Sarid, with a list of recommendations to address school violence. These recommendations came out of a committee composed of leading professors, school principals, Education Ministry officials, teachers' union representatives, and police. The effort took ten months and was adopted under the slogan, No violence in our schools. These recommendations included increasing the number of police in the schools, providing weekly schoolwide forums on violence, giving principals power to punish offenders, decreasing class size, adding school psychologists and grade advisers to organize and implement antiviolence activities, improving the physical appearance and safety of the schools, checking for violence in special education, and setting clear guidelines for teachers who use violence as a means of behavioral redirection. Although this was a program fully supported at its inception, time has shown that while the plan was initiated on a school-to-school basis, the costs associated with statewide implementation were prohibitive (Hoffman, 2000).

In one interesting intervention effort, the police and a school principal joined forces to eliminate the school's drug dealers. In 2000, noticing the increasing number of drug-using students in his school, the Hadassim Youth Village program director, Tzvi Levy, brought in an undercover officer. This was only after he had organized antidrug programs for his 1,800 students through the Al-Sam Anti-Drug Abuse Association. With the undercover officer in place, over a six-month period of time, the officer was able to collect evidence against 22 school-based drug suppliers. The officer that worked at Hadassim was one of 250 undercover detectives working throughout Israel to address and eliminate the problems of drugs and violence among youth.

In keeping with this model, Deputy Commander Suzy Ben-Baruch of the Israel Police Juvenile branch listed four ways that drugs are being dealt with in the schools:

- *Prevention*—The "Safe School" program, similar to DARE in the United States, brings 150 police into schools on a regular basis to work with students.
- *Exposure*—Encouraging schools to expose the problems of violence and drug use in the schools, and not attempting to cover them up.
- *Investigation*—Resources have improved, and services and the ability to track offenders have increased.
- *Bringing cases to court quickly and efficiently*—Open communication between schools and the police is primary.

Students arrested for drug-related crimes will also be brought before a school committee to create a plan to prevent further drug use. Depending on the severity, the school will have the ability to recommend treatment or an antidrug educational program (Gleit, 2000).

Diversity Training

This chapter has introduced the problem of teen violence in Israel and the question of whether or not gangs are a problem there. Hopefully, it has also helped to provide an understanding of the issue of diversity and how differences affect a teen's ability to fit in, adjust to change, and feel part of the larger society. Israeli society does not want teens to choose gangs as a way of belonging. In keeping with the development of programs geared to address violence and drug use among teens, the minister of education established a Unit of Education for Democracy and Coexistence in 1986. This unit's core mission is to develop, promote, and support coexistence (diversity) in the schools. It is a program geared toward a target population of preschool age through twelfth graders plus teachers. "The Department's main areas of focus are

- Education for life in a democratic society
- Education for life in a multicultural society, with emphasis on Jewish and Israeli-Arab relations
- Education for democracy for students who immigrated to Israel

- Educational involvement in current events
- Familiarizing teachers and students with Israeli democracy
- Instituting democratic processes in educational institutions and the educational system; and
- Education toward peace." (Jewish Virtual Library, 2002)

These goals are met through workshops, conventions, and in-service training for youth and youth educators.

Other programs that address diversity are

- *Children Teaching Children*—A pilot program run in conjunction with Givat Haviva, bringing together Jewish and Arab elementary and middle school students and their teachers.
- *Young Archaeologists/Young Painters/Young Sculptors*—A yearlong program with Jewish and Arab students working in the areas of archaeology, sculpture, and painting.
- *Language Studies*—Jewish and Arab high school students work together to pass the oral matriculation examination in English.

The Vilna'i Report did include in its statement that it had been studying successful international programs in an attempt to decrease teen crime behavior. One program was a Norwegian program that addressed the combination of encouragement of pro-social behavior with stiff punishments for violence. This program has been reported to have cut violence in half in Norway in a period of 18 months. The same program has been successfully implemented in England, Scotland, Japan, and South Korea.

CONCLUSION

The lives of Yevgeny and Lior were taken by groups of their peers who were unhappy with a decision or a statement each had made. This teen group behavior could be called gang behavior, and it has raised alarm in Israel. Deputy Commander Suzy Ben-Baruch indicated that increasing numbers of crimes were being committed by youth. "Israel is #1 in teen violence" is not just a headline in the *Jerusalem Post*; it is a reality facing all Israelis. In order for there to be a decrease in this level of teen crime, several factors will need to continue to be addressed. The JDC-Brookdale Institute, 2000, notes

- There appears to be a lack of accountability and documentation for teen offenders. Furthermore, there seems to be a lack of policy with regard to filing of charges or not. In addition, there is also no clear policy for the treatment of incarcerated youth offenders.
- High dropout rates need to be addressed with the minister of education and in-

dividual principals and school administrators. A large number of Israel's teens will go on to military service and postsecondary education.

- School safety continues to be addressed. If a child or adolescent does not feel safe entering school or feels as though they need to join a gang to feel protected, how effective will the educational system be? Teachers and administrators must work together to make school a place where all children feel safe.

- While there have been several programs implemented to enhance acculturation efforts for Arabs, Russians, and Ethiopians, this is still not enough. The government continues to segregate educational, financial, and military efforts, and to that end, they are setting an example that teens and children are following—an example of hierarchy and hatred.

- The Israeli system of ministers is an ineffective system in that no one department is larger or more responsible than another. The problem with the system is the lack of communication among ministers where important issues such as school violence, drug use, and criminal activity are concerned.

The conclusion is that Israel may have a problem with teen gang activity. Over the past several years attempts have been made to address teen violence, whether it was related to gang activity or not. The question of teen gang activity and teen violence will remain in doubt in Israel until a clearer consensus emerges about the nature of the problem of youth violence. Research and dialogue among politicians, educators, the law enforcement community, and scholars can only help in the development of a better understanding of youth violence so that Yevgeny and Lior will not be the first in a line of teen gang tragedies.

REFERENCES

Arnold, M. S. (1999, June 29). "Teen killing, casual style." *The Jerusalem Post*. Retrieved August 16, 2002, from http://www.jpost.com/com/archive/29. June.1999/features/article-23.html.

Benbenishty, R., A. Zeira, and R. A. Astor. "A national study of school violence in Israel." *Wave* 2 (Fall 1999).

The Center for Social Policy Studies in Israel. *Israel: Social-economic review* (Jerusalem, Israel: American Jewish Joint Distribution Committee, 2001).

Central Bureau of Statistics. *Statistical Abstract of Israel* 52 (2001).

———. *Statistical Abstract of Israel* 53 (2002).

Central Intelligence Agency. *The world factbook/Israel* (Washington, DC: Office of Public Affairs, 2000).

Fisher-Ilan, A. (2001, April 1). "Failing the violence test." *The Jerusalem Post*. Retrieved September 1, 2002, from http://cgis.jpost.com/cgi-bin/general/printarticle.

Gleit, H. J. (1999, June 14). "Police: Help needed to fight juvenile crime." *The Jerusalem Post*. Retrieved August 31, 2002, from http://pqasb.pqarchiver.com/jpost/doc.

————. (2000, March 26). "Principal, police join forces to deal with a school's drug dealers." *The Jerusalem Post*. Retrieved August 31, 2002, from http://pqasb.pqarchiver.com/jpost/doc.

Habib, J., D. Ben-Rabi, and D. Argov. *Police intervention in the area of crime prevention among youth*. (RR-376-01-Executive Summary) (Jerusalem, Israel: JDC-Brookdale Institute, 2000a).

————. *Police intervention in crime among immigrant youth* (RR-377-01-Executive Summary) (Jerusalem, Israel: JDC-Brookdale Institute, 2000b).

————. *Police intervention with minors and youth: Summary report* (RR-380-01-Executive Summary) (Jerusalem, Israel: JDC-Brookdale Institute, 2000c).

Harari, R. (2001, September 28). "Focus on Tel Aviv and Jaffa." *The Jerusalem Post*. Retrieved August 31, 2002, from http://pqasb.pqarchiver.com/jpost/doc.

Hoffman, G. (2000, March 10). "Is anyone fighting school violence?" *The Jerusalem Post*. Retrieved August 31, 2002, from http://pqasb.pqarchiver.com/jpost/doc.

Israel Ministry of Foreign Affairs. *Criminal statistics 1988–1999* (Jerusalem, Israel: Central Bureau of Statistics, 1999a).

————. *Demographic characteristics of populations in Israel 1995–1999* (Special Publication 1182) (Jerusalem, Israel: Central Bureau of Statistics, 1999b).

Jewish Virtual Library. *Building bridges: Israeli public policy*. The American-Israeli Cooperative. Retrieved September 1, 2002, from www.us-israel.org/jsource/bridges/one.html.

Lazaroff, T. (2002, May 6). "Pilot program aims to cut teen drug abuse, violence." *The Jerusalem Post*. Retrieved August 31, 2002, from http://pqasb.pqarchiver.com/jpost/doc.

Lefkovits, E. (2001, December 31). "Israel first in violence by 12-year-olds." *The Jerusalem Post*. Retrieved August 31, 2002, from http://pqasb.pqarchiver.com/jpost/doc.

"Setting a better example." (1999, June 18). *The Jerusalem Post*. Retrieved August 31, 2002, from http://pqasb.pqarchiver.com/jpost/doc.

"Sharp rise in teen immigrant crimes, conference told." (2002, February 19). *The Jerusalem Post*. Retrieved August 31, 2002, from http://pqasb.pqarchiver.com/jpost/doc.

Weisman, G. M. *Israel: World Factbook of Criminal Justice Systems—Israel* (Washington, DC: United States Department of Justice, Bureau of Justice Statistics, 1990).

7

ITALY

Bettina Lozzi-Toscano

THE TEEN GANG CONNECTION TO ORGANIZED CRIME IN ITALY

It is difficult to discuss the problem of Italian teen gangs without emphasizing the influence of organized crime because the two are interrelated: the mob finds young recruits from among juvenile delinquents, and teens become seduced by the lure of gang life. Religion, libations, cuisine, and family are staples of Italian culture. However, embedded within this cultural framework is the secretive and violent world of Italian organized crime. Italy has gained the reputation of being the birthplace of organized crime, and subsequently, most of the crimes committed in the country, whether juvenile or adult, are closely linked to the Mafia. As a result, much of the available research on teens and gangs is related to organized crime. Many of the sources reviewed suggest that early juvenile delinquency can be tied to future organized criminal activity. This chapter will focus on the teen gang phenomenon as it relates to Italian organized crime and will discuss the country's legal and political responses to this problem.

The word *gang* has been defined as "a group or association of three or more persons who may have a common identifying sign, symbol or name, and who individually or collectively engage in, or have engaged in, criminal activity, or as a juvenile commits an act that if committed by an adult would be a criminal act" (Chavez, n.d., p. 1). In Italian the word *gang, banda*, translates into a group of friends or a band of thieves. Teen gangs in the Italian experience are different from teen gangs in Latin America or in the

United States. In Italy gang activity is much more tied into the world of organized crime than to what is typically understood as teen "street gangs." Stereotypical youth gangs are usually made up of teens from broken homes, looking for a pseudo family for a sense of belonging. In Italy family is an integral part of the culture. Italian gangs have to offer much more than a sense of belonging to attract members, and organized gangs do just that. These gangs offer status, power, protection, and security and in return demand loyalty, secrecy, and honor.

Due to the increase in organized criminal activity, Italian police as well as policy makers have had to reinterpret the word *gang* to include the element of organized activity. For example, one author defines this reinterpreted understanding of a gang as

A nonideological enterprise involving a number of persons in close social interaction, organized on a hierarchical basis with at least three levels/ranks, for the purpose of securing profit and power by engaging in illegal and legal activities. Positions in the hierarchy and positions involving functional specialization may be assigned on the basis of kinship or friendship, or rationally assigned according to skill. The positions are not dependent on the individuals occupying them at any particular time. Permanency is assumed by the members, who strive to keep the enterprise integral and active in pursuit of its goals. It eschews competition and strives for monopoly on an industry or territorial basis. There is a willingness to use violence and/or bribery to achieve ends and maintain discipline. Membership is restricted, although nonmembers may be involved on a contingency basis. There are explicit rules, oral or written, which are enforced by sanctions that include murder. (Abadinsky, 1994, p. 8)

As a result, Italy has had to reevaluate its policies on juvenile crime. Italy has also expanded its collaborative efforts with other countries with the implementation of prevention programs, community policing, and international aid. Teen gangs are not seen as a separate entity but part of a larger organized element that is increasingly becoming the training ground for future mafiosi.

PROFILE OF ITALY

Italy is located in southern Europe. It is a peninsula that extends into the Mediterranean Sea and is slightly larger than the state of Arizona. Austria, France, Vatican City, San Marino, Slovenia, and Switzerland all border Italy's landmass. It has an estimated population of 57,715,625, of which 4,198,569 are males between the ages of 1 and 14 (Central Intelligence Agency [CIA], 2002). Italy's population is predominantly Italian, although there are small groups of Germans, French, Albanians, and Greeks. Italian is the official language, though German and French are also spoken in some regions. Roman Catholicism is the predominant religion in the country, with some Protestant, Jewish, and Muslim communities emerging.

Government

Italy's government is a republic. The government consists of the president, who is the chief of state; the prime minister, who is the head of government and who has a cabinet; and most importantly a democratically elected parliament. Italy has 20 regions and 94 provinces, and its legal system is based on civil law. There is no federal government or federal system of justice. All criminal laws are included in the penal code of the country. The criminal justice system is part of a state system that operates throughout the nation in local districts and governments. Italy has over twenty political parties, including democratic and communist groups.

Education

Like most European countries, Italy has a government-sponsored education system. More than 90 percent of students attend public schools. The government sets educational policies and develops school curricula. Children are required to attend school from age 6 to age 15, from elementary school through junior high. However, reports have indicated a high rate of school dropout among elementary and middle school children (European Industrial Relations Observatory, 2000).

Once children reach the high school level, they have a choice to attend a four- or five-year specialized program of study. Students can choose between vocational, technical, science, classical, teacher training, and language schools. Comparatively speaking, high school education in Italy is similar to most Western four-year college programs. Italy has forty-seven public universities and some private universities that are run by the Roman Catholic Church.

BASIC POLICIES, LEGISLATION, AND DEMOGRAPHIC INFORMATION

There is a major push within the country to decrease juvenile delinquency and eliminate organized crime. Police agencies are working together with government officials to curtail the school dropout rate as well as increase community policing to combat organized activity. Italy is working toward restructuring the education system as well as the penal system to aid in the fight against organized gang activity.

Most agencies link young people involved in crime to organized activity. Police find it difficult to curtail the growing violence that is engulfing many of the provinces in the country, and law-abiding citizens are torn between their civic duty to report illegal activity and the lure of safety that organized crime offers. Italian citizens look to their police force and politicians to find solutions to this problem; however, conflicts within the legal system as well as within the police force make it difficult to find alternatives.

Italian Police

The police force is divided into three branches, the state police (Polizia di Stato), the *carabinieri*, and the Finance Guard (*Guardia Finanza*). Each branch falls under the authority of the Ministry of Interior, Defense, and Finance. The state police oversee all of the regions and provinces as well as monitor the mountain and maritime police. The carabinieri are responsible for policing local districts as well as for protecting citizens from criminal activity. The Finance Guard is responsible for defending Italy's borders. Their main purpose is to enforce Italian financial law, which includes border patrol and importing/exporting transactions.

The Finance Guard is the primary branch of the police that deals with organized criminal activity, such as drug trafficking and counterfeiting. The carabinieri are responsible for handling juvenile crime, theft, and terrorist acts. The responsibilities of the state police include investigating and analyzing crime scenes and implementing prevention programs. Although each branch has its identified responsibilities, there is considerable overlap in the execution of their roles, complicating communication between the three branches of the police system.

Legal System

The Italian legal system is based on civil law. It encompasses two basic principles, no penalty without a law and no crime without a law (CIA, 2002). The legal system is influenced by ecclesiastical Roman law, which states that an individual is believed to be solely responsible for his or her actions. During Mussolini's reign the Italian legal system was characterized by severe sanctions and authoritarian penalties. Prison sentences were extremely harsh for the most minor offenses. After Mussolini's assassination there were no significant changes made to the penal system, and it has remained virtually the same.

In spite of this, Italy had one of the lowest prison populations in Europe between 1971 and 1991, as reported in the 1991 Instituto Nazionale di Statistica (Italian National Institute of Statistics [ISTAT]). According to some researchers, this relatively low rate of imprisonment is not related to the positive effects of diversion or to alternative strategies for rehabilitating offenders, but to a less-developed system of punishment (Pavarini, 1994). What is even more surprising is the low number of juveniles reported imprisoned in that same year, i.e., 1991 was only 1.4 per 100,000 (ISTAT, 1991).

According to Italian penal code, no teen under the age of 14 can be tried as an adult no matter the severity of the crime (Marongiu and Biddau, 2002). This impacts the organized gang problem because, historically, juveniles under the age of 14 are given much more lenient sentences than their older counterparts, making younger teens much more attractive to organized gangs. Some experts suggest that political corruption and miscommunication within the legal and penal structure of Italian government is partly to blame for this trend of youth recruitment into gangs (Pavarini, 1994).

Gang Demographics

As was mentioned previously, most of the research available on teen gangs in Italy is conducted within the framework of organized crime. There is not a widespread public perception of "youth" gangs in Italy. However, the phenomenon of "criminal organized gangs" is widely recognized, and much of the research reviewed incorporates the element of juvenile criminality. As in most organized gangs, Italian groups recruit mostly young males. Experts have described juvenile crime as a feeding ground for small groups to develop and compete with organized activity (Sullivan, 1997). Teens who start off committing juvenile crime in Italy are vulnerable to recruitment into the dark world of drug trafficking, money laundering, and violence that is characteristic of organized crime. Given that organized crime activity is so embedded in the Italian culture, it seems easy for young teens to become involved in criminal behavior.

There are no statistics available for the percentage of people living below the poverty line in Italy (CIA, 2002). However, studies have suggested that lower socioeconomic status predisposes juveniles to commit crimes (Pfeifer, 1998). In Italy, the increase in juvenile organized criminal activity can be linked to school dropout rates as well as to socioeconomic stressors. Although some studies postulate that teen crime can be connected to civic commitment (the notion that a person's sense of commitment, solidarity, and mutual trust within their geographical area will impact criminal behavior) (Gatti, Tremblay, and Larocque, 2003), most research suggests that juveniles are much more prone to join organized gangs for the prestige and status they offer (Killias, 1989).

HISTORY OF ORGANIZED CRIME AND THE RECRUITMENT OF TEENS

Italy has never been associated with characteristic gang activity, such as drive-by shootings, colors, or visible signs. Italian gang images more closely resemble the *Godfather* stereotype—a group of men sitting in a smoke-filled room making decisions about political bribery, murder, or money laundering. Hollywood and the popular media have had a major influence in how Italian criminal clans, or mafias, are depicted and most people equate mafiosi figures with such characters as Tony from the popular American TV drama *The Sopranos*. However, how Italian gangs developed and how easily teens are seduced by them are embedded in Italy's cultural and political history.

The origin of the word *mafia* is still debated, but most agree that it can be traced back to the Norman invasion of Sicily in the ninth century. Many Italians were captured and enslaved, forced to work on their own farms and lands that had been appropriated by the invaders. As time passed and the Italians grew restless, many fled. The Sicilian people took to the hills and mountains and hid there. This rugged environment became the Sicilian "place of refuge," or mafia. These mafias came to symbolize a unified people banding together against foreign invaders and became societal strongholds for others to depend upon during times of struggle and strife. These people banded together for protection, leadership, and survival. Over time, these clans began to evolve into organized groups that included a leadership structure. Mafias came to signify something patriotic, a group of individuals fighting for their families and their lands.

After Sicily was freed from foreign invaders, these mafia clans integrated their newly formed political structure into neighboring villages, towns, and cities around the island. Due to their clandestine beginnings, mafias continued their secret-society ways and incorporated the same survival mentality within the communities they served. Anyone wanting to become part of the ruling clan had to abide by strict adherence to their rules and beliefs. The most important rule was, and still is, the code of honor, or *omerta* (silence).

Teen Recruitment

In contrast to most Western juvenile gangs, which publicly display their colors, signs, and symbols, Italian gangs continue to exist in secrecy. For the last two hundred years Italian organized gangs have been able to exist in secret and as a result have been able to further infiltrate other regions in the country. The four major mafia organizations are centralized in the regions of Sicily, Calabria, Campania, and Puglia. These four regions are mostly made up of farmers and laborers whose dependence on family and money are essential elements of survival. Teens whose families are in economic need are at greater risk of dropping out of school in order to gain employment to help their families financially. Organized groups feed off this need, and young teens are vulnerable to gang recruitment in order to ensure that their families are taken care of.

Although the Mafia's reputation is notorious and violent, it continues to offer townspeople and business owners the safety and protection it once offered the oppressed villagers during the Norman invasions. Still, Italian youngsters join these mafias, or gangs, for many of the same reasons that marginalized minority youths in other countries join gangs; namely, for structure, status, and protection. Although the gangs demand respect and allegiance, they also promote violence and defiance of authority.

Teen gangs are offshoots of organized crime families, and juveniles are taught from a very young age to protect their own. Whether on a street corner or in school, teens are indoctrinated into the lifestyle from early on (L. Maffezzoli, personal communication, December 2003). More and more Italian gangs made up of eager teens are evolving, and they are emerging from small towns and moving into larger cities. Larger cities like Palermo, Rome, and Naples are starting to see an increase in organized criminal activity (Marongiu and Biddau, 2002).

Italian gangs have always incorporated cultural beliefs into their organizations. Members continue to respect family ties and traditions while simultaneously serving the gangs' needs. This is in strong contrast to more "traditional" gangs, which are made up of abused or neglected children that are looking for a "family" environment. Italian gangs view membership as an extension of their own families, and because of their strict codes of silence for protection, members may feel more secure that their loved ones will be taken care of.

Membership

Membership does have its privileges, and in many of Italy's small towns, teens see gang membership as a route to status and prestige. Delinquency, and especially organized crime, have become the only quick way for many young teens living in poverty to provide for their families. Many of the youths who become criminals leave school and begin learning survival on the streets. Consequently, street life introduces most juveniles to the lure of organized gangs. New members must prove themselves worthy of membership, and with each petty crime, a young teen can begin moving up the gang ladder of power and status. With the protection and immediate rewards teens find with gang membership, most remain loyal to the gang and avoid independent criminal activity. This form of reciprocity ensures group cohesion and loyalty. The Mafia becomes a home away from home, where the young are made to feel important, worthy, and essential to the workings of the organization.

Teens who are recruited by Mafia families start their criminal careers by committing minor offenses. Their crimes secure and sometimes elevate their positions within the "family." In many cases, teen gang involvement is a generational trend that is passed down from grandfathers to fathers to sons. Therefore, in some Italian regions gang, or Mafia, life is as integral a part of a family's structure as is Sunday dinner. Pavarini (1994) stated that Italian structure—i.e., legislation, culture, and family—resembles the layers of an artichoke, which has "a relatively compact heart, covered by layer upon layer of leaves" (p. 55). These young mafiosi are taught to use weapons at an early age and are instructed to hate all authority except the Catholic Church (Mafia history, n.d.).

In comparison to traditional street gangs, which are primarily territorial, Italian street gangs have evolved into highly localized and organized groups. The recruitment of young males is most common because of the traditional Italian family hierarchy. Men are the heads of the household, and females are subservient members of the family. Organized gangs use the Italian family's traditional hierarchical structure to maintain balance within the organization.

ITALY'S POLITICAL AND SOCIAL RESPONSES

In one national survey, Italian citizens identified street crime, particularly crimes committed by young drug abusers, as a top priority (Doxa, 1992). Now, does this trend reflect independent active juvenile criminality in the country, or is it the result of an increase and expansion of gang-related activity? It appears that the combination of a lax juvenile legal system and the prominent influence of organized crime have propelled the Italian government to ask for help from the international community. As with most gangs around the world, Italian gangs have expanded their criminal activity to include drugs and more recently human trafficking (D'Emilio, 2001). Italy has the largest number of heroin addicts after the United States and has the highest rate of heroin overdose deaths per capita (Rudic, 2000).

The social response to the drug abuse epidemic and other youth crime has been to force the government to attempt to reform their police force as well as crack down on organized activity. The Italian government is working on penal reform as well as collaborative programs with other countries. It has joined forces with Russia to combat organized crime and has looked at neighboring countries such as France and Austria to help reestablish effective strategies to address street crime.

Community Policing

Community policing came about as a campaign to restructure policing methods and strategies. Citizens wanted the police force to take a more proactive role in community issues instead of simply responding situationally to specific reports of crimes and events. After much pressure from the police unions as well as public demands, the Italian Parliament passed the Community Policing Law on March 31, 2000. Since Italian police forces first adopted the idea of community policing the homicide rate has been reduced by over 70 percent (Jones and Weisman, 2003).

The community policing program also emphasizes the need for interagency exchanges. The state police will begin implementing community policing programs in other local and regional police forces to collaboratively work toward planning and carrying out crime prevention programs. Since its inception in 2000, community policing has developed outreach programs that include mental health services, drug prevention taskforces, and truancy programs. An important indicator of this program's effectiveness has been the decrease in gang-related violence. With the implementation of education initiatives in late 1997, police-community teams began pursuing and addressing the social and economic causes of teenage gang recruitment. By the end of 1999 gang-related homicides had been reduced to eleven per year. In 2000 there were only nine gang-related homicides in Palermo (Jones and Weisman, 2003).

Collaborative Efforts

Local governments in Italy are working together with the FBI to curtail ports of entry for the drug trade. Juvenile crime associated with drug use or drug distribution is being investigated as part of mob dealings and not as isolated incidents. Gang members are being questioned about their association with organized crime. As a result of this trend, Italy has begun to implement measures to combat the problem of gang activity. Special police squads have been created to dismantle criminal organizations. In one analysis, organized crime was classified as any crime committed by juvenile gangs or other organizations of professional criminals (Albini, 1975). In order to facilitate more police cooperation from other countries, officials are proposing to eliminate internal frontiers in order to combat smuggling and drug trafficking (Fijnaut, 1990).

School administrators together with local community agencies are working toward decreasing the problem of school dropouts. The Italian education and training system does not provide adequate interventions to address the problems of at-risk youth and to prevent school dropouts. Schools and parents are working together to implement guidance and career counseling programs to help students think about future goals beyond their primary education. Policy makers are developing strategies to educate families and youths, suggesting possible alternatives to formal education such as vocational training courses (European Industrial Relations Observatory, 2000).

POLITICAL INITIATIVES AND POLICIES

Since much of the crime in Italy's provinces and regions is committed by organized gangs, policy makers have also looked to other countries with experience in dealing with organized crime for assistance in combating this problem. Italy has started working collaboratively with the U.S. State Department in implementing several initiatives to address gang-related activity. Italy may have given birth to the concept of gangs, but the United States has had the most experience in handling the law enforcement intricacies of organized crime. Because of the history and complexity of Italy's political and legal ties to the Mafia, policy makers and government officials are trying to find alternative strategies to eradicate gang crime.

The Federal Bureau of Investigation (FBI) and the Bureau of International Narcotics and Law Enforcement Affairs (INL), which includes the Drug Enforcement Administration (DEA) and Customs, together with other international agencies, have developed programs to train foreign law enforcement officials in counternarcotics and other law enforcement strategies. The training is specialized and designed to focus on the specific needs of each country. Additionally, joint training is offered in order to foster collaboration between neighboring countries. Programs dealing with financial crimes (i.e., methods for promoting asset seizure and combating money laundering) will continue to expand as police forces and local jurisdictions become more trained and educated.

Finally, Italy is developing research-based programs to improve prevention and treatment services related to young teens to reduce drug- and crime-related activity (United States Department of State, 2002). One such program is the EuroGang Project. The EuroGang network consists of leading European and American researchers in the field. The main objectives of the EuroGang Project are to build a knowledge base regarding youth gangs, construct a common methodological infrastructure for comparative analysis of youth violence, and effectively utilize the knowledge obtained to develop local, national, and international responses to youth crime and violence (Norwegian Institute of International Affairs, 2003). Italy is working with local governments to implement national and community resources to address the increase in gang-related crime. The Italian government is working toward a systemic structural change that will highlight prevention projects for high-risk youths.

Italy, together with the governments of Spain and Japan, is also developing an organizational plan to evaluate its juvenile correctional programs as well as antigang/antiviolence programs (Freeh, 1998). In addition, Italian officials are working together with Italian-American groups in the United States to continue open communication between both governments in order to ensure cooperative actions against gang-related activities. The Italian-American Working Group (IAWG) is one such organization in the United States that is working together with Italian law enforcement to fight against organized crime at the local and international level (Freeh, 1998). This relationship is a cop-to-cop partnership that focuses on strategies and interventions at the basic level of law enforcement.

SOCIAL VIEWS, CUSTOMS, AND PRACTICES

Italian gang membership has remained the same for generations. Stereotypical street gangs have borrowed rituals and symbols from their Italian counterparts (Mangione and Morreale, 1992). There is a hierarchy in Italian gang structure that includes rules, rituals, and traditions. As previously mentioned, Italian culture is very much family-oriented, and in order for Italian gangs to be attractive to teens, they must offer more than the basic element of family life. For many, that difference is in the ability of organized gangs to offer protection, status, and power. Joining a "family" automatically instills a sense of belonging above and beyond personal satisfaction. A member becomes part of a new, "secret" family that wants them for some special characteristic they possess. Belonging to an organized family brings its members much prestige and a sense of elitism because of the power these "families" possess.

Underlining this family structure is the bond that ties members for life, the code of honor. Through informers and antigang investigators, "outsiders" have been able to gain a better understanding of a gang's rituals of initiation. Most organized gangs have a specific ritualistic ceremony through which an initiate enters into a family. For many the ritual includes swearing allegiance to the gang while pricking their fingers and smearing blood on a paper image of a saint ("Camorra Battle," 1997). The symbolism behind the smearing of the blood on a religious image is a reflection of the commitment and allegiance to the gang. Religion is an important part of Italian culture. Over 95 percent of Italians are Roman Catholic (Davis, 2001). The blood is a symbol of complete allegiance. It not only symbolizes a member's willingness to die for the group but also acknowledges that every member of the person's family is tied to this new family and therefore is protected by the gang. This initiation ritual automatically raises a member from a lowly nobody to a prized status that immediately confers honor and respect.

For some Italian teens a search for structure, recognition, status, and protection are enough incentives to attract them to join a gang. Many of these same teens still come home in time for dinner, spend time at home with their families, and go to church on Sundays. The stereotypical Western image of a gang member is usually a misinformed teen searching for a pseudo family for a sense of belonging and excitement. For many Italian teens, Mafia gang life is a place to gain power, status, and reputation. International juvenile crime has been on the rise for several years. Researchers have attributed much of this increase to a global shift within the value system of teens as well as to world politics, media exposure, and changing family dynamics (Brennan-Walshe, 1975). As the face of families change and world events continue to influence everyday life the routine and consistency of organized gangs will continue to attract new devotees.

Joining an Italian Mafia gang is almost like entering a new business: a young recruit starts from the ground level and slowly moves up the ranks. The new initiate starts off as a soldier, the brawn of the organization, doing the dirty work for the family. These members usually are the muscle of the group and are recruited to make sure that others make good on agreements, contracts, or any other dealings already established by the gang. Teens are taught to protect themselves, and they shadow older members as they progress through the ranks. For many, organized crime is a sure and quick road to success (L. Maffezzoli, personal communication, December 2003). Once members prove themselves at the lower levels of the organization, they are moved up the ladder to lieutenant. At this level a member becomes a sort of middle manager, in charge of making sure that the needs of the gang family are being met and that the demands of the boss are being fulfilled. The captains are members that have been within the organization for a number of years and are seen as counselors or confidants to the boss. Captains are in charge of expanding the influence of the Mafia gang into other areas or in other business aspects. Promotions are bestowed as a result of a member's loyalty production. Italian Mafia gangs are run much the way Fortune 500 companies are: promotions are based on personal performance.

As in most gangs, symbols and secret language are a representation of the exclusivity of membership. Members pledge to obey a rigid code of behavior and in doing so are bound by its steadfast commandments of fidelity, silence, and punishment for discrepancies. In order to enforce its rules, organized gangs use a variety of symbols, with "justice" being the ultimate message. For example, if a member breaks the code of silence *(omerta)*, his body may be found with a stone wedged in its mouth. Missing genitals would symbolize disrespect or infidelity to another member ("Camorra Battle," 1997). Italian Mafia gangs do not use colors or clothing as a representation of their "family" primarily because of their code of secrecy. Italian gangsters do not publicly announce their allegiance to their gangs. It is understood and usually spread by word of mouth.

Italy has at least five ruling families in Sicily, Naples, Calabria, and Genova. These established groups have expanded their strongholds and infiltrated bigger cities like Florence and Rome. However, the problem with these Mafia gangs is that their power is reaching beyond the boundaries of the Italian countryside and is moving across countries. Members are being sent to start up other clans in different parts of the world to ensure their place within the spectrum of Mafia gang activity, and with such expansion, law enforcement and government will have an even more difficult time curtailing their illegitimate activities.

FUTURE PLANS

Organized criminal groups, both large and small, have become an increasingly powerful entity in Italy. What were once small territorial street families have grown into full-fledged syndicates trafficking drugs, smuggling goods, and more recently trafficking humans. In the midst of these crime families are the vulnerable teenagers of Italian culture, teens that are recruited to continue the traditions and rituals passed down from one criminal generation to another. Juvenile crime has become the training ground for future initiates, and Italian lawmakers are developing collaborative programs to help minimize gang-related activity.

The Italian government has developed crime legislation to handle organized gang activity and has even added a category of crime of the "mafiosi type" to its classification list. Italian legislators are also working on reformulating the age of criminality to include teens. Presently, the Italian penal code considers any person under the age of fourteen as not mentally competent and therefore not chargeable with a crime. However, if a person between the ages of 14 and 18 is found to be competent, he or she is then considered legally responsible. Teens are given much more lenient criminal penalties (Marongiu and Biddau, 2002). This aspect of the penal code affecting juveniles makes teens more protected from criminal sanction and hence they are increasingly being used as soldiers within crime families.

Italy is looking to develop more collaborative partnerships with other countries to combat the gang problem. Besides the aforementioned programs within local and national governments, Italy is looking to the United States and the FBI for aid. The FBI's international law enforcement initiative called the Legal Attache program is one such partnership. The program assigns personnel to American embassies abroad to help foreign governments solve crimes and train law enforcement officials in antigang and antiterrorism strategies (Freeh, 1998).

The United States' DEA and Customs Department are working together with Italy to combat organized crimes such as money laundering and, more recently, human trafficking. Youth prevention programs and early intervention plans will continue to expand to address the changing profile of juvenile offenders. More interventions aimed at decreasing the school dropout rates as well as expanding community policing programs are also being targeted. Further research is being conducted about juvenile delinquency, bullying, and the development of Mafia-type gangs in order to provide a basis for the development of strategies to decrease the incidents of criminality among the young (Baldry and Farrington, 2000; see also "Bande giovanili," 2000; Castellan, 2001). These changes are being implemented with the hope that an overall systemic restructuring will decrease the incidents of organized activity in a country whose cultural history gave rise to its own *famiglia secreta*.

ACKNOWLEDGMENTS

Mr. L. Maffezzoli is a relative who has personal experience in teen gang activity and his generous participation in this project and his willingness to share insider information about the details of Italian gang life, rituals, and practices immensely enhanced this chapter.

REFERENCES

Abadinsky, A. *Organized crime*, 4th ed. (Chicago: Nelson-Hall Publishers, 1994).

Albini, J. L. "Mafia as method: A comparison between Great Britain and the USA regarding the existence and structure of types of organized crime." *International Journal of Criminology and Penology* 3 (1975): 295–305.

Baldry, A. C., and D. P. Farrington. "Bullies and delinquents: Personal characteristics and parental styles." *Journal of Community and Applied Psychology* 10 (2000): 17–31.

Bande giovanili e violenza degli adolescenti [Child gangs and violence among adolescents]. (2000). Retrieved March 18, 2003, from http://www.brainzaest.it/scuole/medie/labrete/giornale/didattica/bande.htm.

Brennan-Walshe, K. S. "Trends in juvenile crime." *Royal Society of Health Journal* 1 (1975): 6–9.

"Camorra battle leaves 12 dead." *Crime and Justice International* (7 September 1997): 11.

Castellan, S. (2001). Baby gang: Anche in Italia? [Baby gangs: Also in Italy?]. Transcrime, Trentino. Retrieved March 16, 2003, from http://www.questotrentino.it/2001/02/transcrime2_01.htm.

Central Intelligence Agency. (2002). *Italy*. Retrieved February 24, 2003, from http://www.odci.gov/cia/publications/factbook/it.html.

Chavez, G. (n.d.). Gangs: Frequently asked questions—Madison police department. Dane county narcotics and gang task force. Retrieved March 17, 2003, from http://www.ci.madison.wi.us/police/gangfaqs.html.

Davis, J. A. "Italy." In *World Book Encyclopedia*, vol. 10 (Chicago: World Book, 2001), pp. 496–519.

D'Emilio, F. (2001). "Albania: Foreign gangs working with Italian mobs." *Associated Press*. Retrieved February 22, 2003, from http://lists.partners-intl.net//pipermial/women-east-west/2001-January/000720.html.

Doxa. "La precezione della delinquenza." [The perception of delinquency]. *Bolletino della Doxa* (1992, No.19-20): 216–247.

European Industrial Relations Observatory. (2000). Inefficiency of the Italian training system highlighted. Retrieved March 14, 2003, from http://www.eiro.eurofind.ie.2000/02/feature/it0002144F.html.

Fijnaut, C. "Organized crime: A comparison between the United States of America and Western Europe." *British Journal of Criminology* 30(3) (1990): 321–339.

Freeh, L. J. (1998, Summer). "Statement for the record on international crime before the United States Senate Committee on Appropriations Subcommittee on Foreign Operations." Washington, DC. Retrieved February 27, 2003, from http://fbi.gov/congress/congress98/intrcrime.html.

Gatti, U., R. Tremblay, and D. Larocque. "Civic community and juvenile delinquence: A study of the regions of Italy." *British Journal of Criminology* 43 (2003): 22–40.

Instituto Nazionale di Statistica [ISTAT]. (1991). *Statistche giudiziarie [Judicial statistics], 1989*, (No. 33), Rome: Instituto Nazionale di Statistica [ISTAT].

Jones, A., and R. Weisman. Community policing in Europe: An overview of practices in Italy. Retrieved March 18, 2003, from http://acp.org/articles%20-%20expert%20-%our%20opinion/cpineurope/081002-hitaly.html.

Killias, M. "Criminality among second-generation immigrants in Western Europe: A review of the evidence." *Criminal Justice Review* 14(1) (1989, Spring): 13–42.

Mafia history. (n.d.). Retrieved January 16, 2003, from http://www.geocities.com/capitolhill/parliament/3806/mafh.html.

Mangione, J., and B. Morreale. *La Storia: Five centuries of the Italian American experience* (New York: HarperCollins, 1992).

Marongiu, P., and M. Biddau. (2002). Italy. Retrieved January 13, 2003, from http://www.ojp.usdoj.gov/bjs/pub/ascii/wfbcjita.txt.

Norwegian Institute of International Affairs. (2003). The Euro-gang Project. Retrieved March 14, 2003, from http://www.nupi.no/ForskFelles/Eurogang/gang-set.html.

Pavarini, M. "The new penology and politics in crisis: The Italian case." *British Journal of Criminology* 34 (Special issue, 1994): 49–61.

Pfeifer, C. "Trends in juvenile violence in European countries." In *Crime and justice: A review of research* 23, edited by M. Tonry (Chicago: University of Chicago Press, 1998), pp. 255–328.

Rudic, N. "Policing a diverse country." *Crime and Justice International* (February 16, 2000): 5–12.

Sullivan, J. P. "Third generation street gangs: Turf, cartels and netwarriors." *Crime and Justice International* 10 (November 23, 1997): 9–13.

United States Department of State. (2002, March). *International narcotics control strategy report—2001*. Retrieved March 1, 2003, from http://www.state.gov/g/inl/rls/nrcrpt/2001/rpt/8484pf.html.

8

JAMAICA

Lorna Black

INTRODUCTION

For several decades Jamaica has been known as a tropical paradise and has had a reputation as one of the most romantic spots in the Western Hemisphere. Famed for its sun-drenched beaches, warm tropical breezes, beautiful hotels, rich cultural heritage, many places of interest, and reggae music, Jamaica has enjoyed the economic advantage bestowed by the many visitors to the island, making tourism a key sector in the local economy. In recent years, however, Jamaica's reputation as the place to visit has been tarnished by the high levels of crime and violence that have become almost a part of the Jamaican lifestyle.

Jamaica has emerged as a country with one of the highest per capita murder rates in the world. The numbers of serious crimes are at all-time highs, and for a small country the murder rate is relatively high compared to other countries. Obtaining Jamaican crime statistics is not easy. Because of the extraordinarily high crime rates, the Jamaica Constabulary Force (Jamaican police) has stopped routinely releasing crime statistics. According to the Jamaican Constabulary Statistics Department, as reported in *The Sunday Gleaner*, there were 1,139 people murdered in the year 2001 (Crime Review 2001, 2002). This represented an increase of 252 murders over the year 2000, and an increase of 290 over the year 1999. In Jamaica, as in many other countries, the majority of the crimes are committed by young people. Blank and Minowa (2001), in an unpublished study conducted for the World Bank, found that 55 percent of all crimes in Jamaica in 1999 were

committed by individuals who were under the age of 26 years. This is supported by Police Commissioner Francis Forbes, who reported in 2000 that
increasing numbers of young people were committing crimes and becoming
victims of crimes. In 2001, of a total of 3,558 individuals arrested for major
crimes, 1,929 were individuals under the age of twenty-five years (Crime
Review 2001, 2002). Additionally, of the total number of persons sentenced
to adult correctional facilities in Jamaica in 1999, 30 percent were between
the ages of seventeen and twenty-four years (Blank and Minowa, 2001).

Crime and violence are priority concerns in Jamaica; specifically, the issue
of youth and crime is an area that demands attention. In order to effectively
understand the scope of crime and violence in Jamaica, a look at the factors
contributing to crime is essential. Foremost among them is the phenomenon
of gang activities, which has become a significant part of the Jamaican lifestyle during the last 20 years and which has become a growing threat to the
society at large. Another factor is the large numbers of unemployed and
unemployable persons seeking outlets for their frustration, energy, and thirst
for adventure (Levy, 2001). Levy stated that the social conditions and the
economic frustration of no work, lack of viable opportunities, idleness, and
lack of education and training have provided a good breeding ground for
the development of gangs. Additionally, extensive migration during the past
25 years has robbed many young people, many of them young boys, of
good role models and the support that goes with them. Some of their parents have relocated to foreign countries—such as the United States of America, Canada, and Great Britain—as the economic opportunities in those
countries are far superior and more attractive than those available in Jamaica.
These boys have been left behind in Jamaica to be raised by grandparents
or other relatives, or even nonrelatives such as friends and neighbors, giving
rise to the phenomenon known in Jamaica as child-shifting (Blank and Minowa, 2001). According to Levy, this breakdown in parenting and family
values further served to fuel the restlessness that was already evident.

The rise in gang membership and consequent gang activity was further
fueled in the late 1980s and 1990s by the large number of individuals who
were deported back to Jamaica from the United States of America, Canada,
Great Britain, and elsewhere. These individuals, known as deportees, were
Jamaicans who had been convicted of crimes in the foreign countries in
which they resided and served their sentences. They were then sent back to
Jamaica, often with nothing to their names, few friends, and no visible
means of support (Davenport, 2002). The policy of sending foreign citizens
who engage in criminal activities back to the land of their birth has been
adopted mainly by Canada and the United States. These deportees were
often schooled in the culture of gang rivalry, gang war, turf control, and
violence in their countries of residence. Sheridan and Morris (1997) stated
that on arrival back in Jamaica, these deportees quickly entrenched themselves in the existing environment that supported gang and criminal activi-

ties. In some cases, Sheridan and Morris continued, the deportees became the new gang leaders with their ability to introduce management techniques learned from their criminal experiences in North America and Europe. As such, they became the masterminds who directed the locals, the actual perpetrators of the crimes.

A BRIEF PROFILE OF JAMAICA

Jamaica is the third-largest island in the Caribbean and is the largest of the English-speaking islands. It lies about 480 miles (770 kilometers) to the south of Florida and 100 miles (160 kilometers) west of Haiti, in the Caribbean Sea. Jamaica is also known as the land of wood and water due to its lush vegetation and vast water supply. The island is a little smaller than the state of Connecticut in the United States and is made up of coastal lowlands, a limestone plateau, and a group of volcanic hills in the eastern part of the island called the Blue Mountains. Jamaica is 51 miles (82 kilometers) across at its widest point and 146 miles (235 kilometers) from east to west, comprising a total of 4,243 square miles (10,990 square kilometers). The climate is tropical, with hot and humid temperatures, and hurricanes are a natural hazard from about July to November each year.

The people of Jamaica come from many different backgrounds, most having African, European, Asian, East Indian, and/or Middle Eastern ancestry. Most of the population is a mix of several cultures. The population in 2002 was estimated at about 2,680,029, with a growth rate of 0.56 percent (Central Intelligence Agency World Factbook, 2001). Approximately 33 percent of the population is under the age of 15, and roughly 55 percent of the people live in urban areas. The capital of Jamaica is Kingston. The government of Jamaica can be described as a constitutional parliamentary democracy, or constitutional monarchy. This means that the nominal head of the country is the monarch of England, presently Queen Elizabeth II. Her representative in the island is known as the governor-general, who is appointed by her on the advice of the Jamaican prime minister.

Although Jamaica gained full independence from Great Britain in 1962, the position of Jamaica as a former British colony for more than three hundred years is reflected in its language and customs. English is the official language of Jamaica, although many Jamaicans speak a local dialect of English that incorporates African, Spanish, and French elements. The Jamaican dialect, called patois, is an important part of the Jamaican culture and is recognized around the world, along with the native accent. Certain expressions used in the dialect, such as "irie" and "no problem, man," have become familiar through Jamaica's music.

The economy of Jamaica is primarily agricultural, with mining (alumina and bauxite), manufacturing, and tourism other key sectors. About 21 percent of the total Jamaican labor force is engaged in agricultural production with sugarcane as the chief crop. The United States, Europe, Canada, Latin America, and Caricom (Caribbean Common Market) countries are the major trading partners with Jamaica. In Jamaica 61.3 percent of the population are Protestant (Church of God, Baptist, Anglican, Seventh-Day Adventist, Pentecostal, Methodist, United Church, Brethren, Jehovah's Witness, and Moravian); 4 percent are Roman Catholic; and other religions, including some spiritual cults, make up about 34.7 percent (Central Intelligence Agency World Factbook, 2001).

Approximately 85 percent of the people in Jamaica are officially literate, and attendance in school by children between the ages of 6 and 11 is nearly universal since the 1980s (Blank and Minowa, 2001). Most 12 to 18 year olds attend secondary institutions. The University of the West Indies, Mona Campus, located in Kingston, is a major institution of higher learning for the entire Caribbean region, with more than 5,000 students. There are also the University of Technology, the Edna Manley College for the Visual and Performing Arts, the College of Agriculture, Science and Education, the G. C. Foster College of Physical Education and Sports, twelve teacher-training colleges, fourteen community colleges, twenty-nine vocational training centers, a dental auxiliary school, six human employment and resource training centers, and a vocational training development institute.

Gang Vignette

The gang problem in Jamaica is extremely serious, affecting young people, their families, the wider community, and Jamaica's reputation around the world. Rosenberg (2001) provides this revealing story:

When Jermaine awoke to the sound of gunshots he knew exactly what to do—grab his weapon and return fire. "We have to defend our community," the 17-year-old said, "If we don't, they'll kill everyone. They know we don't support the government." He joined other gunmen who engaged the police and army in three days of street battles that erupted in a poor corner of Kingston. . . . Gang violence is as endemic as poverty in Jamaica, a country of 2.6 million people that has a murder rate five times that of the United States. (para. 1)

OVERVIEW AND IMPACT OF TEEN GANGS

During the last twenty years, the increase of gang activities in Jamaica has reached epidemic proportions and gained worldwide notoriety. Gang activity in Jamaica resulted in high levels of crime and drug violence associated with its role as a transshipment point for the South American drug trade. Gangs in Jamaica have accounted for about one-third of all homicides since 1995 (Jamaica Constabulary Force Gang Specialist, personal communication, February 2002).

By the last quarter of 2001 there were approximately 118 identifiable gangs in Jamaica, with an average membership ranging from three to ten individuals (Jamaica Constabulary Force Gang Specialist, personal communication, February 2002). Gangs in Jamaica are classified as active, inactive, and dormant, according to the Jamaica Constabulary Force. An active gang is the term used to describe a gang that is actively participating in criminal activities. Of the 118 identifiable gangs, about 20 percent are considered highly active. This means that their criminal activities constitute large-scale operations across entire communities. Some of these gangs are closely associated with the major political parties. There are also a few gangs with membership of over forty individuals, with some of these gangs maintaining members locally in Jamaica and overseas in countries such as the United States, Canada, and Great Britain.

It is important to note that there is no particular age differentiation in the gangs in Jamaica, as is evident in other countries such as the United States. Membership in Jamaican gangs is not based on age but rather on role and function. According to Moncrieffe (1998), gang members in Jamaica do not join gangs solely for the purpose of participation in criminal activities. They, like gang members in other parts of the world, initially become members of a gang to seek identity and belonging. There are no separate identifiable teen gangs operating on the island. The teenagers are part of the larger, organized gangs operating in the country, and the majority of current youth gangs linked to the larger criminal gangs are made up of youths between the ages of 12 and 15 years (Crime Review 2001, 2002). In Jamaica, where approximately 40 percent of the population consists of children between the ages of 11 and 17, the emergence of these youth gangs as part of the larger, organized gangs and their criminal activities constitutes a serious problem. This is supported by the dramatic increase in crimes committed by the youth (Crime Review 2001, 2002).

The majority of the gangs in Jamaica operate in the inner-city communities, largely in the capital city of Kingston. There are basically two different kinds of gangs operating within Jamaica, both of which cause crime and violence. They are the community and the criminal gangs. The community gang is a group of young males between 12 and 35 years of age who congregate together for the purpose of "solidarity and peer group socializing," and ultimately of defending their turf (West Kingston Report, 2001, p. 8). The implication is that these gangs are formed and maintained by situational factors. Moncrieffe (1998) reported that many of the youths in a particular community simply "drifted to the only accessible and comforting structure available, that is, the gang structures" (p. 23). The typical criminal gang is organized specifically to conduct criminal activities. These criminal activities include involvement in the drug trade, carjackings, and other forms of serious crimes, such as robbery and assault. Levy (2001) stated that there are important differences between the community and criminal gangs. However, Moncrieffe noted that the "differences and their implications are not obliterated by the fact that community gangs commit crimes and that criminal gangs or their members operate at times under the cover of community gangs" (p. 8). The activity levels of these gangs can be categorized as high structure, moderate structure, and low structure (Moncrieffe, 1998).

In 1998 the Ministry of National Security and Justice, Criminal Justice Research Unit, conducted a study of various aspects of gang activity in Jamaica. The study was needed because of the increasing threat to Jamaican society resulting from the criminal activities of the gangs and because of the need to analyze and document "such significant crime phenomena" (Moncrieffe, 1998, p. 4). In the study Moncrieffe (1998) identified three distinct structures of gangs, their activity levels, and their objectives. According to Moncrieffe, the structural levels of the gangs are fairly constant, and give insight into the particular gang's "level of threat, longevity, and ability to proliferate internationally" (p. 15). The three structures are described as high, moderate, and low. Gangs that are active and fall in the high structure category present the most serious threat, and their objective is to obtain financial gains. For the active gangs that are categorized as moderate in structure, the objective is similar to that of the gangs in the high structure category, as they also seek to obtain monetary funds. Gangs that are active and low in structure are low in priority for law enforcement, as their objective is primarily to defend their territory and maintain their power base and reputation.

Additionally, Moncrieffe (1998) states that the activity levels of the gangs seems to correlate to their structure. High-structure gangs are involved in transnational drug trafficking, money laundering, and arms dealing. Moderate-structure gangs are involved in vehicle thefts, extortion of community members, and robberies of banks and businesses. Low-structure gang members are involved in small robberies, sexual assault, and turf wars. However, the activity levels of the gangs can be reduced significantly by a number of factors: intervention strategies undertaken by law enforcement officers, lack of finances, death of a gang leader or core members, and incarceration of members (Moncrieffe, 1998).

HISTORY OF GANG PROBLEM

The formation of gangs in Jamaica can be traced back to the ghettoes of Kingston. These organizations began as street gangs, similar to the gangs in the urban United States. However, they also had ties to the two major political parties in Jamaica, as many were spawned during the political upheaval that engulfed Jamaica in the mid-1970s. Political parties hired gangs of armed street youths to intimidate their opponents in the struggle for power. During this era of political and social turmoil disaffected youths who felt the future held little for them sought empowerment through the respect they gained as armed enforcers for the political parties. To further understand this phenomenon, one must look at Jamaica's political system.

Jamaica has a two-party political system. The two dominant parties are The People's National Party (PNP), which is socialist in orientation, and the Jamaica Labour Party (JLP), which supports free enterprise in a mixed economy. Minor parties have been established, such as the National Democratic Movement (NDM), but they generally have little power, as the Jamaican electorate is fiercely loyal to the two long-established political parties. Voter participation is very high in formal elections in Jamaica, and the country has had several changes of government since it gained its independence in 1962. The two dominant parties, the PNP and the JLP, have each been elected and consequently removed from office by the voters in Jamaica about the same number of times. A politician's survival in Jamaica depends entirely on his/her ability to win repeatedly at the local level. A method of ensuring this very important repeated victory is to create what is known as a garrison constituency and community.

A garrison community is formed by support for a politician within a particular geographical area from carefully screened residents who constitute an unbeatable core of voters for that politician. These people are usually the recipients of favors and other rewards for their loyalty. According to Chevannes (1992), such rewards include housing erected with public funds. This garrison community is usually fiercely loyal to the politician and to the political party he/she represents. Gangs in these communities work to generate unrest by intimidating those in neighboring communities who do not share the same political persuasion. The aim is to intimidate in order to ensure their particular candidate of victory in an election. The stakes are high, as these political strongholds usually benefit from more rewards if their particular political party forms the ruling government.

This history of tribal politics in Jamaica influences the activities of the gangs that evolved out of the political system. There are several hard-core garrison constituencies in Jamaica. The most famous is Tivoli Gardens, located in Western Kingston and closely aligned to the Jamaica Labour Party. Political fights between garrison constituencies during general elections have spilled over into broader, ongoing turf wars. Defense of territory is of paramount importance in the activity level of the gangs. When a new government from either political party is elected, the gang members responsible for any campaign of terror during the election usually leave the island if their party is defeated at the polls.

This was the case in the mid- to late 1970s and the early 1980s, when many members of these gangs from the garrison communities fled to the United States to escape legal problems in Jamaica, while others fled to avoid assassination at the hands of their rival factions in the opposing political party. The activities of these members did not cease upon arrival in the United States. The gangs that were formed for political purposes in Jamaica became involved in the drug trade in the United States and maintained ties to their counterparts in Jamaica (Drug Enforcement Administration, 2002). They became known as posses, adopting the name from films about the old American West, which were popular in Jamaica. These posses developed a reputation for violence because of the grisly murders that they committed to discipline their members and eliminate their competitors (Drug Enforcement Administration, 2002).

The indiscriminate use of violence and flamboyant self-promotion by the Jamaican posses attracted the attention of law enforcement in the United States. Many of the operations of the gangs were eventually closed down, and members were arrested, convicted of various crimes, and sent to prison in the United States. These former gang members eventually became the deportees, who were returned to Jamaica and usually resorted to their old criminal habits for survival, contributing significantly to the upsurge in crimes committed in Jamaica.

SOCIAL VIEWS, CUSTOMS, PRACTICES, AND DEMOGRAPHIC INFORMATION

Of the identified 118 gangs mentioned previously, about 70 to 80 percent are active, small street gangs. Members of these gangs usually commit robberies, thefts, rapes, and some contract crimes, such as shootings, murders, and automobile thefts; or they act as drug couriers throughout Jamaica and sometimes to the United States and Great Britain. There are, however, another 20 percent that are highly active and involved in criminal activity, maintaining strong allegiance to one or the other of the main political parties (Jamaica Constabulary Force Gang Specialist, personal communication, February 2002). The majority of the gang activities are concentrated in the Corporate Area in Jamaica. This area includes the parishes of Kingston, St. Andrew, and St. Catherine, which are more metropolitan than the other parishes. However, gang activities have also spread to other communities across Jamaica, especially those rural areas where the cultivation of marijuana is easily concealed due to the vegetation. Conflicts over control of the marijuana crop have at times led to gang warfare.

Moncrieffe (1998) identified several community gangs that operate in the Corporate Area. Among the gangs operating in this area are Shower Posse and Spanglers Posse. These are gangs that have ties to the two major political parties, have high activity levels, and are known internationally for their drug trafficking and gruesome treatment of their victims (Moncrieffe, 1998). The community gangs in the inner cities are also referred to as "corner crews." The name is derived from their main meeting place, which is usually a particular street corner in the community. According to Bailey, Branche, and LeFranc (1998), the street corner provides a zone of occupation for men, predominantly young men. It is the scene of conflict between and within gangs and between gangs and the police. The theater of the street is also the arena where young men sound out strong messages about themselves through the medium of designer goods, jewelry, their movement and their speech. (p. 12)

The street corner society is a very colorful entity in Jamaican society, especially in lower socioeconomic areas. At any given time, several young men can be seen congregating at their favorite location. The main activities conducted in this locale are "reasoning" sessions, which are usually discussions about the injustices of the established system; smoking (usually marijuana); and playing soccer, dominoes, or ludo (a board game) (Levy, 2001). The street corner is also where unemployed young men congregate, as it offers ways of hustling and working out a way of living. As such, the street-corner society thrives in areas of Jamaica where job opportunities are scarce and where any and every economic opportunity is welcomed.

A function of paramount importance to the community gangs is defending their turf, or the particular geographical area under their control. Since these gangs arose out of the political party conflicts of the late 1960s and 1970s, they thrived on the support and patronage from the politicians whom they supported. It was also during this time that the "dons" emerged. According to Gunst (1995), in the communities controlled by gangs the don figure becomes a role model for young men. The dons are leaders in the communities, usually the garrison constituencies, who wield incredible power ("Making of a don," 2001). To many people who live outside the inner-city communities in Jamaica, the power of the dons to control the community is incomprehensible. Blank and Minowa (2001) found that many parents in these communities often leave the socialization of their young sons to the dons. This is significant, as often the training that they receive is associated with activities that maintain the status and power of the dons.

There are differences of opinion about the role of the dons in the inner-city communities. The dons can be highly respected by the residents in the communities in which they operate. The respect, at times, comes from fear due to the rough justice that is often meted out by the dons. In an interview with one of these dons, published in the *Jamaica Star*, the don stated that his popularity in the community grew partially out of the fact that his business ventures were successful and partially because of the economic assistance that he has been able to give to the members of his community ("Making of a don," 2001). As a result, he felt that the inner-city residents, especially in the garrison communities, respected the dons who, because of their success, become role models for the young people.

The head of the Crime Management Unit (CMU), one of the toughest crime-fighting police units operating in Jamaica, shared a different view of the dons ("Making of a don," 2001). While he recognized that some of the dons give financial assistance to community residents, he is skeptical about where their resources come from, as many of them do not work and do not seem to have any visible means of support. Yet the dons are the epitome of success in the community, driving expensive cars and having several women to travel with them and care for them. The top crime-fighter in Jamaica questions the financial success of the dons and emphasizes that there is a difference between a community leader and a don. He believes that a don uses terror and fear to control the people in the communities, while a community leader does not have to resort to terror tactics, and has earned the respect of the community through long-standing and upright membership.

Jamaica's strategic location in the Caribbean Sea between the Latin American countries and the United States mainland has made it an attractive transshipment port for the drug network operating in South America. In 2001 an estimated one hundred tons of Colombian cocaine passed through Jamaica (Hansen, 2002). According to Hansen (2002), arms dealers from the United States supplied the gangs in Jamaica with high-powered weapons to protect their product. These criminal gangs have more sophisticated weaponry than the local police, and Hansen also believes that this has led to some of the police resorting to assassination of suspected gang members. Amnesty International condemned this abuse of police power (Hansen, 2002). The killing of seven teenagers by the Jamaican police in 2002 was labeled an act of execution by Amnesty International ("Killing of 7," 2003).

The profits from the drug trade are easily visible on the local streets in the capital of Kingston as well as in other communities. The prevalence of gleaming new sport-utility vehicles with dark-tinted windows, and the latest luxury car models, stand in sharp contrast to the burned-out small wooden shacks and homes, which often show the destructive evidence of gang rivalry. For teenagers who have felt the pangs of poverty and who have been raised in deprivation, the attractions of such visible wealth are obvious. Against this backdrop of contradiction, the attraction to become a gun handler at an early age (10 to 13 years) is easier to understand. A youth may be handpicked by a gang leader and given a gun with the instructions to perpetrate a crime against an individual. If the youth successfully commits the crime, it is a way to earn a reputation as a "gunman" and move up in the hierarchy of the gang. It is also a way in which the youth can begin to see hope of deliverance from a life of poverty and economic frustration.

BASIC POLICIES AND LEGISLATION

The problem of serious crime and violence has always been the topic of national debate and much concern in Jamaica. Since the mid-1970s successive governments have established several civilian crime commissions and task forces in response to periods of high levels of serious crime and the ensuing public outcry. These task forces investigate measures that will alleviate the crime problem. Additionally, the Jamaican government has also sought to institute special joint efforts between the police force and the military to combat outbreaks of criminal activity. There is the feeling that reliance on traditional action plans by the different Jamaican governments is a contributory factor to the persistent high-crime problem. In the past new legislation, centralization of law enforcement operations, and more intimidating police practices proved to be nonproductive measures that did not alleviate the problem, but often exacerbated it.

In 1974 the Gun Court, a combination court and prison, was established in Jamaica (Hudson and Seyler, 1991). The purpose of this court was to combat the increase in violent crimes involving firearms and to provide swift passage through the penal system of those crimes that involved the use of guns. The provisions of the Gun Court Act allowed for the detention and prosecution of individuals and authorized a single resident magistrate's court to issue prison sentences to those convicted of illegal possession of firearms or ammunition. The Gun Court carried a mandatory sentence of life imprisonment for gun-related crimes, a harsh stipulation with the intent of discouraging the use of guns. However, in 1983 the Gun Court Amendment Act removed the mandatory sentence of life imprisonment, and also transferred back to juvenile court hundreds of cases involving youths who were under the age of 14 and who had been given life prison sentences under the dictates of the Gun Court Act. Many of these youth were paroled back into society.

Legislators, recognizing the proliferation of organized criminal drug activity by major Jamaican gangs, enacted legislation to address the dramatic increase in drug trafficking. An amendment to the Dangerous Drugs Act, adopted in March 1987, provided stricter penalties for offenses related to the trafficking of illegal drugs. The act empowered the local courts to have jurisdiction over offenses that pertained specifically to cocaine and other hard drugs, and established the maximum penalties that could be imposed (Hudson and Seyler, 1991).

Political Initiatives and Policies

The Jamaican Constabulary Force, the national police, and local urban communities have a long history of tense relations. There is a great mistrust of the police. According to Levy (2001), the behavior of the police force—with its brutal justice—especially toward the youth, has been sanctioned and encouraged by the political establishment. Consequently, the police, by their conduct, have become a major hindrance to some communities in trying to utilize the established official channels designed to deter criminal activity. The emergence of youth gangs has only exacerbated the already tense relationship between the police and the urban communities. Despite the fact that gangs contribute to the high incidences of crime and violence in many poor communities, many members of these communities refuse to cooperate with police inquiries into violence between rival gangs. Rather than seeking justice from law enforcement or assisting where necessary, the residents in the community seek justice through the don figure, who is also perceived as protector and judge in the community.

The mutual distrust and hostility between the Jamaican police and civilians dictate that other initiatives must be in place to adequately address the gang problem. It is clear that the issues of youth and crime are causing great concern in Jamaica, and a number of initiatives are already in place to address the problem of criminal gangs in particular. Among them are frequent publication of a list of wanted persons, the introduction of the Call Gun Hot Line, proactive road traffic law enforcement, and an increase in the number of intelligence-driven searches (Crime Review 2001, 2002). Other initiatives include specialized training for the military, hiring more law enforcement officers, and cooperation between the police force and private firms that utilize security personnel and witness protection services.

Existing Programs and Policies for Youths

The Ministry of Education, Youth, and Culture is the government division formally responsible for youth in Jamaica. The ministry plans and implements health policies and programs directed at youths (Blank and Minowa, 2001). Additionally, there is an active community relations program within the Jamaican Constabulary Force that coordinates programs for the geographical areas that have divisions of the police force. The main programs sponsored by the police force specifically for youth include Police Youth Clubs, Girl Guides and Boys Scouts, and Second Chance. The guiding principle of the Second Chance program is that the youth, the community, and the police will work together to build a civil society. Among the objectives of the Second Chance program is the development of coping mechanisms for youth.

In 2000 the National Center for Youth Development was established by Jamaica. Its purpose is to centralize all services provided by the government agencies and the private sector in order to better monitor and disseminate information that affects youth. In 2001 the National Center for Youth Development began a process of consultation with youth, governmental agencies, the private sector, and members of society at large. The purpose of these dialogues was the development of a new national youth policy to adequately meet the needs of Jamaican youth and to develop strategies to improve attitudes and decrease antisocial behaviors (Blank and Minowa, 2001). In 1997 the Jamaican government also established a "National Policy for Children." The main focus of this policy is the survival, protection, and development of children.

A central focus of youth assistance in Jamaica is the development of training programs. At the core of these training programs is a statutory body under the Ministry of Education, Youth, and Culture called the HEART Trust NTA (Human Employment and Resource Training Trust/National Training Agency). This body is involved in a wide range of training-related activities. Some of these are on-the-job training, work experience, resocialization skills training, sporting programs in school and communities, counseling, and care and protection services. In 1998 youth information centers were established in Jamaica to function as a centralized data bank and resource center for youth. These centers provide information on services that are available in the areas of training, education, health, and counseling for youth.

There are other diverse programs that are designed especially for the youth-at-risk population. The purpose is to develop beneficial programs that will provide youth with attractive alternatives to criminal activity. According to Blank and Minowa (2001), many of the programs that currently exist in Jamaica do not address the wide range of needs of the youth population. However, there is evidence that some of the programs available do work. One such program that has been successful is the Area Youth Foundation, which addresses the youth in Portmore, St Catherine. Teenagers who have joined the Area Youth Foundation have reportedly managed to turn away from the gang culture and embark on professional careers in law enforcement and the media. Other members of this foundation have established businesses of their own. The success of the youth in the Area Youth Foundation program has been recognized because of the program's focus on the arts. This focus on the arts has provided a forum for building the confidence and self-esteem of its participants.

CONCLUSION

The increased violence among young people is one of the most pressing concerns for the government and citizens of Jamaica. Much has been written about the plight of many children and youth living in poverty in the inner-city communities in Kingston (Moser and Holland, 1997). The steady rise in serious crimes since the early 1970s in Jamaica speaks to the need for urgent, serious, and creative attention to the development of prevention measures that will adequately address the underlying factors of poverty and frustration. Jamaicans are aware of the need for the development of long-term strategies for the long-standing crime and gang problem and know that the problems of high crime and violence must be recognized and addressed at their roots. Many feel the issue of partisan political violence, which has always been a constant feature of Jamaican party politics, must be eradicated. Jamaicans are also seeking prevention strategies that are transformative in approach and a system of justice in Jamaica that is consistently credible.

Processes of change in the political and the community systems can make a difference. It will require, however, the participation of the society at large and interventions that improve social conditions and promote nonviolent approaches to conflict resolution.

REFERENCES

Bailey, W., C. Branche, and E. Le Franc. "Street culture and the decay of community." *Caribbean Dialogue* 4 (1998): 2.

Blank, L., and M. Minowa. *Youth-at-risk in Jamaica* (Policy Note, Draft). (Washington DC: World Bank, 2001).

Central Intelligence Agency World Factbook. (2001). *Jamaica*. Retrieved September 10, 2002, from http://www.cia.gov/cia/publications/factbook/geos/jm/html.

Chevannes, B. *The formation of garrison communities*. Paper presented at the Grassroots Development and the State of the Nation Symposium, University of the West Indies, Mona Campus, Kingston, Jamaica, 1992.

Crime Review 2001. "Youth and crime: Areas for attention." *The Sunday Gleaner*, section F1 (3 Febuary 2002).

Davenport, J. (2002). *Gangs in Jamaica*. Retrieved August 31, 2002, from http://www.portmore.org/articles/gangsjamaica.html.

Drug Enforcement Administration. *Jamaica traffickers*. Retrieved March 5, 2002, from http://www.cocaine-facts.org/pages/jamaica_traffickers.html.

Gunst, L. *Born fi' dead: A journey through the Jamaican posse underworld* (New York: Henry Holt & Co., 1995).

Hansen, L. "Profile: Jamaica struggling with increasing gang-and-drug-related crime" [Radio Broadcast]. Washington, DC: National Public Radio, 24 February 2002.

Hudson, R., and D. Seyler. (1991). *Jamaica: National security, Chapter 2D*. Retrieved September 15, 2002, from http://aks.elibrary.com.

"Killing of 7 by Jamaican police labeled execution." *The Miami Herald* (14 March 2003): 12A.

Levy, H. *Corner crews at war and peace in August Town*. Paper presented at the International Criminology Conference, University of the West Indies, Mona Campus, Kingston, Jamaica, January 2001.

"Making of a don." (2001). *The Jamaica Star*. Retrieved September 12, 2002, from http://www.JamaicaStar.com/thestar/20020411/news/news1.html.

Moncrieffe, D. *Gang study: The Jamaica crime scene* (Kingston, Jamaica: Ministry of National Security and Justice, 1998).

Moser, C., and J. Holland. *Urban poverty and violence in Jamaica* (Washington, DC: World Bank, 1997).

Rosenberg, M. (2001, July 15). "Jamaica's gangs entrenched as island's poverty." *Jefferson City News Tribune Online*. Retrieved September 15, 2002, from http://www.newstribune.com/stories.

Sheridan, M., and N. Morris. "A trade in criminals: Canada's policy of deporting lawbreakers helps fuel Jamaica's soaring crime rate." *Maclean's* 48 (February 17, 1997).

West Kingston Report. (2001). Report on the social condition of the inner city of Kingston, Jamaica, bearing on the upsurge of violence that peaked in July, 2001.

9

MALAYSIA

M. Sylvia Fernandez

INTRODUCTION

Crime and juvenile delinquency are serious emerging social issues in developing countries like Malaysia. The effects of poverty, rising unemployment, rapid and unplanned urbanization, exposure to lifestyles and values contradictory to traditional values and behavioral norms, and family breakdown create a conducive environment for the emergence of juvenile delinquency and criminal behavior (United Nations Information Service, 2000; "Responding to Citizens," 1998). Additionally, the priorities set by the political agenda within the country further contribute to this budding problem. Teen gangs are not identified as such in Malaysia; rather, teenagers who engage in criminal activity are identified as juvenile delinquents or gangsters, and this problem is identified as teenage gangsterism ("The social development," 2003).

PROFILE OF MALAYSIA

Malaysia, located in the heart of Southeast Asia close to the equator, consists of a peninsula, West Malaysia, and the northern part of the island of Borneo, East Malaysia. The total land mass of the country covers about 128,430 square miles (332,632 square kilometers) of which two-thirds is forested. This independent federation is a pluralistic society with a population of approximately 23 million people, most of whom live in West Malaysia. The population growth rate is 2.08 percent, with a life expectancy of

67.62 years for males and 73.90 years for females (Malaysia, 2003). Of the total population almost 60 percent are of purely Malay or indigenous descent, 25 percent are of purely Chinese descent, 10 percent are of purely Indian descent, and the remaining 5 percent, classified as other, are of mixed ethnicity. The national and official language of the country is Bahasa Malaysia. English is the language of commerce and of the legal system, with numerous dialects spoken nationwide. Malaysia has a literacy rate of 83.5 percent (Malaysia, 2003). Islam, the national religion, is practiced by nearly all Malays, the majority of Chinese are Buddhists, the majority of Indians are Hindus, and a relatively small portion of Chinese and Indians practice and believe in some denomination of Christianity or other religions.

Due to its location on the early East-West spice trade route, the port cities of Penang, Melaka, and Singapore (before its independence from Malaysia in 1965) were the entry points for diverse political and social influences from around the world. Since the thirteenth century Malaysia has been colonized by the Portuguese twice, and by the Dutch and British, each of whom brought with them their language, religion, architecture, and culture. However, it was during the British era that the greatest economic and social changes took place (Doling and Omar, 2002). One such social change was the emergence of a separate and distinct set of ethnic groups that embraced and continue now to hold on to and practice the lifestyles and cultures of their home countries. The British discovered that the climate in Malaysia was conducive for growing rubber trees and that the lands were rich in tin ore. Unsuccessful in getting the native Malays to leave their farms to work on the rubber plantations or in the tin mines, the British imported labor from their other Asian colonies. The Chinese were brought in to work in the tin mines in the middle of the nineteenth century, and the Indians were brought in to work on the rubber plantations beginning around 1910. Both the Chinese and Indians saw Malaysia as a land of opportunity, and many emigrated there with their families. During World War II and the Japanese occupation of Malaysia nationalism and anticolonialism took root, and a political machine was put into motion that eventually led to Malaysia's independence from Britain on August 31, 1957.

Malaysia is a constitutional monarchy with a parliamentary democracy. The Yang di-Pertuan Agong (sovereign) is elected every five years by, and from, the nine hereditary state rulers of Perlis, Kedah, Perak, Kelantan, Terengganu, Pahang, Selangor, Negeri Sembilan, and Johor. The parliament has two chambers, Dewan Ra'ayat (the house of representatives) and Dewan Negara (the senate). The prime minister, who heads the Dewan Ra'ayat (house of representatives), governs with the consent of the sovereign and chooses the cabinet. The Dewan Ra'ayat consists of 192 elected members who serve for a maximum of five years, and the Dewan Negara consists of 69 members chosen for six-year terms. Each state legislature elects two senators and the sovereign appoints the remaining 43 senators. There is a high court in East Malaysia and one in West Malaysia and a supreme court having jurisdiction over the entire country.

OVERVIEW AND IMPACT OF TEEN GANGS

Malaysia is a developing country, and the political agenda of the country is primarily focused on its economic development and the building of a self-sustaining infrastructure. Consequently, the country's budget allocations reflect funding for the identified economic priorities. Social needs and problems take a backseat, are not readily tracked, and are addressed in a limited way politically and financially (Doling and Omar, 2002). Additionally, the culture of the country and its people places high value and expectation on the family and on education. The family is seen as the core of an individual's personal and moral development. Education is viewed as a privilege and a means to social and economic upward mobility. Although juvenile criminal activity is an emerging concern, presently the issue of teenage gansterism or teen gangs is not identified or seen as a critical social problem.

Social problems with youth in the country are identified and tracked as juvenile delinquency, juvenile crime, and teenage gangsterism, and those youth engaged in these activities are labeled as juvenile delinquents and gangsters. Teen gangs are a rising problem, as evidenced by a striking 62 percent increased incidence of crime involving youth between 1980 and 1995. Statistics for 1990 to 1995 show that of juvenile cases reported, 60 percent involved teenagers ages 16 to 18 years, 35 percent were 13 to 15 years, and the remaining 5 percent were ages 10 to 12 years. (Chief Secretary, 1997; "Social Problems," 2003). As will be discussed in the section on the history of the teen gangs later in this chapter, the type and magnitude of youth violence in recent years is getting more severe and more frequent.

BASIC POLICIES, LEGISLATION, AND DEMOGRAPHICS

When Malaysia was negotiating its independence and determining its social and political structure within a pluralistic society, specific agreements were made among the leaders representing the three primary ethnic groups, namely, the Malays, Chinese, and Indians. Some of the agreements included retention of privileges by the Malays in land ownership and governmental positions to compensate for the "inequality of wealth in favor of the Chinese . . . who controlled much of the industry and trade" (Doling and Omar, 2002, p. 4). In its further attempt to foster nationalism and to equalize the educational, economic, and political arenas for its multiethnic peoples, the government enacted affirmative action policies and legislation favoring the Malays, which in the long run has had the opposite effect ("Ethnic Indians," 2003). Instead of equalizing and bringing together the three primary ethnic groups to form a *Bangsa Malaysia*, a Malaysian national identity, it has served to reinforce and maintain the separateness of each ethnic group.

Some information about the Malaysian educational system, economy, legislation and policies, and the application of affirmative action favoring the Malays within each of these societal institutions, will provide insight into the government's failure to create a one-nation identity. Additionally, the changing family dynamic and structure will provide some understanding of the issue of teen gangs or teenage gangsterism in Malaysia.

Educational System

The educational system is patented after the British system, where students complete a mandatory nine years, including six years of primary (elementary school) and three years of lower secondary (middle school). At this point students must successfully complete a national comprehensive exam. Based on the results of this exam, successful students are placed in a science track, which emphasizes all the specialty areas of math and science, or an arts track, which emphasizes the humanities and social sciences, for two years of *upper secondary* (high school), at the end of which students complete another national comprehensive exam (equivalent to the British O-levels). Only those who pass this exam are eligible to continue on for two years of *preuniversity* education, and at the end of these two years students complete yet another national comprehensive exam (equivalent to the British A-levels). Successful completion of this examination is one of the criteria for admission into local universities.

It is worth noting that during the six years of primary school, standardized achievement tests are administered in years three and five. The school year follows the calendar year, and students attend school year-round, with a two-week vacation approximately every three months. The national education philosophy in the country is "focused towards creating Malaysian citizens who are knowledgeable and competent, who possess high moral standards, and who are responsible and capable of achieving a high level of personal well-being and able to contribute to the harmony and prosperity of the family, the society and the nation at large" (Ministry of Education, 2003, National Philosophy section, para. 1).

In the late 1960s, the government began phasing out English as the medium of instruction in public schools, one subject at a time, until 1970, when Bahasa Malaysia (the official language of the country) became the language of instruction in public schools. In ethnic-specific private schools the language of instruction is the spoken language of that ethnic group. This change was further extended to local universities, where lectures were now being presented in Bahasa Malaysia. The problem with the practice at the university level was that all reference materials and texts were in English, and the process of translating the relevant resources was a slow and tedious one. The outcome was that students entering local universities had to be proficient and fluent in both languages, Bahasa Malaysia and English, in order to get the most from, and succeed in, their education. Furthermore, the practical effect was that university enrollment was limited to Malaysians and other speakers of Bahasa Malaysia, and potential students from other countries were effectively eliminated from attending university in Malaysia. Another drawback to this language practice was that it created a language barrier in trade and commerce between Malaysia and the rest of the world, which was operating in English. The disadvantage of this policy for students—as well as the nation, as a global participant—has resulted in the government rescinding the Bahasa Malaysia policy and once again changing the medium of instruction in public educational institutions.

In the 1990s universities reverted to using English as a language of instruction and developed twinning programs with universities in Australia and the United States to boost Malaysian and foreign enrollment in local universities. Students then had the opportunity to begin their academic programs in one country and complete them in another (Prinita and Cheyney, 1996). Effective 2004, English as the medium of instruction in public schools will be phased back in, beginning with the subjects of math and science (M. Peter, personal communication, March 25, 2003).

The public schools in Malaysia were initially begun by missionaries, for the most part Catholic, and for a long time the principals (headmasters or headmistresses as they are called) were foreign priests, brothers, and nuns. These schools were separated by gender; that is, schools were either solely for boys (with a headmaster for a principal) or solely for girls (with a headmistress for a principal) at all levels except at the preuniversity level, where it was coed. The government sought to reclaim the public schools through legislation that gradually phased out the presence of Christian administrators in the schools and replaced them with Malaysian educators and administrators. Also, the practice of gender segregation was eliminated and replaced with coeducation at all levels of public institutions. For the most part, as was true then and is now, the students as well as the teachers and staff in the public schools are ethnically mixed.

The attempt to create nationalism and to raise the level and numbers of educated Malays and indigenous peoples, as reflected in affirmative action legislation, appeared in many forms within the education system. Examples of such policies and practices include the setting of university admissions quotas based on ethnicity; limiting eligibility for, and access to, financial aid based on ethnicity; pushing the Islamic agenda in public schools at all levels; and having residential schools open only to Malays and indigenous peoples. Some Malaysians, including Education Minister Tan Sri Musa Mohamad, believe that the current structure of the country's education system has ethnically segregated young students in their formative years (Tan, 2001). This resulting educational segregation by ethnicity has kept intact the racial divide between the three primary ethnic groups.

Economy

The government—controlled by the United Malay National Organization—passed the New Economic Policy (NEP) under the Second Malaysia Plan which, consistent with the legislated affirmative action mandates, attempted to increase economic opportunity for the Malays, who were significantly poorer and less educated than the other races. Unsurprisingly, many Chinese opposed the new policies and formed a major political opposition party, which in 1969 won a significant number of seats in national elections. This political upset incited racial riots that swept through the capital city of Kuala Lumpur, and the country was in a state of emergency for two years. In spite of the race riots the government continued its implementation of the NEP, as had been legislated. In an interview with Pereira (2001), Dr. Mansor Mohd Noor, a researcher on race relations at the Science University in Penang (Malaysia), was quoted as saying "the NEP served to widen the gap within a race, that is, lower-income Indians and Malays were sidelined from the high economic growth that Malaysia has enjoyed" (p. 5).

In the 1980s Malaysia launched its industrialization drive that chalked up double-digit economic growth rates and began the influx of people from the rural areas into urban centers to fill newly created jobs. This industrialization drive contributed to an increase in the cost of living. Although individuals had jobs, rural Malay migrants found themselves living in poverty in squatter settlements—a legacy that has been passed on to the next generation. It is estimated that approximately 250,000 Malays live in squatter settlements on the periphery of the Klang Valley, the most developed area in Malaysia. The squatter settlements are the most visible symbol of the widening income gap within the Malay ethnic group. In addition, another 150,000 Indians live in slums around Kuala Lumpur, the capital city (Doling and Omar, 2002).

Legislation and Policies

Tertiary education. Under affirmative action in the Malaysian education system, 55 percent of university admissions were reserved for Malays, with the rest open to non-Malays. Therefore, competition among the non-Malays was great, and highly dependent on one's social and political connections in addition to the requirements of attaining high national examination scores and the ability to meet the financial costs of a university education. The realization of the inequity of this practice has led to an important change. Effective 2003 university admissions are now based on academic merit.

Business practices. In accordance with affirmative action, business loans and government contracts were awarded first to Malays, then to non-Malays. Businesses owned primarily by non-Malay entrepreneurs were required to have a Malay business partner in order to access financial assistance and to secure government contracts.

Changing Family System

In the past, most marriages were arranged, a practice shared by all the primary ethnic groups, and the entire family had a vested interest in the couple staying together and making the marriage work. As each subsequent generation moved away from this practice, the "burden" of making the marriage work began to lie solely with the couple, and the built-in support systems became fewer. Consequently, the divorce rate has increased, resulting in single-parent and blended-family households. The economic boom provided the opportunity for both parents to work outside the home, and often, financial challenges necessitated both parents working to make ends meet, thus leaving children to either fend for themselves or parents to delegate child-rearing to third parties, such as grandparents, maids, and day-care centers ("Juvenile Delinquency," 1996). The once close-knit family in Malaysia has been weakened by modernization, urbanization, and increased labor mobility. Strained family relationships, lack of parental supervision and control, and the absence of role models within the family contribute to the rise in youth violence and crime, and in juvenile delinquency ("The Social Development," 2003).

HISTORY OF TEEN GANGS

Malaysian culture is such that high value and expectation is placed on the family and on education. Successes and failures are a reflection not only of the individual but more so of the family. The nuclear and extended families are seen as the support systems and the primary influences in the development of an individual. Parents have the responsibility to ensure that their children are raised with appropriate values, are educated, and become productive members of society (Doling and Omar, 2002). A misbehaving child or a problem teenager is seen as a blemish on the family; therefore, a tight rein is maintained on children, and problematic behaviors are squelched or not discussed at all. In the past, corporal punishment was widely used as a method of enforcing discipline and control both at home and at school.

In Malaysia, education is seen as a privilege, not a right; therefore, a great deal of attention is paid to formal education, and parents are quite involved in the academic lives of their children. The challenge to successfully complete national comprehensive examinations compels parents to enroll their children in programs that provide academic tutoring and enrichment outside of regular school hours. Between the tutoring and enrichment programs, and extracurricular activities at school, students have very little idle time, and do not typically participate in criminal activity. It is a fairly small number of children and teenagers who actually have idle time and are thus free to engage in delinquent and criminal behaviors.

Adult gangs have a long history in Malaysia. When the waves of immigrants from China and India came to Malaysia during the British era, they quickly recognized the need to protect themselves and their interests from opportunistic social predators. To this end, they brought with them existing gangs from their home countries. These gangs tended to operate primarily underground while offering the working immigrant the security—protection—offered by the gangs. This was the introduction of ethnic gangs in Malaysia that still continue to be active today. The visibility of teen gangs is negligible in the history of Malaysia as an independent nation. Teen gangs are a fairly recent phenomenon.

The ethnic isolationist policies of the government—as evidenced in the educational system, in business practices, and in the economy—have contributed to the rise in violence among disenfranchised youth. The present generation has limited knowledge of the 1969 race riots, demonstrates no real fear of violence and its consequences, and comes from homes marred by divorce. Many have no real sense of ownership or purpose in life and turn to gangs to live out their dreams or resort to drugs to cope with their present lives.

Youth violence and gang activity has been evident in recent years, but it has yet to raise alarm, and it doesn't seem like anyone is paying attention. According to Pereira (2001), in 1997 a teenager died and several others were injured in a gang clash. In 1999 several people were injured and six cars damaged in a gang clash. In June 2000 three samurai-sword-wielding youths slashed a food-stall worker. Netto (2000) reported several incidents of student-on-student assaults.

Behaviors that were once brushed off as "the usual school fights," lack of discipline, or bullying are now labeled "gangsterism." What makes it gangsterism is that the assault is not by an individual acting in the heat of the moment but rather that the assaults are planned, organized, and carried out by a group. For example, in May 2000 Butterworth (in the state of Kedah) police arrested 14 teenage boys for punching and hitting 4 fellow students with sticks. According to the police, the perpetrators believed the victims "ratted" on them to a teacher for cutting class. In another incident in Ipoh (in the state of Perak), 16 boys beat their 17-year-old classmate until he was unconscious because they believed he stole from the class fund and wanted to get a confession out of him. For the most part, teen gang activities are focused on extortion, protection money, and drug dealing (M. Peter, personal communication, March 25, 2003).

To summarize, it would be fair to say that Malaysia's youth today are a product of an ethnically segregated educational system; of an economic system that has created two classes within communities, the haves and have-nots; and of a policy designed to nurture Malays that has only benefited a handful. In the strong push for the Malay and indigenous peoples' economic development through affirmative action policies, the Chinese and Indians have been inadvertently neglected. This inequity has created significant dissatisfaction and disillusionment among young Chinese and Indians, some of whom have turned to gangs to vent and act out their frustrations through criminal activity.

In an interview with Netto (2000), Ravinder Singh, a consumer rights activist, stated that the problem of school violence and teenage gangsterism began about 15 years ago and has gotten progressively more serious and more frequent. The issue has been, and continues to be, ignored by school principals and district education officers, who do not want to admit to such problems in their schools for fear that the negative publicity would tarnish their image. The current debate on the causes of this rising problem ranges from the banning of corporal punishment in schools to automatic advancement of academically weak students to the next grade, to the low self-esteem of students needing academic remediation. The outcome, regardless of the identified causes, is teenagers who are lost and frustrated with schoolwork and who do not feel respected by their teachers and peers. To them the only way to gain recognition and feel a sense of belonging is to join a gang. In ethnically mixed public schools, students join gangs to protect themselves from fellow students.

POLITICAL AND SOCIAL RESPONSES

Although the problem of teen gangs is still relatively small, there are proactive measures that are being taken by the criminal justice system to curb the further spread and growth of the problem. Specific crime prevention strategies come under the purview of police functions and community-based involvement. Police functions include proactive preventive measures to advise commercial and financial institutions on upgraded methods for improving their security systems, as well as on ways of reducing their risk of becoming potential targets of vandalism and criminal attacks. Through the media the public is advised to take measures to minimize crimes of opportunity. Police officers are assigned to schools as guest speakers on topics addressing the various components of the criminal justice system and on specific criminal matters. Community-based involvement is widespread and effective in crime prevention, detection, and treatment and rehabilitation of juvenile offenders. Voluntary civic organizations, societies, clubs, and associations have responded positively to prevention initiatives. Examples of specific programs include the formation of "Vigilante Corps," whose objective is to assist in maintaining the peace and security in outlying rural areas, and Neighborhood Watch groups, aimed at fostering closer relationships among the multiethnic communities and instilling a sense of responsibility based on mutual respect, trust, and confidence ("Some Background," 2003). A youth-relevant role of these watch groups is to enforce curfews for teenagers. On weekdays the curfew is set at 10:00 P.M. and on weekends it is set at 12:00 A.M.

Political Initiatives and Policies

During the Sixth Malaysia Plan (1990–1995) various youth development programs were implemented to nurture youth. Such programs include job skills upgrade training, increasing participation in sports and cultural activities, leadership training, and activities to inculcate high moral values and ethics in youth. To meet the rising challenges to traditional values and culture, these programs focus on molding a generation of youth who are educated, united, democratic, liberal and tolerant, competitive, ethical, and scientifically and technologically progressive. A higher emphasis will be placed on developing a resilient youth community and strengthening the family institution and role of parents in inculcating moral and spiritual values in youth. The government recognizes the family as the basic societal unit and as the primary source of nurturing and care; to this end there will be a national focus on going back to the basics of family: family life and values (Chang, 2000; Yahaya, 2000).

As Malaysia moves toward achieving its goal of being a fully industrialized society, under the Seventh Malaysia Plan, the government will establish a high-level interagency committee to ensure that the country's economic progress is not negated by social problems. Policies and strategies will be formulated for social and family development, the coordination and integration of programs to minimize the occurrence of social problems, and the development of solutions to overcome potential problems. Efforts will be undertaken to equip families to face the challenges of rapid economic development as well as maintaining stability and harmony within the family. Specific strategies will be developed to accomplish these goals (Chang, 2000).

Balanced development is a priority of the Seventh Malaysia Plan's national development program. This means delineating strategies for generating sustained rapid economic growth while ensuring that the benefits of economic growth are equitably shared among Malaysians of all ethnic groups (Yahaya, 2000). The government acknowledges that it needs to strengthen community institutions, particularly those geared directly toward youth, and to increase youth participation in those institutions, in its effort to prevent crime and juvenile delinquency. Special mechanisms will have to be developed to deal with young delinquents and provide them with improved economic and social rehabilitation opportunities through noninstitutional, community, peer-group, and family-based approaches in order to facilitate their reintegration into mainstream society (United Nations Information Service, 2000).

SOCIAL VIEWS, CUSTOMS, AND PRACTICES

Given that teen gangs are not identified as a critical social problem, there is very little public discussion and equally as little written about the issue. Due to the cultural values espoused in the country, it is the family and school that have the primary responsibility for taking the first shot at addressing the problem. In a minimal way the government does recognize the emergence of a problem with teen gangs and has identified a general omnibus framework for addressing youth social concerns. However, specific long-term strategies and timelines for implementation are yet to be defined, especially as they relate to teen gangs.

PLANS FOR ADDRESSING TEEN GANGS

The Seventh Malaysia Plan, released in 1996, under which Malaysia is currently operating, has set a priority goal of becoming an industrialized nation by the year 2020. The government will encourage the privatization of many industries, mainly to enhance the Malays' participation in the economy and to create more programs to help Malay entrepreneurs. Giving more privileges to the Malays will only continue to increase the conflict between the primary ethnic groups, making racial segregation more evident than it already is now (Jaffar, Thome, and Cinco, 1996). The rise in ethnic-specific teen gangs and the dissatisfaction between the primary ethnic groups is now driving the government to make changes that were not planned for initially. As discussed earlier, changes in the educational system and the development of youth-centered programs are proactive measures to curb the escalation of this problem.

From an empirical standpoint, research is needed to gather evidence of the personal and social costs of industrialization and economic advances in Malaysia, including the loss of personal and social values. The research findings can then shape legislation, policies, and programs that address the problem. Additionally, the findings can provide a structure for developing programs to cultivate a generation of youth who are personally and socially healthy and responsible.

REFERENCES

Chang, S. T., Representative of Malaysia to the United Nations (2000, March). Statement made on agenda item 100: Social development, including questions relating to the world social situation and to youth, aging, disabled persons, and the family. Retrieved March 9, 2003, from www.undp.org/missions/malaysia/speech1.htm.

Chief Secretary, Ministry of National Unity and Community Development, Malaysia. (1997, March). "Ringkasan eksekutif laporan isu-isu social masa kini" (Executive summary report on current social issues), paper presented at the Sessi Percambahan Fikiran Megenai Isu dan Masalah Sosial diNegri Johor (Brainstorming Session on Social Issues and Problems), Kota Tinggi, Johor, Malaysia.

Doling, J., and R. Omar. "The welfare state system in Malaysia." [Electronic version] *Journal of Societal and Social Policy* 1(1) (2002): 33–47.

Ethnic Indians in Malaysia live life on the razor's edge. (2003). Retrieved March 23, 2003, from www.indianexpress.com/ie/daily/20010317/iin17048.html.

Jaffar, H. A., Thome, R., and Cinco, G. (1996). ISKL's Group Reports—2096. Kuala Lumpur, Malaysia. Retrieved March 9, 2003, from www.cwrl.utexas.edu/~burniske/uv96/ISKLGR3.html.

Juvenile delinquency on the rise in Malaysia. (1996). Kuala Lumpur, Malaysia: Muslimedia. Retrieved March 9, 2003, from www.muslimedia.com/ARCHIVES/sec98/juvenile.htm.

Malaysia. (2003). Retrieved March 9, 2003, from www.indbazaar.com/country/country.asp?name=140.

Ministry of Education. (2003). National Philosophy. Retrieved March 9, 2003, from www.moe.gov.my/english/kpm/frinfcorp.htm.

Netto, A. (June, 2000). "Malaysia: Violence rises with gangsterism in schools." *Inter Press Service: World news*. Retrieved March 9, 2003, from www.oneworld.org/ip2/june00/06_04_010.htm.

Pereira, B. (2001, March 23). Widening gaps within races. *Straits Times Singapore*.

Prinita, J. I., and Cheyney, M. (1996). Education. Retrieved March 23, 2003, from www.cwrl.utexas.edu/~burniske/uv96/ISKLGR2.html.

Responding to Citizens. (1998). Retrieved March 23, 2003, from www.oecd.org/pdf/M00004000/M00004723.pdf.

The social development situation and prospects of Asia and the Pacific into the twenty-first century: Summary. Meeting paper no.1, part 3 of 4, Social Development Division, United Nations ESCAP. Retrieved March 23, 2003, from www.un.org/depts/escap/sps/paper1c.htm.

Social Problems in Malaysia. (2003). Retrieved March 9, 2003, from www.ypkdt.org.my/ypk/social-problems.htm.

Some Background on the Criminal Justice system of Malaysia. (2003). Retrieved March 9, 2003, from www.lectlaw.com/files/int15.htm.

Tan, J. (2001, March 31). Learning to live in Malaysia. *Straits Times Singapore*.

United Nations Information Service. (2000, March). ESCAP convenes regional seminar on assessment and classification of adult offenders and juvenile delinquents in Bangkok, 13–15 March 2000. Press Release No. G/10/00. Retrieved March 9, 2003, from www.unescap.org/unis/press/g_10_00.htm.

Yahaya, M. K. Y. Deputy Permanent Representative of Malaysia to the United Nations. (2000, October). Statement made on agenda item 37: Implementation of the outcome of the World Summit for social development and of the special session of the General Assembly. Retrieved March 9, 2003, from www.un.int/malaysia/GA/GA/GA31Oct00.html.

10

PAPUA NEW GUINEA

Sinclair Dinnen

INTRODUCTION

In Papua New Guinea (PNG), juvenile gangs, while an urban phenomenon of relatively recent origin, have become a major source of fear and insecurity. The first section of this chapter provides some essential background information about the country. A brief outline of some of the key features of traditional Melanesian societies is followed by an overview of developments since PNG gained its independence in 1975. Subsequent sections address the growth of juvenile gangs, the official responses these have provoked, and the principal characteristics and dynamics of the modern gang.

PROFILE OF PAPUA NEW GUINEA

Papua New Guinea occupies the eastern half of New Guinea, the world's second-largest island, with a total land area of 178,770 square miles (463,000 square kilometers) and a sea area of just over 1,150,000 square miles (3 million square kilometers). To the east of the mainland lie a number of smaller islands, the largest of which are Bougainville, New Britain, and New Ireland. The country's topography is varied and demanding, ranging from the imposing mountains and high valleys of the central highlands to the vast tracts of lowland swamps and the profusion of low-lying islands and scattered atolls. An extensive and largely unmarked land border is shared with the Indonesian province of Papua (Irian Jaya) to the west, while sea borders separate PNG from Australia to the south and the Solomon Islands to the east.

Traditional Societies

The early inhabitants of New Guinea migrated from Asia approximately fifty thousand years ago. Prior to colonial incursion, the predominantly Melanesian population led a subsistence lifestyle, using rudimentary agricultural, hunting, and fishing techniques. Traditional societies were small-scale and relatively self-contained. The largest permanent political units typically consisted of 200 to 300 persons living in villages and rising to several thousand in parts of the more densely populated highlands. These units consisted of groups within which organized warfare would not normally take place (Chowning, 1977). Social relationships were based on kinship, with the rights and obligations of each individual derived from their membership in the extended group. Patterns of land inheritance, special knowledge, and personal property could be either patrilineal or, as in many coastal and island societies, matrilineal. Men tended to be dominant, even in matrilineal societies. Reciprocity was an important element of Melanesian morality and was embodied in the ceremonial exchange of food and gifts. Gift exchange was a means of maintaining social control, a vehicle for trade, a way of demonstrating leadership, and a strategy for consolidating alliances.

Melanesian societies were "stateless" in the sense that they had no centralized political or administrative organization equivalent to a government that could weld together those sharing a common language and culture. These were relatively egalitarian societies, and legitimacy was dispersed widely, at least among the adult males. While subject to a great deal of variation, leadership status was more usually achieved than inherited. The reputation and standing of the Melanesian "big-man" was achieved through individual prowess in warfare, in organizing trade, or in ceremonial exchange. Building and maintaining leadership involved the continuous and skillful manipulation of resources and relationships. Warfare was endemic in many places (Berndt, 1962). In practice, hostilities were typically followed by elaborate peacemaking ceremonies (Meggitt, 1977; Strathern, 1971).

Independence and the Challenges of Development

Papua New Guinea was granted full political independence on September 16, 1975, after a somewhat brief and inconsistent period of colonial administration, initially by Britain and Germany and subsequently by Australia. Today it is one of the most socially diverse and fragmented countries in the world. Approximately eight hundred languages are spoken among a population of just over 5 million people. English, *Tok Pisin* (Melanesian Pidgin), and *Motu* (the *lingua franca* of the Papua region) are the official languages. The structures and belief systems of traditional Melanesian societies have demonstrated persistent strength and viability amid the rapid changes that took place during the colonial and postcolonial periods. Despite the overlay of the institutions of the modern nation state, there is still little sense of national unity or shared identity. Primary allegiances continue to be implanted in local language groups and small kin-based associations. The spectrum of modern PNG society ranges from village-based life dependent on a combination of raising subsistence and cash crops to life in the bustling and multiethnic environments of the growing towns of Port Moresby (the national capital), Lae, Madang, Wewak, and Mount Hagen. Some 85 percent of the population continue to derive their livelihood from rural agriculture, while 15 percent live in urban areas.

Papua New Guinea is richly endowed with natural resources, including timber, marine life, oil, gas, gold, copper, and other minerals. Despite this, economic and social development during the past three decades has been disappointing and uneven. This has often been attributed to mismanagement and poor governance on the part of PNG's political and bureaucratic elite, as well as to the adverse impact of external economic shocks. It is also a reflection of the lack of preparation for independence from which the new nation was launched in 1975. Port Moresby is still cut off from the other main centers of population by road and is accessible only by sea or expensive air travel. In addition, significant logistical challenges are presented by the demanding domestic topography.

In the decade after independence, approximately one-quarter of internally generated revenue came from the Panguna copper mine on Bougainville Island. By 1989 this single mine accounted for nearly 10 percent of the country's gross domestic product. In the same year the mine was closed down as a result of armed rebellion by local landowners, who were aggrieved by the levels of compensation. This rebellion grew rapidly into a secessionist struggle between Bougainville nationalists and the PNG security services and their local allies. The closure of the mine and the nine-year civil war that followed was a major economic blow to PNG, as well as the source of enormous suffering for the people of Bougainville (May and Spriggs, 1990; Regan, 1998).

PNG's small and fragile formal economy has not kept pace with the rapidly growing youthful population and has been incapable of absorbing the large number of annual school dropouts. With an annual growth rate of 2.6 percent, approximately half of the population is under twenty years old. The economy's export orientation has increasingly linked the country to the fluctuations of regional and international markets. Levels of public debt have risen to unsustainable levels as successive governments have sought to finance their policies through loans from commercial banks, multilateral financial agencies, and bilateral donors. Rising corruption among political leaders and other public officeholders has also been implicated in the poor and declining performance of the public sector.

While classified as a low- to middle-income country by international standards, PNG's main social indicators are now closer to those of low-income countries. Poverty has grown significantly, particularly in rural areas. Essential infrastructure, such as roads, is in a chronic state of disrepair in many places, while the provision and quality of basic government services, including health and education, have declined progressively in rural areas. Life expectancy and adult literacy rates are substantially below those in neighboring countries in the South Pacific and Southeast Asia. Infant mortality and crude birth and death rates are all above the average in the region. Moreover, the incidence and spread of HIV/AIDS has grown alarmingly in recent years, adding greatly to the pressures of an already overstretched health service. By 2002 PNG was ranked 133 out of a total of 173 countries evaluated under the United Nations Development Programme's Human Development Index (UNDP, 2002).

Crime and Lawlessness

Escalating lawlessness has emerged as one of the most pressing challenges facing the young nation. Euphemistically termed the law and order problems, growing levels of violent crime and social disorder are symptomatic of larger processes of social and economic transformation (Dinnen, 2001). As well as impacting citizens on a personal level, crime is a significant disincentive to commercial activities and foreign investment.

The popular term for the violent activities of gangs of adolescent boys and young men is *raskolism*, and this provides the most notorious face of these law and order problems. Crimes attributed to raskol gangs range from minor assaults, carjacking, housebreaking, and highway holdups to armed robberies, gang rapes, and murder. The term raskols, first coined in Port Moresby in the mid-1960s during the final decade of colonial administration, reflects the ambivalence felt then toward juvenile offenders, whose offenses were predominantly minor and acquisitive and rarely involved violence (Harris, 1988). This early ambivalence has long since disappeared and been replaced by an endemic fear of raskolism. Foreign governments issue security warnings for their citizens contemplating travel to Papua New Guinea. The violence associated with contemporary raskolism, often involving the use of firearms and sexual assaults, has generated much adverse publicity for PNG and lies behind high levels of personal insecurity among many citizens, particularly urban dwellers and women.

Violence is, of course, neither new nor unique to PNG. The prevalence of intergroup or "tribal" fighting among many Highlands New Guinea societies is well documented, as is the incidence of "payback" killings and rapes. Prowess in warfare has historically been an acknowledged route to prominence and leadership for ambitious young men in many societies. It is also important to acknowledge the violence inherent in the broader processes of colonization that have had such a dramatic and transformative impact on the peoples and societies of Melanesia. The early stages of colonial "pacification" that aimed to suppress violence and warfare among and be-tween indigenous groups were themselves dependent on the threat and use of violence (Rodman and Cooper, 1983). There are also issues of structural violence of more recent origin that are shared with many other developing and transitional countries. These manifest themselves in the growing levels of poverty, inequality, and social exclusion associated with the integration of small and fragile postcolonial economies into larger international markets dominated by powerful nations and transnational corporations.

The spread of lawlessness in PNG parallels broader patterns of social and urban development. Organized crime is concentrated in the expanding ur-ban centers, where public and private wealth is concentrated. Quantifying the extent of these problems is difficult given the scarcity and unreliability of available statistics. Criminal justice data primarily reflect the situation in the urban areas, where less than 15 percent of the total population lives. They, nevertheless, suggest a significant growth of crime, with a 65 percent increase in the number of serious offenses reported to the police over the last decade (World Bank, 1999). The highest proportion of reported serious crimes occurs in Port Moresby. Mount Hagen (Western Highlands Prov-ince) and Lae (Morobe Province) rank second and third, respectively. With a population conservatively estimated at more than 313,000 (UNDP, 1999, p. 175), Port Moresby has been described as one of the most dangerous cities in the world (Zvekic and Alvazzi del Frate, 1995). Between 1996 and 1998, the capital alone accounted for a recorded total of 232 murders, 3,361 robberies, 2,131 breaking and enterings, 556 cases of causing griev-ous bodily harm, 816 serious sexual assaults, 585 drug offenses, and 307 cases of illegal use of firearms (Sikani, 1999, p. 18). Figures from 2000 indicate that Port Moresby accounted for 55 percent of all reported rob-beries, 64 percent of vehicle thefts, 28 percent of drug offenses, 28 percent of murders, and 21 percent of serious sexual assaults (Australian Agency for International Development [AusAID], 2000).

Although they originated and continue to be concentrated in the urban centers, gangs are now found in many rural areas as well. Rural raskolism, however, is more akin to banditry and often takes the form of armed holdups of passenger and commercial vehicles traveling slowly along poorly main-tained highways and feeder roads (Reay, 1982). Rural crime of this kind tends to be episodic and is most likely to occur during the harvesting of cash crops, such as coffee, when buyers are traveling the Highlands with large amounts of cash. More-permanent gangs operate with relative impu-nity in the larger towns. At a macrolevel, urban raskolism has developed in a context where access to the small, formal economy is severely restricted and criminal opportunities are greatest. Crime has arguably become the sin-gle largest component of the informal urban economy. A recent survey es-timated that 18 percent of Port Moresby's inhabitants rely on crime as their principal source of income (Levantis, 1998). Corruption and malfeasance

Table 10.1
Population Growth of Port Moresby, Papua New Guinea

Year	Indigenous Population
1966	31,985
1970	42,616
1971	59,563
1975	92,500
1981	142,100
1986	198,500

Note: From *Colonial Town to Melanesian City: Port Moresby 1884–1974*
  (p. 85), by N. D. Oram, 1976, Canberra: Australian National University. Subsequent population data added. Reprinted with permis-
  sion.

among the political elite and the inability of successive governments to de-
liver "development" have furthered the rise of raskolism, providing a powerful motif in the rhetoric of disadvantage espoused by many among the
swelling ranks of the urban and rural poor.

THE GROWTH OF RASKOL GANGS

One of the most striking aspects of the phenomenon of raskolism is the
relatively short period of time over which it has emerged as a major law-
and-order problem. Unlike their counterparts in many other parts of the
world, juvenile gangs in PNG have no lengthy history. Prior to the early
1960s there was little concern expressed by Australian colonial authorities
about either crime or juvenile offenders. By the mid-1970s, however, fear
of the burgeoning raskol problem had become prevalent.

Juvenile gangs appeared against a background of rapid urban growth that
followed the removal of colonial restrictions on indigenous movement. The
abolition of these restrictions opened up the main towns—formerly the preserve of the European elite—to large-scale migration from rural areas. Between 1966 and 1971 the population of Port Moresby grew at an annual
rate of 11.7 percent (Oram, 1976, p. 84). Figures from this period indicate
the scale of Port Moresby's expansion.

As in many migrant populations, there was a preponderance of young
single males (Oram, 1976). In 1971, for example, 48 percent of the indigenous male population of Port Moresby comprised young men under the
age of 30. While the sex ratio among the indigenous population has become
more balanced with the passage of time, early migrants were predominantly
male. Thus, there were 282 men to 100 women in 1961, 184 men to 100
women in 1966, and 159 men to 100 women in 1971.

The first gangs were primarily mechanisms for coping with the stress and cultural dislocation experienced by young male migrants in the alien urban environment. Young men from the same areas of origin and sharing the same language would spend time together and occasionally engage in minor crime. Criminal activities at this time appear to have been largely confined to theft of cash, food, and, of course, beer (Parry, 1972). The decriminalization of alcohol consumption in 1962 was another ingredient in early gang formation and, according to one observer, constituted the "spark which ignited the flame" (Harris, 1988, p. 8). Alcohol, primarily in the form of beer, was considered a prestige item and associated with modernity. Drinking alcohol became a rite of passage for many young men wishing to prove to their peers that they had become "officially modernized" (Marshall, 1982, p. 5).

From the mid-1970s urban arrest figures indicated an increase in the volume of acquisitive crime. This increase has been attributed to the gradual spread of raskol activities from low-visibility urban settlements to the more respectable Port Moresby suburbs (Harris, 1988, p. 11). It also reflected a growing sophistication in criminal organization, including the involvement of better-educated gang members, which enabled a "process of vertical integration of gangs into larger criminal networks" (Harris, 1988, p. 13). Raskolism developed from being primarily a means of support and identity among young migrants to a vehicle for material sustenance and advancement. A process of consolidation occurred in the late 1970s and early 1980s, involving an often violent struggle for domination in particular neighborhoods between the larger criminal groups. The incidence of payback rape and other serious assaults committed in the course of intergang conflict heralded a significantly more violent phase in the evolution of urban raskolism (Dorney, 1990, pp. 304–305). By the late 1980s Port Moresby gangs were reported to have become "efficient criminal organizations which operate with little fear of apprehension" (Harris, 1988, p. 1).

While much everyday street crime remains relatively minor, the frequency of serious criminal violence has increased in recent years, as the following figures demonstrate.

Criminals have become sophisticated in their planning and execution of operations to rob payrolls, banks, business houses, and cash-in-transit. It is apparent that many such operations are inside jobs involving the active collusion of employees in the targeted premises. Evidence also suggests a deepening nexus between raskol elements and certain political and other prominent figures who employ criminal muscle for electoral, commercial, or security purposes.

The increasing use of firearms has added greatly to the personal insecurity induced by raskolism. Homemade guns produced in illegal "gun factories" are widely available and relatively cheap. Recent years have also witnessed a significant growth in the availability of more-expensive high-powered weap-

Table 10.2
Increase in Reported Levels of Serious Crime (1990 and 1999)

Serious Crime	1990	1999	Difference (%)
Murder	429	425	−1
Serious sexual offenses	1,072	1,444	35
Robbery	2,028	3,061	51
Break and enter	2,856	2,568	−10
Fraud (>K1,000)	112	344	207
Total	6,497	7,842	21

Note: From *Annual Report*, by Royal Papua New Guinea Constabulary, 1990 and
    1999; Port Moresby: Author. Reprinted with permission.

ons. Some of these are believed to be the product of a drugs-for-guns trade,
in which high-quality marijuana grown in PNG is exchanged for weapons
from Australia. This trade appears to be concentrated in the islands of PNG's
Western Province, which constitute part of the sea border with northern
Australia (Inguba, 1999). While gangs are involved in the distribution of
marijuana to local markets, it is believed that the drugs-for-guns trade is
more likely to involve dishonest business and political leaders acting in association with foreign criminals. Other high-powered weapons are the products of thefts from the armories of the PNG police and defense force, while
yet others are sold or rented out illegally by corrupt members of these so-
called protective forces. Police raids conducted during curfew operations
between November 1996 and January 1997 were reported to have netted
more than 45 pistols, shotguns, and automatic assault weapons, as well as
fragmentation grenades (*National*, January 22, 1997). The increasingly bra-
zen character of criminal activities also serves to escalate individuals' fears.
Robberies and carjackings often occur in crowded parts of town in the middle of the day. One of the most disturbing aspects of contemporary raskolism is the high number of sexual assaults against women and girls. Although
raskol gangs are by no means the only source of sexual violence, they have
become closely associated with the practice of "pack rape," involving multiple rapists. In addition to planned rapes, many sexual assaults appear to be
crimes of opportunity, committed in the course of another crime (e.g.,
housebreaking) or when a victim is found on her own.

The most visible manifestation of the fear generated by raskol crime lies
in the barbed-wire fencing and elaborate security provisions that now dom-
inate the urban landscape. Offices, hotels, restaurants, business premises,
government offices, schools, and the residences of the urban elite are heavily
fortified against criminal intruders. Private security is one of the few booming industries, and uniformed guards and dogs are ubiquitous in all the main

towns. Such private provision is, of course, unavailable to the poor, who are largely dependent on the security provided by extended families and *wantoks* (members of the same clan or tribal group). After nightfall the streets are deserted, with none of the markets or busy street life found in neighboring Asian countries. Certain parts of Port Moresby have acquired reputations for being unsafe and remain effectively "no-go" areas for strangers. These include most of the settlements where the poor and unemployed are concentrated. For women and girls, security considerations remain a significant constraint on freedom of movement, even during the day.

Concerns about criminal violence have been a major factor behind the failure to develop a tourist industry along the lines of other South Pacific countries, such as Fiji and Vanuatu. These concerns have adversely affected commerce at all levels, from large international investors to ordinary villagers unwilling to risk transporting their produce to urban markets. Private employers have recently ranked theft and crime as the most significant obstacle to doing business in PNG (Institute of National Affairs [INA], 1999). Insurance premiums are prohibitively high, as are additional costs, such as the provision of private transportation for employees working late. For expensive expatriate labor, Papua New Guinea is viewed as a hardship post.

OFFICIAL RESPONSES TO RASKOLISM

Public debate on crime in Papua New Guinea has been a familiar law-and-order one. Growing concerns have been accompanied by demands to strengthen the police, increase penalties, and expand the prison system. More-challenging questions relating to the factors and processes contributing to crime have generally been sidestepped in favor of short-term reactive responses, with the emphasis on deterrence and punishment. Even here, there has been a marked gap between the tough rhetoric espoused by political leaders and the actual implementation of policies. What is clear is that the modern criminal justice system, as it has developed in PNG, has proven to be no match for the growth and increasing sophistication of criminal enterprise. The institutional weaknesses of the principal agencies—police, courts, and prisons—have been the subject of numerous reviews and are currently the focus of intense reform projects funded by the Australian government. While the factors behind these weaknesses are complex, the end result is that the criminal justice system, as it currently operates, provides little effective deterrence to serious crime (Dinnen, 2002).

As the frontline agency, the police have demonstrated little capacity for conducting criminal investigations. The chances of being arrested for major crime remain relatively small. In 2000, for example, there were 5,205 serious crimes reported in Port Moresby and only 1,936 arrests made. This suggests that in the national capital, there is an almost two-in-three chance of not being arrested for the worst offenses (AusAID, 2001). Where arrests do occur, subsequent prosecutions often fail through lack of sufficient police evidence. In addition to their technical deficiencies, the police have an extremely poor record in the area of community relations. This reflects, in part, their colonial origins as a paramilitary force whose primary role was doing the government's work and only secondarily controlling crime. Police officers and their families continue to live apart from the wider community in barrack-style accommodations. Ambivalent attitudes toward the police have been reinforced by serious allegations of police brutality against individual suspects, and in some cases entire communities. Pending litigation and the rate of new litigation against the police have reached extraordinary levels in recent years. Claims cover matters such as illegal police raids, false imprisonment, wrongful arrest, assault, and police killings. More than half of all litigation against the state arises from actions against the police (PNG Department of Attorney General, 1999).

The shortcomings of state policing have contributed to the massive growth in private security. Likewise, they lie behind the practice of using legal provisions intended originally for emergency situations as standard responses to serious outbreaks of crime. Such measures, provided under the constitution and other legislation, have included states of emergency, curfews, and special policing operations. They usually entail restrictions over movement in the designated area, as well as an increase in police powers. In justifying the imposition of a state of emergency in Port Moresby in 1985 in response to a series of brutal gang rapes, the then–prime minister stated that the "police can no longer—using their normal powers—control it." Reactive responses of this kind are designed to restore order in specified areas and, in practice, often entail heavy-handed police raids against settlements and other communities suspected of harboring raskols and stolen property. Such displays of militaristic strength belie the actual capacity of the PNG police to respond to crime in a more routine manner.

The 1985 state of emergency set in motion a pattern of state responses to localized outbreaks of crime that has been repeated many times in subsequent years. An increase in raskol activities—or the perception of such—leads to mounting public pressure for government action. Official responses typically include the announcement of a package of repressive measures (only a few of which get implemented), and in the most serious situations the imposition of a curfew. Order and public confidence are temporarily restored until the next buildup, when similar responses are demanded, and so on.

Police raids conducted during such operations give rise to numerous complaints and, increasingly, civil suits against the state. Serious assaults may take place, and property that cannot be accounted for by the production of receipts is likely to be seized as possible evidence or may even be stolen by individual officers. These are deliberately punitive strategies aimed at coercing acquiescence from recalcitrant communities. Police often justify such methods in terms of their own frustrations about lack of community support and having to work through a cumbersome, inefficient, and inadequately resourced justice system. The inevitable consequence is a further deterioration in police-community relations.

Repressive measures have only a temporary and superficial impact on crime. Once the curfew is lifted, crime rates begin to rise again. There is also a real risk that curfews lose even their short-term benefits when used too frequently or extended over long periods of time. They are also extremely costly exercises and invariably impact already overstretched police budgets. They may also serve inadvertently to strengthen criminal organization. Wanted criminals will either maintain a low profile for the duration of such operations or move to other areas unaffected by the restrictions. By displacing criminals in this way, these measures may have contributed to the dispersal of criminal networks to other parts of the country.

Induction into raskol membership often includes having violent encounters with police. Police violence in the course of pursuit and arrest, or during questioning, is depicted as routine by criminal informants, often being referred to colloquially as the "panel beat shop"(reference to shops where panels of cars are beaten back into shape). Stories about police beatings—whether real or imagined—provide young criminals with an important way of building reputation among their peers, as well as a means of eliciting sympathy from the wider community. Similarly, incarceration has become another rite of passage in the raskol world. Gangs thrive inside PNG's largest prison at Bomana, outside Port Moresby. Periods of imprisonment increase solidarity within particular groups, as well as nurture personal associations and future collaboration among the groups.

There is no state-provided social security or welfare in PNG, and the poor and indigent are reliant on the support provided by relatives and wantoks. While there has been much talk about developing youth programs, training programs, and employment generation, little real progress has been made. The government department responsible for such matters—the Department of Home Affairs and Youth—has been consistently underfunded and carries little political weight in the hierarchy of government. In practice, official responses to the growing problem of juvenile crime have been overwhelmingly of the repressive law-and-order kind. Young offenders are treated little differently from adult offenders in every aspect of the formal justice system. Diversionary schemes exist in theory but are rarely used, owing to lack of adequate supervisory resources. Critical reforms in juvenile justice have been delayed for over ten years because the Juvenile Courts Act of 1991 has yet to come into force.

In Port Moresby and the other larger towns, youth groups compete with each other for contracts to cut grass and carry out other menial public works for the urban authorities. The money raised from such activities is extremely small once it has been divided among individual members, so such groups tend to have short life spans. Churches, which constitute the single most important element of PNG's nascent civil society, have had a long engagement with youth groups, including those operating on the fringes of urban society. This includes ministering to young offenders in prison and running a number of institutions for juveniles, such as Boystown in Wewak. Evangelical crusades appeal directly to marginal youths, and evangelical preachers have played a key role in attempts to initiate dialogue between criminal leaders and state officials. These occasions, exemplified in "gang retreats," bring criminal and political leaders together for informal discussions about law-and-order issues, particularly those pertaining to youths.

The churches have also played an important role in some of the most innovative attempts to address raskol crime in recent years. These attempts include the phenomenon of gang surrender, which reached its peak in the mid-1990s. Gang surrender is a strategy for exiting crime and is, in part, an informal response to the excesses and deficiencies of the criminal justice system. Initiated by the churches, groups of gang members surrender themselves and their weapons at public ceremonies. Gang members ask for forgiveness for their crimes and for help with rehabilitation and reentry into noncriminal society. The latter usually entails small income-generating schemes, such as poultry projects, that will enable the group to leave crime for a legitimate livelihood. Churches or individual pastors often act as brokers for surrenders. As such, they are instrumental in persuading the group to surrender and, in return, assist in securing access to desired economic or training opportunities. In the past, such strategies received considerable support, and magistrates were likely to be sympathetic to defendants who had voluntarily renounced their criminal pasts. This support has gradually diminished, however, as violent crime has continued to grow and as beleaguered town dwellers have become more skeptical of such strategies.

THE RASKOL GANG

The raskol gang demonstrates some important continuities with older forms of Melanesian social organization. Contrary to their depiction in media accounts, raskol gangs appear to be relatively fluid entities with minimal formal structure and rules of membership. In the mid-1990s four major criminal conglomerates operated in Port Moresby. These were Bomai, Koboni, Mafia, and 585. Although the gangs were territorially based, there was little evidence of territorial or other significant patterns of intergang conflict. The organization of the criminal underworld, like that of the Melanesian clan, is essentially segmentary. Each of the four major conglomerates consisted of an indeterminate number of loosely associated subgroups that had their own names and leaders and, in practice, exercised a high degree of autonomy. The continuous variation in the size and configuration of criminal groups—generally following the fortunes of individual leaders—parallels that of traditional political organization. While the conglomerates can trace their origins back to smaller and ethnically homogeneous groups, the associated subgroups ensure that they reflect the ethnic heterogeneity of the urban milieu. Active members range in age from early teens to mid-twenties. Most, though by no means all, have dropped out of school or, more precisely, have been pushed out as a result of their parents' or guardians' inability to pay the required fees.

Difficulties with the notion of raskol gangs as strictly bounded entities are illustrated by the relative ease of entry to and exit from criminal groups. Entry into particular criminal groups appears to be quite casual, with none of the formal initiation rites noted by earlier observers (Harris, 1988; Utulurea, 1981; Young, 1976). A prospective recruit might be invited to participate in a criminal venture, and his performance informally assessed by colleagues. The more usual pattern of entry entails a process of incremental involvement commencing at an early age over a long period of time. Leaving the group appears to be equally casual. An individual might tire of the criminal lifestyle and dangers involved and gradually withdraw from active service. Alternatively, he might acquire family responsibilities or full-time employment or undergo religious conversion. David Matza's (1964) notion of "delinquent drift" appears to be applicable in this context. In practice, gang members are often unable to state with any precision the number of members in their particular criminal entity. This highlights the essentially indeterminate character of raskol organization.

A number of observers have remarked on the similarities between modern criminal leaders and traditional "big-men" (Goddard, 1992, 1995; Harris, 1988; Kulick, 1993; Schiltz, 1985). The leader of each of the four main criminal conglomerates is known as the father, indicating the highly personalized bond that exists between criminal leaders and their followers. Success for the modern criminal leader, as with his traditional counterpart, depends in large measure on his ability to engage in a process of skillful manipulation of resources and relationships. Whereas the Melanesian big-man built his power and prestige through the accumulation and ceremonial exchange of traditional items of wealth, the criminal leader constructs his power base around acquisitive crime and the strategic distribution of proceeds among followers and kin. An important object of distribution in both cases is to engender social credit and, in the process, enhance individual reputation and personal bonds of loyalty. As Schiltz (1985) remarks:

[D]istributing spoils from robberies . . . enhances one's name. By giving generously one builds up social credit, and making people obligated is the most elementary form of creating bonds of domination/subordination. Port Moresby rascals know these age-old political strategies just as well as those village men who try to make a name for themselves by giving away pigs or shells. (p. 147)

A notable feature of raskol enterprise is its manifest failure to provide lasting material prosperity for even its most successful practitioners. For the latter, success is largely a consequence of how they distribute the proceedings of crime and thereby build and consolidate the loyalty of followers. In this respect, raskolism provides another variation of a familiar Melanesian quest for standing and prestige.

As well as demonstrating important continuities with the past, raskolism represents a response to new circumstances arising from the dramatic social and economic transformations of recent times. As such, it has important similarities with the plight of marginalized youth in other parts of the developing world. Many of the young men and boys drawn to raskolism express a deep resentment and anger at what they view as the injustice of their peripheral role in society. This anger is directed at government (or the state), political leaders, public servants, and other members of the salaried elite because of their conspicuous consumption and unwillingness to share their wealth. This failure to share is viewed as a major breach of indigenous notions of reciprocity and exchange, and engenders powerful feelings of betrayal.

Whereas the phenomenon of raskolism is often explained in official discourse as the almost inevitable, if unfortunate, outcome of insufficient job opportunities, young criminals express a broader sense of grievance that is directed at the inequitable distribution of available material and social resources, including jobs. A recurring sentiment among urban youths is that of having been tricked or cheated out of their right to participate fully in the development of their country. Many of these youngsters are second- or third-generation urban dwellers whose ideas and expectations have been shaped by their exposure to formal education and other aspects of global culture from an early age. While commentators often suggest that unemployed youths should return to rural villages and live off the land, this is simply not an option for many youngsters. Their rural connections may be tenuous at best, and they often have neither the skills nor the inclination to live in a village.

Juvenile gangs in Port Moresby are made up of young men from many different ethnic backgrounds, whose identities are closely tied to the city or that part of it where they have grown up and reside. Their vehicle of communication is more likely to be the generic *Tok Pisin* (Melanesian pidgin) than a local language or dialect. As such, they represent "one of the few enduring social structures in which regional and tribal divisions are blurred and broken down" (Harris, 1988, p. 2). Having embraced the idea of the modern world, they are excluded from the means for participating in it. To add to their sense of grievance, they are labeled raskols and hounded by a criminal justice system that appears to take little interest in the infractions of the elite. Youth leaders often seek to legitimatize raskolism, as both a means of drawing attention to their plight and a way of negotiating a legitimate place in the development stakes. In this rendition it becomes a form of collective action, using the threat of criminal violence as a bargaining tool for securing equal participation in capitalist development. Such sentiments are reflected in the following letter from a Port Moresby gang that was read aloud at a gang retreat:

Just for your information, we must let you know that we, the neglected and rejected, with birthrights and nationalities, sons of this country, out here on the streets will cause problems wherever we go. It is very clear that nobody cares for us. That's why we in turn must make you turn back and look at us, that we are still there [sic]. (Letter from "Criminals of KGK Koboni of Horse Camp," July 6, 1991, on file with the Foundation for Law, Order and Justice, Port Moresby.)

There is also a distinctly retributive dimension to raskol violence that connects with culturally embedded notions of reciprocity and exchange. From this perspective violent crime is aimed at punishing those who have failed in their obligations to the young and, in the process, forcing them back into more appropriate exchange relations. Schiltz (1985) refers to this as the "equalizing dimension" of raskolism:

From the point of view of the gangs, however, modern society represented by the state is an opponent who is unwilling to enter into exchange relations with them and thus enable them to compete for, and participate on an equal basis in, the nation's wealth and social processes. . . . [T]he "equalizing dimension" . . . expresses itself in the violent confrontation of rival powers who exchange blows, rascal gangs versus the state. (p. 149)

Contemporary raskolism is no longer simply a vehicle for assisting the difficult personal adjustments involved in the transition from rural to urban environments. In the eyes of many of its practitioners it has become an instrument for challenging perceived injustices and negotiating a more equitable social order. An unfortunate irony is that it is fellow members of the urban poor who are most vulnerable to the depredations of raskol violence. They are unable to afford the elaborate security provisions available to their more affluent counterparts. At the same time, the ambivalence toward raskols expressed in many urban settlements reflects the fact that the rhetoric of disadvantage articulated by criminal leaders is shared widely in such communities.

From its inception the raskol gang has been a predominantly male preserve. The masculine subculture of the juvenile gang reflects deeper currents of male dominance and sexual antagonism found in many Melanesian cultures. While the technology of so-called tribal fighting has changed dramatically as a result of the introduction of modern weapons, the violence of young warriors continues to be an expression of a potent masculinity. The conventional virtues of the tribal warrior—physical strength and courage, loyalty to comrades, and the capacity to outwit the enemy—remain those of the contemporary raskol. While the constitution and other PNG laws enshrine Western notions of human rights and formal equality between the sexes, violation of the rights of women remains widespread. Research by the PNG Law Reform Commission, among others, establishes that violence toward women is prevalent in modern Papua New Guinea and is by no means confined to those who are labeled raskol (Toft, 1986; Toft and Bonnell, 1985).

Raskol gangs have become an important vehicle for the initiation of young urban men into the ambivalent urban space. As well as drawing on older Melanesian models of masculinity, they take inspiration from the models provided by global culture. Prominent among the latter are the macho heroes of the action movies that are shown regularly in settlements, villages, private homes, cinemas, and video outlets. The violent masculinity of Rambo and his endless imitators is reflected in the popular culture of urban youth. Militaristic clothing is highly valued, as are dreadlocks or shaven heads and, of course, the ubiquitous dark glasses. Media images from distant conflicts, including the so-called war against terrorism, are scrutinized with great interest and used selectively to replenish a vibrant street style. In late 2002 Osama Bin Laden T-shirts became the latest accoutrement of young male fashion in Port Moresby—until complaints forced stores to withdraw these items. This phenomenon is not confined to deviant youths but is also embraced by younger members of the police and military forces. Members of the police mobile squads deployed on Bougainville at the start of the conflict continued to display facial camouflage and wear special combat fatigues for many months after they had returned to policing duties on the mainland. The same aggressive masculinity that underlies the behavior of tribal warriors and urban raskols informs the responses to them by the law enforcement agencies of the modern state.

REFERENCES

Australian Agency for International Development [AusAID]. (2000). *Royal Papua New Guinea Constabulary (RPNGC) Evaluation Report*, July–December.

———. (2001). *A Review of the Law and Justice Sector Agencies in Papua New Guinea.*

Berndt, R. M. *Excess and restraint* (Chicago: University of Chicago Press, 1962).

Chowning, A. *An introduction to the peoples and cultures of Melanesia*, 2d ed. (Menlo Park, CA: Cummings, 1977).

Dinnen, S. *Law and order in a weak state: Crime and politics in Papua New Guinea* (Honolulu: University of Hawai'i Press, 2001).

———. "Building bridges: Law and justice reform in Papua New Guinea." *State Society and Governance in Melanesia Discussion Paper 02/02* (Canberra: Australian National University, 2002), pp. 1–18.

Dorney, S. *Papua New Guinea: People, politics and history since 1975* (Sydney: Random House, 1990).

Goddard, M. "Big-man, thief: The social organization of gangs in Port Moresby." *Canberra Anthropology* 15(1) (1992): 20–34.

———. "The rascal road: Crime, prestige and development in Papua New Guinea." *The Contemporary Pacific* 7(1) (1995): 55–80.

Harris, B. M. *The rise of rascalism: Action and Reaction in the Evolution of Rascal Gangs* (Discussion Paper 54, pp. 1–52). (Port Moresby: Institute of Applied Social and Economic Research, 1988).

Inguba, S. "Bilateral cooperation in cross-border crime." In *Australia–Papua New Guinea: Crime and the bilateral relationship*, edited by B. Boeha (Port Moresby: National Research Institute, 1999), pp. 48–53.

Institute of National Affairs [INA]. *Factors contributing to the lack of investment in Papua New Guinea: A private sector survey* (Port Moresby: Institute of National Affairs, 1999).

Kulick, D. "Heroes from hell: Representations of 'rascals' in a Papua New Guinean village." *Anthropology Today* 9(3) (1993): 9–14.

Levantis, T. "Tourism in Papua New Guinea." *Pacific Economic Bulletin* 13(1) (1998): 98–105.

Marshall, M., ed. "Introduction: Twenty years after deprohibition." In *Through a glass darkly: Beer and modernisation in Papua New Guinea* (Monograph 18, pp. 3–13) (Port Moresby: Institute of Applied Social and Economic Research, 1982).

Matza, D. *Delinquency and drift* (New York: John Wiley & Sons, 1964).

May, R. J., and M. Spriggs, eds. *The Bougainville crisis* (Bathurst, NSW: Crawford House Publishing, 1990).

Meggitt, M. J. *Blood is their argument: Warfare among the Mae Enga Tribesmen of the New Guinea Highlands* (Palo Alto, CA: Mayfield Publishing, 1977).

National. (1997, January 22) Retrieved from http://www.thenational.com.pg/.

Oram, N. D. *Colonial town to Melanesian city: Port Moresby 1884–1974* (Canberra: Australian National University, 1976).

Papua New Guinea Department of Attorney General. Brief to Minister for Justice, Hon. Kilroy K. Genia MP, 1999.

Parry, G. L. "Organized juvenile crime in Port Moresby." *South Pacific Bulletin* 22(1) (1972): 43.

Reay, M. "Lawlessness in the Papua New Guinea Highlands." Vol. 2 of *Melanesia Beyond Diversity*, edited by R. J. May and H. Nelson (Canberra: Research School of Pacific Studies, Australian National University, 1982), pp. 623–637.

Regan, A. J. "Causes and course of the Bougainville." *Journal of Pacific History* 33(3) (1998): 269–285.

Rodman, M., and M. Cooper, eds. *The Pacification of Melanesia* (Lanham, MD: University Press of America, 1983).

Royal Papua New Guinea Constabulary. *Annual report* (Port Moresby: Author, 1990).

———. *Annual report* (Port Moresby: Author, 1999).

Schiltz, M. "Rascalism, tradition and the state." In *Domestic violence in Papua New Guinea* [Monograph 3], edited by S. Toft (Port Moresby: Law Reform Commission of Papua New Guinea, 1985), pp. 141–160.

Sikani, R. "Criminal threat in Papua New Guinea." In *Australia-Papua New Guinea:*

Crime and the bilateral relationship, edited by B. Boeha (Port Moresby: National Research Institute, 1999), pp. 12–35.

Strathern, A. M. *Rope of Moka: Big-Men and ceremonial exchange in Mount Hagen, New Guinea* (Cambridge: Cambridge University Press, 1971).

Toft, S., ed. *Domestic violence in urban Papua New Guinea*. Occasional Paper 19 (Port Moresby: PNG Law Reform Commission, 1986).

Toft, S., and S. Bonnell, eds. *Marriage and domestic violence in rural Papua New Guinea*. Occasional Paper 18 (Port Moresby: PNG Law Reform Commission, 1985).

United Nations Development Programme [UNDP]. *Papua New Guinea human development report 1998* (Hong Kong: Government of PNG and UNDP, 1999).

———. *Human development report 2002. Deepening democracy in a fragmented world* (New York: Oxford University Press, 2002).

Utulurea, G. "Gangs in Port Moresby." *Point* 1 (1981): 109–117 (*Point* is published semiannually by the Melanesian Institute for Pastoral and Socio-Economic Service, Goroka, PNG).

World Bank. *Papua New Guinea—Improving governance and performance* (Washington, DC: World Bank, 1999).

Young, F. D. *Pasin Bilong Rascal: Juvenile crime in Port Moresby*. [Research Report 209]. (Port Moresby: Psychological Services Branch, Public Service Commission, 1976).

Zvekic, U., and A. Alvazzi del Frate, eds. *Criminal victimisation in the developing world* (New York: United Nations Interregional Crime and Justice Research Institute, 1995).

11

PUERTO RICO

Edil Torres Rivera and Loan T. Phan

INTRODUCTION

Puerto Rico is a small island in the Caribbean with a population of 3.8 million people living in an area smaller than Rhode Island (U.S. Census Bureau, 2002). For more than five hundred years, this island nation has endured colonial governments, first under Spain's monarchy and, in the last one hundred years, under the United States. A number of Puerto Rican historians are convinced that the gang problem in Puerto Rico is due to political ambiguity and a long history of human rights violations of inmates in the Puerto Rican prisons (Picó, 1998). The problem of gangs in Puerto Rico is not widespread, and a number of experts believe that it is not a big problem. This is supported by the fact that the only literature about gangs that can be found in Puerto Rican libraries is the product of newspapers and not academic literature (De Jesús Mangual, 2002; Serrano, 2002).

HISTORICAL BACKGROUND

Puerto Rico, as a United States territory, exhibits a similar diversity of cultural characteristics in its society to that which exists in the United States. However, Puerto Rico is a colony of the United States and, as such, experiences immense political ambiguity, which has impacted how Puerto Ricans define themselves legally and economically (Fitzpatrick, 1987; Quintero Rivera, González, Campos, and Flores, 1960; Rivera Ramos, 2001). Puerto Rico centers around the future status of the country: attaining U.S. state-

hood; continuing to be an *estado libre asociado*, or commonwealth; or becoming a free republic. In other words, Puerto Ricans are somewhere
between being American and being Latino (Flores, 1993). This ambivalent
status has created unique problems for many Puerto Ricans with respect to
their identity, especially for those from lower socioeconomic status (Cordasco and Bucchioni, 1973; Fitzpatrick, 1987; Marino, 2002; Quintero Rivera, 1976; Quiñones Vizcarrondo, 1989).

Puerto Rican history spans some 500 years, from its discovery by Chris-
topher Columbus on his second voyage, November 19, 1493 (Díaz Soler,
1994; Fitzpatrick, 1987; Scarano, 1993). When Columbus arrived in Bor-
inquén, or Borikén (the name given to the island by its inhabitants), he
found a group of natives that the Spaniards would later name *Los Tainos*,
but anthropologists and historians now believe were part of the Arawak
culture (Díaz Soler, 1994; Scarano, 1993). The native Arawaks of Puerto
Rico and the Dominican Republic had a political and economic system that,
according to many historians, was more advanced than that of all native
Indians from the other Antilles (Gómez Acevedo and Ballesteros Gabriois,
1978; Sued-Badillo, 1989). The Arawaks disappeared one hundred years
after the colonization by the Spaniards (Burdette, 1976; Gómez Acevedo
and Ballesteros Gabriois, 1978; Sued-Badillo, 1989).

Puerto Rico was not colonized immediately after it was discovered.
Rather, the island was colonized by the Spaniards in 1509, when Juan Ponce
de León arrived (Scarano, 1993). This period in the history of the Puerto
Rican nation was also marked by confusion and indecision on the part of
the Spanish government about how island matters would be administered
and by whom (Scarano, 1993). Fernándo de Aragón, the king of Spain, was
in dispute with Columbus's family, which resulted in confusion about how
the island was to be governed. The confusion would not end until 1511,
leaving the new colony in political uncertainty for its first two years.

Spain's interest in Puerto Rico did not last long, as the reserve of gold
on the island was exhausted by the second half of the sixteenth century.
Spain became more interested in Mexico and Peru, as they found fortune
in the form of gold and silver in those territories. However, in 1700 Spain
was compelled to protect its crown possessions in America; and consequently, a strategic function was assigned to Puerto Rico. This function
would elevate Puerto Rico to a key position in the defense of Spanish treas-
ures in the Americas. A pattern of political ambiguity was thus established
for Puerto Rico; that is, Spain would lavish a great deal of attention and
importance on Puerto Rico for periods of time and later would ignore the
island completely. This pattern would not cease until the next colonization
of Puerto Rico by the United States in 1898 (Díaz Soler, 1994; Scarano,
1993).

In the latter part of the nineteenth century, Puerto Rico was recognized
for its production of coffee. This period in its history was known as the

Golden Age, when urban development and material prosperity flourished. Nonetheless, the political reality of Puerto Rico was to remain as it was. Spain was unwilling to grant the reforms desired by the majority of the Puerto Rican people.

In addition, Puerto Ricans attained progress in the arts and education, and these achievements contributed to the formation of a national identity (Scarano, 1993). In the nineteenth century, for the first time the customs and characteristics of the native Puerto Ricans made their way into the Creole literature. The characteristics that later would define a Puerto Rican identity appeared in a number of publications and the nationalistic feelings of the Puerto Rican people became obvious (Scarano, 1993).

Following the Spanish-American War in 1898, the Treaty of Paris made Puerto Rico a possession of the United States, which served to extend the period of political ambiguity, as the colonial position of Puerto Rico continued. Since the invasion of Puerto Rico by the United States in 1898, Puerto Rico has remained a neocolony within the United States' political system; that is, Puerto Rico belongs to, but is not a part of, the United States. Nevertheless, Puerto Ricans have been United States citizens since 1917. The colonialism of Puerto Rico is defined by the island's economic dependency on the United States economy and by the politics surrounding the island's relationship to the United States (Meléndez and Meléndez, 1993).

In 1947, under the Jones Act of 1917, Puerto Ricans were given the right to elect their own governor. In 1948 Don Luis Muñoz Marín, the first governor, was elected by popular vote. Under his leadership a new political status was instituted—the *Estado Libre Asociado de Puerto Rico*, or E.L.A. (Free Associated State of Puerto Rico or Commonwealth). This status was approved by the Congress of the United States and became law on July 25, 1952. This status provided Puerto Rico with some autonomy in its government, but it was still governed by United States federal laws. This, according to Meléndez and Meléndez (1993), maintained Puerto Rico as an unincorporated territory of the mainland.

The island has two additional ideologies related to the political status of Puerto Rico that help to perpetuate political and ethnic confusion among the islanders. First, there is a small but very vocal group that demands the independence of the island, led by the Independence Party (*Partido Independentista Puertorriqueño*, or *PIP*). Second, there is the group that advocates statehood for Puerto Rico or its annexation to the United States (*Partido Nuevo Progresista*, or *PNP*). "The problem of status is not a simple matter of government, but rather a deeply rooted problem of identity" (Fitzpatrick, 1987, p. 31). Therefore, Puerto Ricans must face the challenge of understanding complex differences in race, socioeconomic status, gender, values, and beliefs in order to appreciate their own identity (Silén, 1973; Vázquez, 1991).

In 1996, for the fifth time Puerto Rico came under the administration of *El Partido Nuevo Progresista* (The New Progressive Party), which is the party that advocates statehood for the island. The movement for annexation to the United States is not a new phenomenon, but one that has existed since the turn of the twentieth century (Meléndez, 1988). For Puerto Rico, some of the consequences of strengthening the relationship with the United States, however, involve confusion about Puerto Rican ethnic identity, adjustment in values and beliefs, and violent behavior (Fitzpatrick, 1987; Mintz, 1973; Vázquez, 1991). Meléndez (1988) supported this same point of view in his disagreement with Maldonado Denis (1972), who saw the annexation movement as one of a middle class that was assimilated into American culture and that was without any sense of national identity. Meléndez (1988) continued to explain his argument: "Under such analysis, it is argued that the absence of a national identity is the result of cultural imperialism and the lack of national bourgeoisie. The contemporary statehood movement becomes predominantly a cultural phenomenon, largely determined by the assimilation of Puerto Ricans, particularly by the economic elites" (p. 4). According to De Vos and Romanucci-Ross (1975), crises in identity occur when people must choose between conflicting group loyalties.

A number of social scientists have placed the blame for the genesis of gangs in Puerto Rico on the ambivalence of Puerto Ricans about their identity. This view is supported to some degree by the social dislocation and underground economics in Puerto Rico. As a result of the colonial status of the island, many Puerto Ricans possess little control over their own economic viability (Aguilar Aguilar, 1997; Bourgois, 1995; Weisel, 2002). The average per capita income for Puerto Ricans is eight thousand dollars and the unemployment level is about 14 percent—and has never been lower than 13 percent in recent history (U.S. Census Bureau, 2002). Therefore, some sociologists and mental health professionals argue that gangs and, in particular, criminal activities are not necessarily a choice, but a way to survive in such situations (Bourgois, 1995; Torres-Rivera, Wilbur, Phan, Maddux, and Roberts-Wilbur, in press).

THE GANG PROBLEM

The United States Drug Enforcement Administration estimates that the second-most-used route of drug dealers to the United States is via the Caribbean—and Puerto Rico and the Virgin Islands in particular (Fiske, 2002). Puerto Rico is the initial point of entry because of the location of the island and the lack of customs inspections between Puerto Rico and the United States. This traffic in drugs is considered to be a contributor to the development of gangs in Puerto Rico. Gangs control over one thousand points of drug trafficking on the island. Cocaine in Puerto Rico is less expensive than in any other place in the United States. This, in combination with the economic decay of the island, has made cocaine trafficking an attractive motivator to juvenile gangs in the public housing projects. Puerto Rico has the second-highest number of homicides in the United States, with the majority being gang related. The British Broadcasting Corporation (BBC) reported that, in 1990, under the protection of the Columbian drug cartels or organizations, large amounts of heroin were imported into Puerto Rico and distributed free of charge among drug dealers to assess the market reaction on the street. The result was the creation of a large number of drug addicts and an underground economy using drugs, not money, as a means of exchange (Bourgois, 1995; Fiske, 2002). A significant number of Puerto Rican youth participated in the use and dealing of heroin and other drugs as a result of this decision to test market heroin in Puerto Rico. In order to corner their share of the market for dealing street drugs, youths gangs were formed and consolidated. Both the Puerto Rican media and social scientists contend that the strong emergence of juvenile gangs was a function of this underground economy created by the decision to test market heroin in Puerto Rico (Cordero, 2002). These drug-related teen gangs were part of the larger problem of importation, sale, and distribution of drugs into Puerto Rico. Making clear distinctions between youth gangs involved in organized drug crime and other kinds of youth gangs was made more difficult as a result.

In addition to the difficulties in trying to understand the origins of the gang phenomenon, defining what is a gang and what is not further adds to the complexity. For example, the National Youth Gang Survey Trends relied on self-definitions and police officers to define what a gang is and who is a gang member (Egley, 2002). For a number of Puerto Ricans these definitions are distorted and misleading (Aguilar Aguilar, 1997). In fact, the problem of gangs is more a symptom of economic malaise and lack of identity. Regardless of how complex this problem may be, no one can deny that organized groups do exist and that criminal activity in Puerto Rico is alarming.

While the literature about gangs in the United States presents a number of definitions and types of gangs (Harris, 1988; Vigil, 1988; Weisel, 2002) based on the media and conversations with some gangs members, some believe Puerto Rican gangs should be defined as cultural groups because they have strong ties with the community, and to a large degree many of the gang members are related to each other by blood, close friendship, or chosen family (*compadrazgo*). It is not uncommon for drug dealers who happen also to be gang leaders to finance festivities and other community activities.

Therefore, people are accepted into gang membership not through an initiation, as such, but through kinship and compadrazgo. Puerto Rican gangs are family-based, many members having close blood relationships.

Leadership is maintained in a single family, and gang roles are inherited. This is different from the way gangs gain members in the rest of the United States. Another characteristic of Puerto Rican juvenile gangs is that sexes are seldom mixed within one gang. However, on occasion, female gang leaders will take over gangs temporarily while the male leaders are in custody or in jail.

Puerto Rico does not have direct laws that specifically deal with juvenile gangs, but rather has what is known as Law 183, which was amended in 1995. This law deals only with juvenile offenders, and not gangs; therefore, as stated earlier, the problem is not addressed specifically as a gang problem by the government.

Since Puerto Rico is a country with an identity crisis, the problem of juvenile gangs is also confusing, as evidenced by the contradictory information about the existence of gangs. Likewise, even obtaining names of gangs can be tricky on the island. In a number of neighborhoods and public housing projects specific names are not given to the local gang. As a rule, they are called by the name of the project or the family controlling the location. Although juvenile gangs are not officially recognized by the Commonwealth of Puerto Rico, both juvenile and adult gangs can be found in Puerto Rico, as well as in the United States. There also is a strong indication that juvenile gangs in Puerto Rico originated with the organization of the adult prison gang known as Los Ñetas (Picó, 1998). Some of the best-known gangs will be discussed briefly. Most of the information comes from local media and from talking with people who live in public housing projects and are loosely associated with gangs or gang members.

SPECIFIC GANGS

Los Ñetas

The gang known as Los Ñetas originated in the Puerto Rican prison system in the 1970s as a result of substandard conditions and inmates needing protection from prison guards (National Drug Intelligence Center, 2001; Picó, 1998). Los Ñetas has spread to the U.S. prison system and into many Puerto Rican communities on the mainland, mainly in Connecticut, Florida, Massachusetts, New Jersey, New York, Pennsylvania, and Rhode Island. While this is not a juvenile gang per se, a number of historians and sociologists claim that the youth gang movement in Puerto Rico branched out from this particular group (Picó, 1998). In the public housing projects of Puerto Rico the colors of this group are displayed with pride, since it is a belief among those of low socioeconomic status that all Puerto Ricans may end up in jail at any given time in their lives. Los Ñetas uses drug trafficking as its major source of income, and is also involved in other criminal activities, including extortion, intimidation, robbery, assault, money laundering, weapons trafficking, and murder (National Drug Intelligence Center, 2001).

El Grupo 25 de Enero del 1981

El Grupo 25 de Enero del 1981, like Los Ñetas, had its beginnings in the Puerto Rican prison system. The biggest difference is that this group was formed to defend itself *against* Los Ñetas. Information on this gang cannot be found in any academic book or in the media, and only those with direct links to inmates have knowledge of this group. Its story has been an oral tradition that inmates and their families pass down from generation to generation, and disclosure to outsiders is not permitted (Picó, 1998).

El Grupo 27

El Grupo 27 is a true juvenile gang and is related to El Grupo 25 de Enero del 1981. It is composed mainly of youths who have spent time in juvenile halls and have, or had, family members connected to the original group. It is mainly a local group that primarily engages in illegal activities such as selling cocaine, heroine, and marijuana in the public housing projects.

Other Groups

The local newspapers (*El Nuevo Dia* and *Primera Hora*) and, in particular, the tabloid *El Vocero* mentioned the following groups as gangs that included, but were not limited to, juveniles. The following groups originated from the south of the island:

a. Los Tiburones is a local group about which little information can be found.
b. Las Avispa is a group that mainly participates in criminal activities linked to car theft. Most of the participants are related to one another.
c. The group known as Los Martinez was made up of family members who engaged in criminal activities and terrorized the neighborhood with their violent acts.

Size. The majority of gangs in Puerto Rico have a small number of members because their chief membership includes family members and people related by compadrazgo. Generally, juvenile gangs are composed of about ten or eleven members, most of whom are related by blood, and a few friends who are not really part of the organization, but who hang around the periphery.

Organization. Unlike adult gangs such as Los Ñetas, Puerto Rican juvenile gangs have a very loose organization, which is mainly operated by one person, without delegates. The other family members who are part of the gangs are primarily drug distributors or runners. If the boss is absent, the daily activities of the gang come to a complete stop.

Gang-Related Crime and the Public Housing Projects of Puerto Rico. While it is difficult to find hard statistics about how many juveniles join gangs and/or are involved with criminal activities, it has been established that juvenile crimes tend to represent 23 percent of all crimes in Puerto Rico (Gonzalez Valentin, 2002). The average age of juvenile felons in Puerto Rico is 15.2 years. About 80 percent are males. Most young delinquents come from single-parent households and about 18.1 percent live in public housing projects and are gang-involved. Nine out of every ten minors were unemployed at the time they reached the judicial system and 32.8 percent were school dropouts. Puerto Rico's murder rate is more than three times higher than that of the United States. Smaller cities in Puerto Rico sometimes have higher gang homicide rates than either Chicago or Los Angeles, even though the majority of crime occurs in the San Juan area. For example, Ponce, the second largest city in Puerto Rico, with a population of about two hundred thousand, recorded twenty-one gang homicides for the first half of 1989, a rate higher than that found in Chicago or Los Angeles during the same period.

A number of these crimes are committed in public housing projects by juvenile gangs. In 1990 the government of Puerto Rico decided to bring to an end the crimes in the public housing projects by mobilizing the National Guard around the public housing projects. Additionally, the government put gates and fences around the public housing projects in an attempt to keep drug dealers and crime inside. However, this action created a worse problem as the drug dealers became even more entrenched and the juvenile gangs more powerful (Gonzalez Valentin, 2002). Today a number of social scientists are still debating whether the actions of the government in 1990 actually helped to alleviate the juvenile and gang-related problems or just added to the magnitude of the problem (Gonzalez Valentin, 2002).

SOLUTIONS TO THE JUVENILE GANGS PROBLEM FROM A PUERTO RICAN PERSPECTIVE

Puerto Rico does have a number of programs similar to those in the United States to address the juvenile gang problems on the island; namely, prevention programs in the school such as Drug Abuse Resistance Education (DARE), after-school activities sponsored by the Police Athletic League, and other federally funded programs. Church and community organizations also have programs that assist in prevention and, in addition, take care of juvenile gang members. However, the most effective programs appear to be those that prepare juveniles to get a job or provide vocational training that will help them become self-sufficient. Programs such as "escuela de la comunidad," or community-based education, have been adopted even by U.S.-based programs in Puerto Rico (i.e., AmeriCorps, see http://www.americorps.org/joining/direct/direct_pr.html) (Garcia Blanco and Colon

Morera, 1993). Nonetheless, the success of such programs is directly linked to a number of variables that are not under the direct control of the Puerto Rican people.

FUTURE OF JUVENILE GANGS

It appears that the future of juvenile gangs is directly related to the ability of Puerto Rico as a country to deal with its economic problems. Additionally, addressing the youth gang problem requires addressing the ambiguity of identity of Puerto Ricans, who are pulled in two directions: their own national identity and their identity as United States citizens. During the two years since a new political administration took over, public figures have been accused and convicted of corruption (Dolores Hernández, 2002; Pérez, 2002). Given that most of the country is bankrupt, Puerto Rican juveniles may not see much of a future outside of a life of crime. The values of a society are those reflected in the children of that society, as Picó (1998) clearly stated in his ethnographic study of inmates. Without a system that approaches juvenile delinquency and crime from an emic (insider's) perspective, the values of Puerto Rican society will continue to erode.

The manner in which the Puerto Rican government has ignored the problem of juvenile gangs clearly reflects the symptoms of colonialism. While colonialism is a difficult concept to define, for the purpose of this chapter it makes sense to define colonialism to include the domination of a group of people by foreign leaders, injury to cultural pride, the inability of the colonized people to have control of their own political destiny, a degree of economic exploitation, and a denial of human rights. This comprehensive definition is essential because in order to restore a people's dignity, radical changes must occur and people must be allowed to feel empowered by their actions. Thus, gang behavior can be understood as the lingering effects of colonialism (Fanon, 1965; Memmi, 1996), particularly for the Puerto Rican children, who first were forced to endure the effects of European colonization and later the effects of the United States imperialism (Meléndez and Meléndez, 1993). Some believe the only way to deal with the complex problem of crime and gangs is by helping Puerto Ricans be Puerto Ricans without subordination from another country.

REFERENCES

Aguilar Aguilar, M. A. (1997, August). *Las pandillas y su image* [Gangs and their image]. Retrieved September 1, 2002, from http://www.geocities.com/CapitolHill/Senate/9131/pandilla.html.

Bourgois, P. *In search of respect: Selling crack in el barrio* (Cambridge: Cambridge University Press, 1995).

Burdette, B. *The Puerto Ricans: On the island, on the mainland, in Connecticut* (Storrs, CT: University of Connecticut, 1976).

Cordasco, F., and E. Bucchioni, eds. *The Puerto Rican experience: A sociological sourcebook* (Totowa: Littlefield Adams & Co, 1973).

Cordero, G. "Imparable la oleada de asesinatos en la isla" [Unstoppable the wave of homicides in the island]. *El Nuevo Día* (22 July 2002): p. 40.

De Jesús Mangual, T. "Desarticulan pandilla de 'gatos negros' " [Put out of commission the gang 'the black cats']. *El Vocero* (12 July 2002): p. 56.

De Vos, G., and L. Romanucci-Ross. *Ethnic identity cultural continuities and change* (Mountain View, CA: Mayfield Publishing Company, 1975).

Díaz Soler, L. M. *Puerto Rico: Desde sus origenes hasta el cese de la dominación Española* [Puerto Rico: From its beginnings until the end of the Spanish domination]. (United States of America: Editorial de la Universidad de Puerto Rico, 1994).

Dolores Hernández, C. "Si yo fuera tío Sam" [If I were uncle Sam]. *El Nuevo Día* (25 July 2002): p. 96.

Egley, A., Jr. (2002, February). *National youth gang survey trends from 1996 to 2002.* Retrieved September 1, 2002, from http://www.ncjrs.org/txtfiles1/ojjdp/fs200203/txt.

Fanon, F. *A dying colonialism.* Translated by H. Chevalier (1959; reprint, New York: Grove Press, 1965).

Fiske, P. "El negocio de las drogas" [The drugs business]. *BBC Mundo* (1 September 2002): pp. 1–6.

Fitzpatrick, J. P. *Puerto Rican Americans: The meaning of migration to the mainland,* 2d ed. (Upper Saddle River, NJ: Prentice-Hall, Inc., 1987).

Flores, J., ed. *Divided borders: Essays on Puerto Rican identity* (Houston, TX: Arte Público Press, 1993).

Garcia Blanco, A. M., and J. J. Colon Morera. "A community-based approach to educational reform in Puerto Rico." In *Colonial dilemma: Critical perspectives on contemporary Puerto Rico,* edited by E. Meléndez and E. Meléndez (Boston, MA: South End Press, 1993), pp. 157–169.

Gómez Acevedo, L., and G. Ballesteros Gabriois. *Culturas indigenas de Puerto Rico* [Indigenous cultures of Puerto Rico] (Rio Piedras, Puerto Rico: Editorial Cultural, Inc., 1978).

Gonzalez Valentin, M. B. (2002, September 30). Juvenile Delinquency Statistics Unreliable . . . Targeted, La Perla Residents Say They Are Under Siege By Police. Retrieved March 26, 2003, from http://www.puertorico-herald.org/issues/2002/vol6n40/JuviStats-ens.html.

Harris, M. G. *Cholas: Latino girls and gangs* (Brooklyn, NY: AMS Press, 1988).

Maldonado, Denis M. *Puerto Rico, mito y realidad* [Puerto Rico, myth and reality], 2d ed. (Barcelona: Ediciones Peninsula, 1972).

Marino, J. "Puerto Rico's new war on poverty." *The Washington Post* (4 September 2002): pp. A1–A3.

Meléndez, E. *Puerto Rico's statehood movement* (Westport, CT: Greenwood Press, 1988).

Meléndez, E., and E. Meléndez, eds. *Colonial dilemma: Critical perspectives on contemporary Puerto Rico* (Cambridge, MA: South End Press, 1993).

Memmi, A. *Retrato del colonizado* [Portrait of the colonized], translated by J. Davis (1966; reprint, Buenos Aires, Argentina: Ediciones del la Flor, 1996).

Mintz, S. W. "Puerto Rico: An essay on the definition of national culture." In *The Puerto Rican experience: A sociological sourcebook*, edited by F. Cordasco and E. Bucchioni (Totowa, NJ: Littlefield Adams & Co., 1973), pp. 26–89.

National Drug Intelligence Center. (March 2001). *New Jersey drug threat assessment.* Retrieved July 10, 2002, from http://www.usdoj.gov/ndic/pubs.669/over view.htm.

Pérez, S. "De la ficción a la realidad" [From fiction to reality]. *El Nuevo Día* (23 July 2002): p. 88.

Picó, F. *El día menos pensado: Historia de los precidiarios en Puerto Rico (1793–1993)* [The day that you less thought about it: History of the inmates in Puerto Rico (1793–1993)] (Rio Piedras, Puerto Rico: Ediciones Huracán, 1998).

Quiñones Vizcarrondo, F. *El cerebro Puertorriqueño* [The Puerto Rican brain]. (Caguas, Puerto Rico: Imprenta Cartagena, 1989).

Quintero Rivera, A. G. *Worker's struggle in Puerto Rico* (New York: Monthly Review Press, 1976).

Quintero Rivera, A. G., J. L. González, R. Campos, and J. Flores. *Puerto Rico: Identidad nacional y clases sociales (Coloquio de Princeton)* [Puerto Rico: National identity and social classes]. (Rio Piedras, Puerto Rico: Ediciones Huracán, 1960).

Rivera Ramos, E. *The legal construction of identity: The judicial and social legacy of American colonialism in Puerto Rico* (Washington, DC: American Psychology Association, 2001).

Scarano, F. A. *Puerto Rico: Cinco siglos de historia* [Puerto Rico: Five centuries of history]. (México: McGraw-Hill Interamericana, S. A., 1993).

Serrano, O. J. "Arrestan a traficantes" [Arrests dealer]. *Primera Hora* (13 July 2002): p. 2.

Silén, J. A. *Historia de la nación Puertorriqueña* [History of the Puerto Rican nation] (Rio Piedras, Puerto Rico: Editoriales Edil, Inc, 1973).

Sued-Badillo, J. *La mujer indigena y su sociedad* [The indigenous woman and her society] (Puerto Rico: Editorial Cultural, 1989).

Torres-Rivera, E., M. P. Wilbur, L. T. Phan, C. Maddux, and J. Roberts-Wilbur. "Counseling Latinos (a) with substance abuse problems." *Journal of Addictions and Offender Counseling.* In press.

U.S. Census Bureau. (2002). *Population division. Small area income and poverty estimates. Estimates for 1997 for Puerto Rico.* Retrieved September 7, 2002, from http:/www.census.gov/hhes/www/saipe/puertorico/puertall97.html.

Vázquez, J. M. "Puerto Ricans in the counseling process: The dynamics of ethnicity and its societal context." In *Multicultural issues in counseling: New approaches to diversity*, edited by C. C. Lee and B. L. Richardson (Alexandria, VA: American Counseling Association, 1991), pp. 185–194.

Vigil, J. D. *Barrio gangs: Street life and identity in southern California* (Austin, Texas: University of Texas Press, 1988).

Weisel, D. L. *Contemporary gangs: An organizational analysis* (New York: LFC, Scholarly Publishing LLC, 2002).

12

TAIWAN

Julia Yang

INTRODUCTION

Taiwan has experienced rapid social, political, and cultural changes in recent years. Many extreme reactions of adolescents, and thus, antisocial behaviors, are foreign and puzzling to their families and the educational authorities. While youth gang members are not involved in serious delinquency, the social impact of youth gangs in Taiwan schools and community is intense, especially when compared to the Confucian moral teaching everyone is expected to practice. Youth gang prevention and intervention efforts in Taiwan began less than a decade ago. Because of the multiple factors contributing to youth gang behaviors, counteractive measures by educational and judicial systems in Taiwan vary, ranging from primary prevention in schools to safe schools, legal education, special charter schools, and interventions for juvenile delinquents. Paradoxically, while the firm hierarchical structure associated with traditional Confucian values alienates some Taiwanese youth, school-based interventions are positively received and regarded as indispensable in responding to the needs of youths at risk.

This chapter attempts to describe the history and demographic makeup of Taiwan's youth gangs in relation to their social backgrounds and gang-related behaviors, as well as the prevalence of at-risk youths in Taiwan's schools. Social, political, and educational responses to gang problems are discussed in light of Confucian values in the family, and associated educational and cultural changes. Although many new interdepartmental initiatives targeting gang-involved youths are now available, the effects of such structural interventions have yet to be studied.

Youth gang status is difficult to define, and comprehensive direct services targeting gangs have yet to be developed in Taiwan. A prescriptive, school-based at-risk adolescent identification and intervention model used with high-risk adolescents who exhibit gang-related behaviors has proven to be useful in the meantime. This intervention model is based on the cognitive moral (Gibbs, 1993, 1996; Gibbs, Potter, and Goldstein, 1995) and interpersonal-skills approaches (Goldstein, 1993a, 1995). The model has been predominantly applied in the secondary school setting as a prevention measure.

DEVELOPMENT OF TAIWAN YOUTH GANGS AND DEMOGRAPHIC INFORMATION

Although youth gangs have existed in Taiwan for more than half a century, it was only in the late 1990s that Taiwanese society became aware that youth gangs were connected to various crime organizations and that they had marked their turf in junior high and high schools (Chai and Yang, 1999). Around the mid-1990s statistics on Taiwanese juvenile delinquency indicated that the age at which youths committed their first crimes was dropping, the number of female juvenile delinquents was rising, and the variety of crimes was also increasing (Chai and Yang, 1998). Taiwanese society first woke up to the existence of youth gangs when more than a hundred gang members, acting collectively, appeared at the funeral of a crime organization leader in 1997. It was reported that each member wore a black suit and sunglasses and carried a cell phone. Since then, gang culture has often been glorified by the media.

In recent years, gangs have lost most of their leaders due to governmental efforts at gang busting and incarceration. The need to recruit and mentor the next generation of gang members has increased. Schools, therefore, function as sites for gang recruitment and socialization. Youth gang members are perceived to be "low cost," loyal, and brave and are given more-lenient court sentences if arrested than older adult gang members.

Similar to the description of the New York Chinese gangs by Huff (1993), most Taiwanese gang members are bonded in strong camaraderie. Those targeted for recruitment are often lonely, vulnerable, and culturally marginal youths. The more elaborate traditions of gang member selection and induction with religious rituals (i.e., taking oaths; burning money to appease deceased ancestors' souls; and drinking wine mixed with blood before the altar of Kwan, the historical hero of justice in secret societies) have been replaced by simple registration in exchange for immediate material rewards. Direct evidence of youth gang membership is, therefore, difficult to identify. The presence of youth gang behaviors, nevertheless, poses a direct threat to communities and schools. As empirical data of the prevalence of youth gangs in Taiwan are extremely scarce, the following discussions are based on research by the author on high-risk adolescents and their self-reported perceptions of and affiliations with gangs and gang-related behaviors.

Participation, Activities, and Motivation

In a national survey study of 1,605 twelve- to eighteen year-old youths, 5.2 percent of the youths admitted that they were presently affiliated with a gang group (Yang, 1997a). About 10 percent of the school students and 26 percent of the youths in juvenile correctional facilities indicated they had been gang members in the past. They reported that most gang activities (e.g., hanging out in pubs and chatting on the Internet) were not seriously delinquent. Nevertheless, according to experts on youth crimes, critical gang-related youth behaviors in Taiwan include substance abuse, dropping out of school, teen pregnancy, robbery, school violence, theft, motorcycle racing, group fights, and coercion of younger students in schools (Chai and Yang, 1995; Yang, 1996). Because handguns are not readily available to youths in Taiwan, the most common deadly weapon used is a knife. Gang graffiti is created by using knives to leave deep marks on cars, tires, and public properties. Knives are also used in intra- and inter-gang group fights. Motorcycle racing has also resulted in the deaths of gang members or the random killing of innocent bystanders.

When asked about their perceptions of gang participation, 81 percent of youths in school and 54 to 59 percent of youths identified as juvenile delinquents indicated that peer pressure and the absence of family bonding were the main factors that perpetuated gang participation. Most youths surveyed perceived gang participation as a way of seeking protection, and fewer perceived school failure as a factor contributing to gang involvement. The Taiwanese youths' perceptions are slightly different from American professionals' perceptions of the causes of gangs. In the National Youth Gang Survey by Spergel and Curry (1993), respondents from criminal justice and community-based agencies perceived the main causes of gang problems as stemming more from family breakdown and school failure and less from peer influence and the need to seek protection.

Characteristics

With a database accumulated from several national surveys of 5,200 adolescents in Taiwan, an analysis was made of social background factors of youths self-reporting involvement in risk behaviors compared with peers who denied involvement in risk behaviors (Yang, 1996). The results revealed a consistent pattern of background information about the youth gangs and gang-related behaviors. Behaviors associated with school gangs included school violence, substance abuse, dropping out, theft, gambling, robbery, suicide, and hazardous motorcycle racing. The factors significantly differentiating the adolescents with self-reported risk behaviors included being male, being an only child, parents' marital breakdown, not living with parents or living with father alone, poor school performance, and low socioeconomic status (SES). They also reported having more friends and family members with risk behaviors.

In a later study of factors predictive of at-risk behaviors in adolescents, juvenile delinquents scored significantly higher than their peers in all four areas of cognitive distortions as measured by the Chinese and standardized version of the How I Think scale (HIT) (Gibbs, Barriga, and Potter, 1992; Yang, 1998). The four areas of cognitive distortion are self-centeredness, mislabeling/minimizing, assuming the worst, and blaming others. Cognitive distortions are beliefs about reality and others that cannot be confirmed by events or experiences. Such distortions are thought to stem from a self-centered bias or a preoccupation with moral judgment and social-perspective-taking. Results of reliability data and validity measures correlating cognitive distortions with self-reported antisocial behavior were found to be favorable (Barriga and Gibbs, 1996; Barriga, Harold, Stinson, Liau, and Gibbs, in press; Liau, Barriga, and Gibbs, 1998).

Prevalence of Youth Risk Behaviors and Youths at Risk

Risk factors often considered in relation to juvenile criminal behaviors are gender, socioeconomic status, age, intelligence, family structure, school performance, and race (Hsiu, 1993). Definitions of at-risk youths change over time, as they reflect social or cultural values and economic or political priorities in a given cultural context. As factors contributing to youth behaviors are multifaceted, the term "at risk" is descriptive of a set of factors in personal, family, school, and community contexts that may lead some adolescents to have a higher probability than their peers of engaging in high-risk behaviors or experiencing the consequences of such behaviors. Examination of both social system variables and personal cognitive variables provides a useful framework for developing an understanding of adolescents' behaviors and beliefs and how these factors can further help differentiate subgroups, such as at-risk and non-at-risk youths (Yang, 1996).

Prevalence of Youth Risk Factors and Behaviors. Table 12.1 summarizes percentages of selected background characteristics and risk behaviors of adolescents in schools and in juvenile delinquent programs (Yang, Liu, and Liang, 2000). It is clear that the delinquent respondents reported having more risk factors and risk behaviors than respondents who were attending school. An examination of the percentages for each factor, or behavior, allows us to see which youths are at risk due to family breakdown, school failure, smoking, running away from home, truancy, and fights, just to name a few.

Table 12.1
Youths' Self-Reported Percentages of Risk Factors and Risk Behaviors

Risk Factor	School Respondents	Juvenile Offender and Delinquent Respondents
	N = 1562	N = 117
	%	%
Parent Marital Breakdown	14.4	50.4
Single Father	3.5	14.5
Single Mother	6.4	22.2
School Failure	4.8	40.2
Low SES	5.3	27.4
Friends with Risk Behaviors	1.6	5.1
Family with Risk Behaviors	.3	1.7
Smoking	3.8	52.1
Gambling	5.8	12.0
Cheating	12.1	17.9
Running Away from Home	1.1	24.8
Truancy	1.0	27.4
Addictive Internet Use	4.3	10.3
Late Night Activities	4.4	17.1
Theft	2.6	7.7
Fights	11.3	27.4
Substance Abuse	0	3.4
Detention/ Suspension	2.4	35.0
Robbery	.6	1.7

Note: From Prevelance of Taiwan-Chinese At-Risk Adolescents in the Urban Cities (NSC No. 88-241-H-017-002), by J. Yang, L. C. Liu, and T. C. Liang, 2000, Taipei, Taiwan: National Science Foundation.

Prevalence of Youths at Risk. To avoid over- or underestimating youths' risk status, Yang (1996) and Yang, Liu, and Liang (2000) devised a checklist to assist teachers in early identification of at-risk students and an empirical scale for students to assist counselors in clinical assessment of risk status. The development of these instruments was based on a common risk factor conceptualization model; namely, that risk factors behind various risk behaviors are interrelated and most likely occur together (Yang, 1996, 2002; Yang, Liu, and Liang, 2000). Relatively weighted points for each risk factor of the checklist were calculated to allow teachers to better assess student risk status. Norms for identifying risk status of both at-risk and non-at-risk groups were established using the empirical scale for students based on this study. A total of only 2.9 percent of the school respondents were found to score equal to or higher than the average juvenile delinquent respondents on the empirical scale.

Table 12.2
Prevalence of Taiwanese Juvenile Offenders, Juvenile Delinquent and School-Based High-Risk Adolescents (1998)

	Number of Individuals	Prevalence Rate
Juvenile Offenders	19,082	.88%
Juvenile Delinquents	227	.01%
School-Based High-Risk Adolescents (estimate based on a sample of 1,526)	64,149	2.95%
Youth Population (12 to 18 years old)	2,175,364	

Note: From Prevalence of Taiwan-Chinese At-Risk Adolescents in the Urban Cities (NSC No. 88-241-H-017-002), by J. Yang, L. C. Liu, and T. C. Liang, 2000, Taipei, Taiwan: National Science Foundation.

In her study on the prevalence of at-risk youths Yang estimated that for the total population of the three major cities in Taiwan from which the sample was drawn 3 percent of adolescents in schools were at risk. (Yang, Liu, and Liang, 2000). A summary of total youth population, percentage of youth crimes, and delinquent youths is presented in Table 12.2.

It is noteworthy that the 1998 rate of juvenile offenders in Table 12.2, when compared with a rate of 1.21 percent in 1993, indicated a significant decrease (Chai and Yang, 1998). Methods of estimating the prevalence of youths at risk often vary according to the type and number of factors studied. Pen (1995) estimated that 7 percent of Taiwan's junior high school students were considered high risk, based on single risk behaviors. Dryfoos (1990) estimated that 10 percent of American youths are considered very high risk, with multiple risk factors; another 15 percent were at risk with two to three risk factors; and 25 percent were at the midlevel of risk status with a single factor. In Yang's study, the rate of 2.9 percent of high-risk adolescents in schools is rather conservative. The identified 2.9 percent of adolescents should be targeted for tertiary gang prevention and intervention; that is, according to Goldstein (1993c), efforts to "reduce the reoccurrence of or impairment from conditions that have already taken place" (p. 477).

CULTURAL CUSTOMS AND SOCIAL RESPONSES

In a society such as Taiwan's, which has moved rapidly from the premodern (agricultural) to modern (industrial) and within the last few decades to the postmodern era, people are bound to experience conflicts between the new and the old, the industrial and the traditional, the Westernized and the indigenous (Carlson, Chan, Change, Kurato, and Yang, 1999; Miller, Yang, and Chen, 1997; Yang, 1997b). Tension between the changing needs of youth and families in a modern Taiwan and the persistence of the old traditional ways of doing things is reflected in the present state of cultural customs in the Taiwanese educational and political systems. Following are examples of how the traditional values of family and education could become systemic hurdles for Taiwanese youths who experience family breakdown or school failures.

Cultural Values in Families

The philosophy of Confucianism, strong family ties, and kinship are the core influences of Taiwan culture. Family sociologists agree that the Confucian values of hard work, education, and the familial role structure persist and impact Chinese families in spite of Western cultural influences. Social progress and modernity inevitably result in altering social and relational structures as well as necessitating a new value system for social adjustment and integration (Yang, 1997b). Familial support roles and functions, the traditional cornerstone of Taiwanese social interdependence, are being restructured. The traditional (ideal) patrilineal kinship ties are being challenged, as is the stability of family relationships. This stability, interpersonal intimacy, and social support traditionally provided by families are challenged when youths resist the subordination they are prescribed to follow. In the traditional Taiwanese family, such subordination of youth to parents and family is regarded as virtuous.

While parental marital breakdowns and the lack of parental bonding are factors contributing to youths' risk behaviors universally, Taiwanese youths may be exceptionally troubled. A Taiwanese cultural norm that insists on certain family ethics prescribing proper hierarchical relationships and harmony by honoring these ethical principles is at odds with the increasing reality of marital and family breakdown. In the face of problems with their parents and family, Taiwanese adolescents who experience such marginality are left to their own devices and the influences of older peers encountered outside the family.

Cultural Values in Education

Confucian dominance is best exemplified by Taiwanese educational philosophies that guide and teach individuals about how to live and behave in all life settings, such as family, school, work, and community. Such social and moral traditions emanating from Confucianism persist, having both positive and negative impacts on the present Taiwanese educational system. Education is culturally regarded as the only way to achieve success in political, social, familial, vocational, and financial life. Such philosophical idealism is not sensitive to diverse needs and is resistant to changes. Problems of inadequate educational resources and opportunities remain unchallenged and unchanged. Some individuals experiencing school failure and who drop out are not provided access to reenter education due to their gender or low class status, and are subject to many forms of oppression in their work and communities. The concept of career development over a lifetime is irrelevant in Taiwan's educational system. School-to-work transition is thus not facilitated at any stage if a youth leaves the schools.

For example, current Taiwan education is compulsory for only nine years, and there are not enough high schools to accommodate all junior high school graduates. It is understandable then that a certain proportion of adolescents will be deprived of receiving high school education. College is not a choice for many youths who do not see education as relevant to employment or for those who experience earlier barriers in learning. This is especially true during times of economic recession. To maintain the affluent lifestyle most of their parents were able to afford, these adolescents, without basic skills or work competencies, have elected alternatives that violate the traditional values or the social norm.

From the postmodern perspective, adolescents are not only the recipients of cultural influences but also contributors to their own cultural patterns (Pedersen, 1995). Taiwanese youths, via their extreme reactions, are challenging the practicality of education and struggling daily with the rigid parameters of their learning and discipline in schools. Subcultures that allow expression of their anger via aggression and experiment can contribute to many antisocial behaviors. Consequences of the system failures, and the impact on these adolescents who are at risk of school failure or dropout, are serious. While rejected by both the education system and families (most likely, school failure would become a family shame for these individuals), adolescents are left with very few options other than seeking solidarity among gang members, thereby helping to ensure acceptance, support, recognition, and sometimes protection.

Social Responses

To meet the family and community expectations, schools utilize tracking measures to ensure a high rate of high school or college entrance. Teachers in the Confucian tradition are expected to be first mentors, then counselors, advisers, and finally teachers. Now with a sense of helplessness, they have narrowed their roles to subject teaching, not knowing how to deal with the behaviors of many of today's youth. When families are blamed for poorly preparing the youths for effective learning and for creating problems in the community, they, in turn, blame the schools and communities for not providing their children with appropriate education and resources. Communities are condemned by families and schools for providing age-inappropriate and tempting materials and activities for youths. Once young people are regarded as problematic, the effects of such labeling can often lead the adolescents at risk to more negative reactions and then to more risk behaviors as they become outcasts of schools, the communities, their own families, and thus their culture.

To date, policy gaps that allow the problems of youth gangs to grow worse over time continue to exist between the judicial and educational systems. Paradoxically, education is indispensable in a cultural context such as Taiwan's, where education is strongly stressed as the only avenue for vocational and political advancement. Obviously, the school is not primarily responsible for the degradation of the youth subculture. However, the public continues to rely on the schools to counter the worst aspects of youth popular culture and to fortify students with expectations of high standards and sound moral judgment.

POLITICAL AND EDUCATIONAL RESPONSES

In the past three decades Taiwan—in responding to economic productivity; political liberation and democratic progress; natural disasters; and recently, national defense and security concerns—has undergone many societal and political changes. Many social reforms have taken place in response to these rapid changes among laborers, women, the military, farmers, artists, and, in general, human rights activists. Some of these reforms have resulted in positive changes in policies and legislation in the areas of minority rights, gender equity, special education, and social welfare. It is interesting that as our youths continue to confront challenges in all aspects of their lives, education is one of the last societal issues to be addressed.

Educational Reform

Since 1994, following a national commission chaired by Nobel Award recipient Yuan Tseh Lee and his associates, educational reform led by national leaders in Taiwan has begun to reexamine issues in education based on the needs of all learners and to make recommendations for school restructuring. Goals and proposed areas of educational changes were developed from grassroots strategies such as public hearings. The goals of education reform, formulated from this commission, are based on the principles of democracy, humanism, internationalization, technological advancement, and pluralism (Lee, 1996). In the last five years the education reform commission's agenda of serving all students has just begun its articulation in student development, curriculum reform movements, and assessment as related to high school and college entrance. Strategies for implementing these changes appear to be top-down (i.e., consistent with the social hierarchy prescribed by Confucian teaching) and have been hampered because the Taiwan education system has shown neither the capacity nor the will to change. Interesting but confusing interactions are now happening among the stakeholders, education commission, and resistant schools.

Political initiatives related to prevention and interventions with at-risk youths are direct results of these educational reforms, including the two National Six-Year Youth Guidance Plans (1991–2003). The government, when sponsoring initiatives, often offers decisive support and directions in guidance-curriculum development, grants for professional development, paraprofessional training, and school counseling research. Although school counselor positions have been mandated in all schools at all levels in Taiwan since the 1970s (Stickel and Yang, 1993), there has been no public legislation decreeing who should hold these positions; that is, there is no appropriate certification for school personnel to guide professionalism and professional development. Presently, the highest governing unit for school counseling in the Taiwan Ministry of Education is still called the Council of Moral Discipline. Ironically, when youths need political support in Taiwan, traditional Confucian values in the centralized social order may be a significant obstacle to the development of youth services and support for youth service professionals.

GANG IDENTIFICATION, PLACEMENT, EDUCATION, AND MONITORING

Youth gang prevention and intervention efforts in Taiwan began less than a decade ago. A new collaborative framework including justice, interior, and educational approaches has been formed, driven by educational efforts and new legislation and policies. In 1999 new legislation enabled the Ministries of Justice, Education, and the Interior to collaborate for the first time to establish residential alternative schools to accommodate youths who need protection and special supervision while they continue their schooling (Yang, 2002a). The following briefly highlights the major initiatives and concludes with a summary of promises and challenges.

Juvenile Delinquent Education. Two correctional facilities for juvenile delinquents under the regional judicial courts were converted into quasi-school settings in 1999 by the Ministry of Justice. The purpose was to humanize treatment and maximize opportunities for the young offenders. An alternative curriculum was designed and tested before the changes were implemented. Teachers with counseling and social work backgrounds were added to the staff for the first time.

Juvenile Probation Services. Probation offices are available under the local district judicial courts working with the police force, schools, families, and communities to monitor high-risk youths and their behaviors.

Alternative Schools. The first independent residential alternative school was established in 1999 to accommodate female at-risk youths referred by local or regional district judicial courts. Altogether, by 2004 there will be six independent alternative schools serving about 700 youths from 15 cities. There are currently four collaborative alternative schools serving 400 students from 13 cities.

These recent initiatives share core values in serving at-risk youths. Some examples are a focus on education, community-focused law enforcement, legal education, teaching social skills to replace antisocial behaviors, developing community allies and support, and a focus on job-related programs. Operation of these initiatives will require close cooperation among government and community agencies. There have been some disputes over budgets and resources, ownership of problems, and problem-solving strategies. Continuity and longevity of such collaboration can be challenged by macro factors such as the economy, and organizational and political leadership structures. Public policy is needed to enact a centralized organization for gang prevention, control, and intervention.

GANG PREVENTION: A MODEL OF SCHOOL-BASED VIOLENCE PREVENTION

Ideally, gang and violence prevention is aimed at reducing risk factors and introducing or increasing protective factors for youths in community, school, and family settings. School-based violence prevention programs can be utilized to meet the primary and secondary levels of intervention as suggested by Goldstein (1993c). Primary prevention is designed to reduce the incidence of certain risk behaviors, and secondary prevention and intervention are targeted toward at-risk populations showing early signs of the condition in question. A school-based violence prevention program is most effective when it is theory driven, with research based in needs assessment, well-tested interventions, and outcome evaluation. In this section we will describe a countrywide model of a violence-prevention program with a focus on early identification and small group intervention for at-risk adolescents. Accountability of this program was demonstrated through its use of the following procedures: common risk factor conceptualization as described earlier, a checklist and empirical risk assessment scale for teachers and students, implementation of a social-skills training program, and outcome evaluation.

Over a span of three years, more than 9,000 junior high school students from 44 schools were first evaluated by their homeroom teachers using the teacher's checklist. These students were rated on an empirical scale; about 1,200 were identified as at risk. They participated in a six-week small-group social-skills training curriculum led by the school counselors. The curriculum was based on the models first brought to Taiwan by the cognitive psychologists Goldstein (1995) and Gibbs (1996). Ninety school counselors were trained to assist in the identification of students' risk status, using a mutual help format and small-group leadership techniques. Social skills were taught to the adolescents via problem-solving situations. Parental consent, as well as the authority mandate for student and counselor activities, was secured with the country education commissioner. Students from each participating school were recommended for primary, secondary, or tertiary prevention or intervention. Each school, in return, agreed to allow most of the students identified for secondary intervention to participate in the small groups.

A countywide program evaluation was then conducted with 2,300 junior high students from which 360 students were recommended to participate in the social-skills training program (Yang and Hwang, 1999). Effectiveness of program development and implementation was examined in part in the areas of at-risk student identification, content and design of the social-skills training curriculum, and counselor and student perceptions of curriculum process and outcome. Multiple posttest instrumentation and data collection methods, including direct interviews with counselors and students, were used in this study.

Positive student behavioral changes were observed. Changes in students' cognitive distortions were significant after the curriculum implementation. Results of the program evaluation overall confirmed the program feasibility and were successfully used for further budget requests for future program needs. Subsequently, the countywide identification and intervention of at-risk adolescents continues to receive funding support, and two other yearly reports on the countywide projects have been produced by the county office. The program is currently undergoing the sixth year of implementation.

Processes and outcome of this project confirmed that the identified predictive risk factors can help the counseling services in schools focus upon the at-risk group for timely intervention. It is clear that school administrators, counselors, teachers, and researchers can collaborate to identify and reduce youth risk factors and intervene by strengthening resiliency factors in adolescents who are identified as at risk.

FUTURE PERSPECTIVES

Today, education in Taiwan faces a profound test of its commitment to serve all students, including youths with gang status or behaviors. Although educational authorities have put forth many efforts and resources to improve the methods of dealing with troubled youths, effects of recent interventions have yet to be determined. Conflicts between contemporary social changes and the traditional Taiwanese cultural demands for youth to be subordinate to family and school will continue to alienate youth and lead to more youth gang involvement. Education, although going through massive restructuring in response to Taiwan's educational reform, still plays a critical role in preventing youth gangs and related violence.

A review of literature suggests that the difficulty of defining risk status for an adolescent stems from changing societal priorities and cultural patterns and values. Theory and research-based violence-prevention initiatives can assist in the early identification of and intervention with youths at risk for gang behaviors.

While there is great potential in early identification and counseling for high-risk youths using school-based prescriptive programming (Goldstein, 1993b, 1993c, 1995), challenges with the present youth gangs remain to be addressed in Taiwan. These challenges include developing interdepartmental yet centralized and organized strategies in gang identification, tracking, and prevention/intervention.

REFERENCES

Barriga, A. O., and J. C. Gibbs. "Measuring cognitive distortion in antisocial youth: Development and preliminary validation of the How I Think Questionnaire." *Aggressive Behavior* (1996).

Barriga, A. O., J. R. Harrold, B. L. Stinson, II, A. K. Liau, and J. C. Gibbs. *Cognitive distortion and problem behaviors in adolescence* (Columbus, OH: Ohio State University, in press).

Carlson, J., A. C. N. Chan, J. W. T. Change, Y. Kurato, and J. Yang. "The influence of technology on families: An Asian perspective." *The Family Journal* (1999): 231–235.

Chai, D. H., and S. L. Yang. "The study of hazardous motorcycle riding." *Criminology Journal* (1995): 1–30.

———. "Taiwan youth crimes: Problems and resolutions." In *Adolescent counseling and guidance in Taiwan and USA*, edited by J. Yang (Taipei, Taiwan: Ministry of Education, 1998), pp. 1–26.

———. "Gangs in schools: Problems and resolutions." *Journal of Student Guidance Bimonthly* 65 (1999): 8–17.

Dryfoos, J. G. *Adolescents at risk: Prevalence and prevention* (New York: Oxford University Press, 1990).

Gibbs, J. C. "Moral-cognitive intervention." In *The gang intervention handbook*, A. P. Goldstein and C. R. Huff. (Champaign, IL: Research Press, 1993), pp. 159–185.

———. *EQUIP training with Taiwan junior high school counselors.* Presented at a workshop sponsored by National Kaohsiung Normal University, Taiwan, 1996.

Gibbs. J. C., A. Q. Barriga, and G. Potter. *The How I Think Questionnaire.* Unpublished manuscript, 1992.

Gibbs, J. C., G. B. Potter, and A. P. Goldstein. *The EQUIP Program: Teaching youth to think and act responsibly through a peer-helping approach* (Champaign, IL: Research Press, 1995).

Goldstein, A. P. "Interpersonal skills training interventions." In *The gang interven-*

tion handbook, edited by A. P. Goldstein and C. R. Huff (Champaign, IL: Research Press, 1993a), pp. 87–158.

———. "Gang intervention: A historical review." In *The gang intervention handbook*, edited by A. P. Goldstein and C. R. Huff (Champaign, IL: Research Press, 1993b), pp. 21–54.

———. "Gang intervention: Issues and opportunities." In *The gang intervention handbook*, edited by A. P. Goldstein and C. R. Huff (Champaign, IL: Research Press, 1993c), pp. 477–494.

———. "Counseling at risk youth." In *The 1995 Symposium on Counseling and Guidance in the U.S. and Taiwan*. (Taiwan: Ministry of Education, 1995).

Hsiu, T. J. *Causation of adolescents' criminal behaviors*, 2d ed. (Taipei, Taiwan: Wu-Nan Publishing, 1993).

Huff, C. R. "Gangs in the United States." In *The gang intervention handbook*, edited by A. P. Goldstein and C. R. Huff (Champaign, IL: Research Press, 1993), pp. 3–20.

Lee, Y. C. *Report on Taiwan education reform: Recommendation of goals, principles and strategies* (Taipei, Taiwan: Ministry of Education, 1996).

Liau, A. K., Barriga, A. Q., and J. C. Gibbs. "Relations between self-serving cognitive distortions and overt vs. covert antisocial behavior in adolescents." *Aggressive Behavior* 24 (1998): 335–346.

Miller, G., J. Yang, and M. Chen. "Counseling Taiwan Chinese in America: Training issues for counselors." *Journal of Counselor Education and Supervision* 37(1) (1997): 22–34.

Pedersen, P. "Cross-cultural applications of counseling theory and practice." *Proceedings of Counseling and Guidance in Taiwan and USA 1995 Symposium* (Taiwan: Ministry of Education, 1995), pp. 59–68.

Pen, C. H. "Youth at risk behaviors and counseling interventions." *Proceedings of Counseling and Guidance in Taiwan and U.S.A 1995 Symposium* (Taiwan: Ministry of Education, 1995), pp. 25–38.

Spergel, I. A., and G. D. Curry. "The national youth gang." In *The gang intervention handbook*, edited by A. P. Goldstein and C. R. Huff (Champaign, IL: Research Press, 1993), pp. 359–400.

Stickel, A. S., and J. Yang. "School guidance and counseling in the United States and Taiwan: Parallels and beyond." *The International Journal for the Advancement of Counseling* 16 (1993): 224–244.

Yang, J. *Social, cultural and psychological traits of at-risk adolescents: Foundation of diagnosis* (Taipei, Taiwan: Psychological Publishing, 1996).

———. "Taiwanese youths' perceptions of gang crime." (Research Report No. 2–2) (Taipei, Taiwan: Ministry of Education, 1997a).

———. "Technology and cultural change: Implications in counseling Taiwan Chinese families." In *Conference Proceedings of the 6th International Conference on Counseling in the 21st Century* (Beijing, China, 1997b).

———. "Factors predicting at risk adolescents: An empirical study." *National Kaohsiung Normal University Journal* 9 (1998): 93–117.

———. "Claiming social justice for youth at risk: Best practices." *Symposium on Best Models of Alternative Schools for Youth at Risk* (Taiwan: Ministry of Education, 2002a).

Yang, J., and P. Y. Hwang. *Effects of at-risk adolescents identification and a social skill development curriculum of junior schools: A county wide program evaluation* (Taiwan: Tao-yuan County, 1999).

Yang, J., L. C. Liu, and T. C. Liang. *Prevalence of Taiwan-Chinese at-risk adolescents in the urban cities* (NSC No. 88-241-H-017-002) (Taipei, Taiwan: National Science Foundation, 2000).

13

TRINIDAD AND TOBAGO

Joanna E. Headley

INTRODUCTION

Trinidad and Tobago make up a Caribbean twin island nation with an exciting cultural mélange of old and new, Eastern and Western, traditional and contemporary. The calm Caribbean waters, the surf, white sands, green mountains, and seasonal outflows from South American rivers are all hallmarks of Trinidad and Tobago. However, the tranquillity of this beautiful island nation has recently been compromised.

The level of violence in Trinidad and Tobago due to teen gang activity has escalated over the past ten years. Violence, crime, and delinquency within the 10- to 19-year-old population have been the focus of growing concern for the government and the general public of Trinidad, as well as throughout the other Caribbean islands. According to the Central Statistical Office [CSO], Trinidad and Tobago ended the year 2001 with a record murder rate of 151 cases. This represented an increase of 11 murders over a 1994 high of 140 cases, a statistical increase of 7 percent over seven years. Drug and gang activity accounted for most of the murders. In looking at the profiles of those engaged in the criminal activities, one sees that they are mostly young men in their teens and early twenties who are poorly educated and seemingly unemployable.

The issue of teen gangs and drug dealing is a difficult one. It would not be unreasonable to make a link between Trinidad and Tobago's recent political turmoil, poverty level, the prevalence of American media, and the increased murder rate. Schools have also been vulnerable to the violence and criminal acts of the teen gangs, especially because the school system in Trinidad and Tobago is highly influenced by social class and status. After completing a series of complicated examinations, students are divided into government-run schools or prestigious private schools. This division often causes resentment and hostility in the government-run schools, which house most of the indigent or poorer students. In essence, the length of time in school, coupled with the activities and behaviors that these students engage in on a daily basis, allow one the opportunity to detect early signs of deviance (Deosaran, 2002). Students who commit small infractions such as being tardy, skipping classes, fighting, or destroying property often end up committing more serious offenses after school (Hoge and Andrews, 1996).

Currently, one in every three youths in the government-run schools is afraid to go to school because of fear of being hurt, attacked, or bullied (Deosaran, 2002). Therefore, "the school should be viewed as central to the understanding of delinquency" and teen gangs (Jensen and Rojek, 1997, p. 281). Trinidad and Tobago's young people are subjected to many influences outside of the school system. Belonging and a sense of purpose are influences that have made some teens consider joining the Jamaat Al Muslimeen, a group of Muslim extremists that staged a coup attempt in Trinidad on July 27, 1990. The country was astounded to learn how many teens and youths were recruited for this violent mission. The problem of teen gangs in Trinidad and Tobago has definitely made an impact on society; however, the country's gang scene pales in comparison with other more highly publicized and organized gangs worldwide.

PROFILE OF TRINIDAD AND TOBAGO

Trinidad and Tobago is located at the southern end of the Caribbean archipelago, 7 miles (11 kilometers) from Venezuela on the shoulder of South America. Trinidad is approximately 1,864 square miles (4,828 sq km) and Tobago is approximately 120 square miles (300 sq km), a total of 1,980 square miles (5,128 sq km). The island nation came under British control in the nineteenth century and was granted independence in 1962. Trinidad is one of the most prosperous islands in the Caribbean due to its petroleum and natural gas production and processing. Comparatively speaking, Trinidad is slightly smaller than the state of Delaware.

Population

The population of Trinidad and Tobago in 2001 was 1.3 million, with a labor force of 600,000 (CSO, 2001). The island consists of a melting pot of multiethnic and multicultural groups: African descendants constitute 39.5 percent of the population; those of East Indian descent, about 40.3 percent;

multiracial (mixed), about 18.4 percent; white, about 0.6 percent; and Chinese, Syrian, Lebanese, and others, about 1.2 percent (CSO, 2001).

Government

The government in Trinidad and Tobago is a parliamentary democracy, similar to that of the United Kingdom, where the prime minister is head of government and the president is the chief of state. Two main political parties constitute the government: the People's National Movement (PNM) and the United National Congress (UNC). Recently, there has been political turmoil in Trinidad and Tobago due to the results of the last election. The two main rival parties, PNM and UNC, both received an electoral vote of 18. A new election was scheduled in October 2002: The PNM then won a landslide victory over the opposition (UNC) for Trinidad and Tobago's new government.

Economy

Trinidad and Tobago has earned a reputation as an excellent investment site for international businesses. However, the high unemployment rate (12.8 percent) remains one of the main challenges for the government. According to the Central Statistical Office (2001), 21 percent of the population is below the poverty line and there is a 40 percent unemployment rate among the 15- to 24-year-old age group. The gross domestic product (GDP) in 2000 was $11.2 billion or $9,500 per capita.

Education

Primary and secondary education is free and compulsory. However, there are fees for private primary school. A child is required to be in school from the age of 3 or 4 years old to 16 or 17. The secondary education of students is strongly related to social class (Deosaran, 1992). Students are streamed into either government secondary schools or private schools. The literacy rate in Trinidad and Tobago is approximately 98 percent.

OVERVIEW AND IMPACT OF TEEN GANGS IN TRINIDAD AND TOBAGO

There is nationwide concern about the crime and teen gang situation and its impact across the Caribbean. However, "attempts at systematic sustained research in criminology have only recently begun" (Deosaran and Chadee, 1997, p. 37). In the past, Caribbean research into crime, teen gangs, and delinquency was politically driven (Deosaran and Chadee, 1997) and, therefore, underfunded. This scarcity of past research and databases, coupled with the government's instability, has prompted local scholars and policy makers to join efforts to plan strategic interventions to deal with the problem of youth deviance in Trinidad and Tobago.

The Meanings and Types of Gangs

The gangs in Trinidad and Tobago deviate from the usual stereotypical images of gangs in the United States. In Trinidad, the term "gang" refers to a particular group of individuals that "collectively possess similar aims and values, which may be formal or informally organized to engage in certain activities which can be deemed illegal and unlawful" (McCree, 1998, p. 156).

Jankowski (1991) noted that gang members possess similar personality or character traits, which he summed up in the expression "defiant individualism." This incorporates six characteristics of personality: competitiveness, social isolation, self-reliance, wariness of others, a survival instinct, and an outlook that justifies cheating and stealing as a natural way of life. The Institute of Social and Economic Research (ISER) at the University of the West Indies (St. Augustine, Trinidad campus) carried out a comprehensive study of the community of Laventille (a mostly poor community on the outskirts of the capital city, Port-of-Spain) in order to identify and examine the nature and extent of criminal behavior due to gangs. McCree (1998) identified a gang continuum comprising four main types of gangs: soft, semi-hard-core, posh, and hard-core (see Table 13.1). These gang types vary in size, composition, nature of activities, length of time in existence, scope of operations, and level of organization.

Soft gangs comprise mainly young people in the 10- to 16-year-old age group. These youths are often involved in vandalism, graffiti, petty larceny, and stealing fruits. This type of gang is not usually violent, but can engage in acts of intimidation, senseless fighting, and destruction.

Semi-Hard-Core gangs are made up of unemployed youths and adults whose activities include more serious crimes of larceny, such as burglary, assault, breaking and entering, and robbery. The members of such gangs may possess weapons and are capable of wounding and murdering to achieve their goals.

Posh gangs include members of the middle and upper class, largely the entrepreneurs and professional elite who engage in white-collar crime and the drug trade. The posh elite may use weapons and can resort to murder. Even though this gang's leader is not a teen, teens are recruited. The status and social class of the posh gang allow it to lure teenagers and young adults into the group with the promise of a better life, without financial hardship. These new recruits often do the "dirty work" for the posh gang.

The **Hard-Core** gang includes members from the working class and the

Table 13.1
Typology of Gangs

Type of Gang	Membership	Means	Activities
Soft	Teenagers	Stones, sticks, sling-shots, knives	Stealing fruit Vandalism
Semi-Hardcore	Unemployed youths, adults	Guns, knives, cutlasses or machetes	Burglary Assault and robbery on individuals
Posh	Social elite, professionals	"Cooking the books" Guns, murder (complicity)	White-collar crime Drugs
Hard-Core	Unemployed/working class	Guns, contract killings, kidnappings, Molotov cocktails, dismemberment	Robbery (organizations) Drugs Rape

Note: From *Annual Statistical Digest* (No. 41), Central Statistical Office, 1997, Port-of-Spain, Trinidad and Tobago: Central Statistical Office.

unemployed. Its activities range from bank robberies to rapes and murders. The hard-core gang often engages in extreme violent acts such as Mafia-style drive-by shootings, dismembering of limbs, kidnapping, and contract killings (McCree, 1998). Both the posh and hard-core gangs employ and recruit teenagers and young adults, and they are heavily associated with the drug trade. The hard-core gang differentiates itself primarily by the character of the violence it inflicts on enemies and victims (McCree, 1998). The semi-hard-core, the posh, and the hard-core can, in reality, overlap in activities and group members. The overlap is evident in the Jamaat al Muslimeen group. Members of this Muslim gang can be described as either semi-hard-core or hard-core in nature, depending on the activities in which they choose to participate.

Gang Behavior

Gang formation and behavior is different in Trinidad and Tobago from that in the United States. The Los Angeles Crips, Bloods, and Esses were initially formed as a means of group protection. Their activities consist mainly of defending their turf or streets, selling hot merchandise, hanging out and partying, and dealing drugs. The gang scene seems to appeal to youths who need a sense of belonging and family. The other gang members serve as a substitute family. Membership in this type of gang is somewhat consistent and sustained. On the other hand, Trinidad's gangs are more short-lived and are formed to engage in a particular activity or as a means to a particular end.

The larger, more organized gangs tend to be formed or become active when a "need" arises, such as for an attempted coup, a drug trade, kidnapping or hostage-taking, robbery, or murder. These gangs actively recruit teens and young adults with the promise of material gain, financial security, protection from the law (Jankowski, 1991), respect from the community, and an abundance of sexual partners. Another aspect that makes teen and youth recruitment so profitable to these large gangs is that they are less of a liability, because they are not prosecuted as harshly as adults. The smaller, less organized gangs tend to be formed in times of financial emergencies. They are often formed in the schools or in a particular neighborhood. These youths usually become financially strapped just before the carnival, or festival, season in Trinidad. They commit several robberies and burglaries to get money to pay for their carnival costumes and to entertain themselves at the parties.

In its formation and behavior patterns, the Muslimeen group is slightly different from the other gangs in Trinidad. The Muslimeen is a consistent and sustained group formed around its religious affiliations. Abu Bakr, the group's leader, entices his young male followers with the promises of schooling abroad in Libya, monetary security, fame, and religious absolution from any illegal or unlawful activities.

McCree (1998) identifies the major reasons for criminal behavior and the formation of gangs as "the role of poverty, social and status deprivation, social disorganization, values and family background, and identity formation of the individual" (p. 159). He further notes in his research that the need for money is the most prominent reason for teen gang formation and criminal behavior.

Impact of Teen Gangs on the Country

Gangs and criminal behavior have had a negative impact on the country. Gang wars continue to fuel murder sprees and Mafia-style warfare. Many citizens who live in the area of constant gang wars feel unsafe and traumatized. Many families in lower-income communities fear their children will be enticed by a gang. The battle against poverty definitely plays a significant role in teen gangs and teen recruitment in Trinidad and Tobago. In essence, gangs offer young men access to jobs and opportunities that they are unable to get in the community. The lack of these vital resources leads to frustration, and young men can be driven to prove their manhood by taking up risky activities that will earn them status, respect, and resources. Some in the media have linked this cycle of frustration and high risk to gangs and criminal behavior in the country and the prevalence of robbery/homicide and rape ("Editorial: A Distressing Record," January 2, 2002). Another negative impact of gangs has been on the tourist industry. Between 1995 and 1999 tourist arrivals in Trinidad and Tobago increased by 38 percent, the highest growth figure recorded for any country in the southern Caribbean. However, between 2000 and 2002, tourism tapered off and began to decline. The perception is that for a small country, Trinidad and Tobago has far too much crime and gang activity.

Legislation and Demographic Information

While the overall unemployment rate in Trinidad and Tobago is 12.8 percent, there is a 40 percent unemployment rate among the 15- to 24-year-olds (Deosaran and Chadee, 1997). The police divisions with the highest crime rates are the Northern division, which encompasses the Laventille area, Arima, St. Joseph, Arouca, Tunapuna, and Maloney; the Port-of-Spain division, which consists of Besson Street and Belmont; and the Southern division, which consists of San Fernando, Princess Town, and Marabella. The crime rates in these areas are closely related to the gang scene, where extensive power struggles for control of turf and the drug trade take place.

Teen gang and juvenile offenses reported by the Central Statistical Office (1997) for persons under 16 years of age indicate that there were 322 offenses by juveniles in 1986; in 1995 the number had decreased to 287 offenses and rose to 405 offenses in 1996. For the ten-year period 1986 to 1996, the total number of juvenile offenses was 3,394, an average of 339 offenses per year. The court records show that "destitution" (no parent or other fit person to provide for youth) accounted for more than 30 percent of juvenile offenses. Further, 809 of the 3,394 offenses for this ten-year period were "beyond control." It is noteworthy that while the average "beyond control" figure for the ten-year period was 80.9 per year, in 1995 alone it was 147 (CSO, 1997; Deosaran and Chadee, 1997). See Tables 13.2 and 13.3.

Legislation Related to Teen Gangs

The punishment of youths is subject to law (Children Act, 46:01) and usually is part of a judicial process in which a probation report is significant. Youths are sometimes sent to juvenile homes through "orders" for safety or through what is in effect a sentence (Deosaran and Chadee, 1997). For example, the Children Act (46:01) states:

An offender charged in Court with an offence punishable of an adult by imprisonment, and the offender is ten years of age or upwards but less than sixteen years. The Court may order him to be sent to a certified Industrial School.

Table 13.2
Offences Committed by Juvenile Offenders[1] 1987–1996

Period	Total Number of Offenses[2]	Destitution[3]	Assault and Battery	Larceny	House Breaking and Larceny	Throwing Missiles	Obscene and Annoying Language	Beyond Control	Drugs	Wounding	Armed with a Weapon	Sexual	Other[4]
1987	288	89	12	1	27	2	4	44	2	—	1	1	86
1988	363	129	12	3	31	1	11	28	11	4	7	3	104
1989	330	81	—	1	43	4	—	59	7	2	5	—	103
1990	297	103	—	—	40	—	1	47	5	4	7	3	58
1991	294	132	—	1	35	—	1	81	2	1	2	—	13
1992	278	102	—	2	42	1	2	75	7	2	3	2	17
1993	268	79	2		42	11	2	75	2	9	8	—	15
1994	262	57		—	31	1	5	86	7	4	6	—	26
1995	287	44	2	4	26	—	2	147	9	3	6	—	13
1996	405	86	—	18	33	10	15	129	27	21	8	6	16

Note: From *Annual Statistical Digest* (No. 41), Central Statistical Office, 1997, Port-of-Spain, Trinidad and Tobago: Central Statistical Office.

[1]Persons under 16 years of age

[2]Types of offences and actions taken by court will correspond with the number of offences and not the number of offenders

[3]Having no parent, guardian, or other person to provide for him or her

[4]Includes offences not given

Table 13.3
Action Taken by the Juvenile Court 1987—1996

	Total Number of Offenders	Bonded	Fined	Probation	Corporal Punishment	Sent to Orphanage	Sent to Industrial School	Reprimanded and Discharged	Fit-Person Order[1]	Dismissed	Discharge Section
1987	280	8	—	57	—	32	36	11	95	43	6
1988	357	5	2	86	—	52	43	8	94	67	6
1989	314	5	—	85	—	30	43	8	85	53	21
1990	273	13	1	66	—	25	53	4	77	36	22
1991	290	3	—	70	—	28	52	6	98	37	—
1992	278	6	4	60	—	22	56	—	66	55	9
1993	245	3	5	79	—	12	44	13	48	64	—
1994	245	8	—	101	—	8	24	14	32	75	—
1995	280	11	—	112	—	8	43	16	33	65	2
1996	393	9	—	68	—	25	34	39	92	80	46

Note: From *Annual Statistical Digest* (No. 41), Central Statistical Office, 1997, Port-of-Spain, Trinidad and Tobago: Central Statistical Office.

[1]Legal guardian

Section 83 states the offender can also be whipped or ordered to pay a fine and/or damages. For the older youths (16 to 18 years), the following laws (Chapter 13:05, Section 7) apply:

(1) Where a person is convicted of any offence other than murder, or for any offence which he is liable to be sentenced to imprisonment:
    (a) the person should be between sixteen and eighteen years of age, and
    (b) that by reason of his mode of life it is expedient that he should be subject to detention for such term and under such instruction and discipline as appears most conducive to his reformation and the repression of crime, the Court may, in lieu of sentencing him to the punishment provided by law for the offence for which he was convicted, pass a sentence of detention under penal discipline in the Institution for a term of three to four years.

HISTORY OF THE GANG PROBLEM

When compared with the United States and Jamaica, Trinidad and Tobago's gang history is not extensive. The first ganglike uprising in Trinidad and Tobago, familiarly referred to as the Black Power Revolution, occurred in February 1970 as a result of the deteriorating social and economic conditions in the nation at that time. Its leaders demanded government action to solve problems such as unemployment and social discrimination. After a series of riots that resulted in many injuries, burned buildings, and several deaths, the government declared a state of emergency. Further riots were banned, a dusk-to-dawn curfew was imposed, the press was censored, and several leaders were arrested. Army troops banded together and mutinied in support of the black power rioters, seizing the nation's arsenal and holding several hostages. The islands' government received arms and ammunition from the United States and suppressed the rebels.

During the 20-year period following 1970, Trinidad's gang scene was inconsequential, composed of small school gangs that bullied and intimidated other students. These gangs were formed on the basis of both neighborhood and personal affiliations. Other gangs were formed and organized in certain lower-income areas of the country. They shared a neighborhood and a mutual sense of poverty. This mutuality gave them a reason to come together to form a neighborhood gang. Similarly, some young men met in the juvenile homes, jails, or the prison system and organized to form a gang when they were released. This type of gang organization is based on personal affiliations.

Another factor in Trinidad's society that generated gangs was the influx of immigrants from smaller islands in the Caribbean. Drugs, a lack of money, and a craving for a higher social status fueled these small gangs. On July 27, 1990, the Muslimeen gunmen attempted a coup. They stormed Trinidad's parliament and the nation's television station and held several government parliamentarians and civilians hostage (Deosaran, 1992). Many people were killed and injured, and the downtown section of Port-of-Spain was destroyed with Molotov cocktails. Although the Muslimeen, like the black leaders in the 1970s, are not considered a typical gang, their activities can be characterized as hard-core gang behavior.

The most notorious and "true" gang in Trinidad and Tobago's history was the Dole Chadee gang. Dole Chadee, also known as Nankisson Boodram, was obsessed with power and money. He always wanted to be in full control and felt that money could buy anything, and this desire to be the head honcho contributed to his eventual demise by execution. He was found guilty of four of the most brutal murders in Trinidad's history. Chadee first became known in 1983, when he was charged with the murder of St. Clair McMillan, known as Rammer the Jammer, but the case was soon dropped because the court lacked evidence. Chadee had many run-ins with the law, including for stealing cars, assembling to gamble, and possessing marijuana and cocaine. Several charges were brought against him for trafficking narcotics and counterfeiting United States currency (Joseph, 1999).

The Scott Drug Report in 1987 linked Chadee with Colombian drug cartels. Chadee formed his hard-core gang with young relatives and personal and neighborhood affiliations. He easily recruited his young members with the lure of increased social status and responsibilities, financial security, and an endless supply of drugs, women, and fame. Gangland killings became almost routine in the late 1980s.

In 1993 Chadee and his gang were charged again for the murder of Jamaat al Muslimeen member St. Clair McMillan. Dole once again evaded the law after the main witness in the murder case was "mysteriously" kidnapped and shot in the head. With his power increasing, Dole Chadee's hometown, Williamsville, became known as his turf and empire; his gang of youths patrolled the area with 24-hour surveillance. Later that year, Chadee's nephew, who was part of his gang, was gunned down, and police feared more gang violence would ensue.

On January 10, 1994, Dole Chadee and his gang carried out a Mafia-style murder of four members of a family in Williamsville. The parents and two young children were shot execution style, in the back of the head. Chadee and the members of his gang were arrested (Joseph, 1999a). In October one of the members of Chadee's gang who had participated in the Baboolal murders gave a deposition that was accepted by the courts before he was brutally murdered. Clint Huggins, even in death, played the most crucial part in getting Dole Chadee and the eight other perpetrators convicted for the murders of the family (Wilson, 1996). Another gang member, Levi Morris, was granted a life sentence for turning state's evidence. Clint Huggins's deposition and Morris's testimony sealed the fate of the accused members. On June 4, 1999, Dole Chadee and his accomplices were hanged, marking the end of a ruthless gangland boss and drug lord.

In August 1998 a teenage gang, with members ranging in ages from 13 to 16 years old, stabbed and killed a 19-year-old youth in northwest Port-of-Spain over a bottle of ink used for making tattoos ("Youth Gang," 1998; McCree, 1998). The name of this headline-making teenage gang was the Gambinos. Such gangs continue to be a disturbing trend in Caribbean society. According to a study of teenage gangs, it was found that 16 percent of 10- to 12-year-olds, 21 percent of 13- to 15-year-olds, and 18 percent of 16- to 18-year-olds reported being a members of gangs, (McCree, 1998; "The Gambinos," 1998).

SOCIAL VIEWS, CUSTOMS, AND PRACTICES

To increase and maintain their membership, gangs employ a combination of tactics, such as force or intimidation, enticement, recreation, material and financial security, protection, job opportunities, and social status within the community (Jankowski, 1991; McCree, 1998).

Gang Leaders. Globally and historically, gang membership tends to be male dominated (Cain, 1995). Gang leaders are often chosen based on "manhood" tests, such as who commands the most fear and respect from others. This test identifies the "bad boy" of the group; the one with the worst reputation. Another custom or practice that gangs use to delegate a leader is to automatically choose the one who possesses a firearm. Hence, the male with the firearm is perceived as the bad boy to be feared—the one with the power.

Recruitment. Gangs in Trinidad and Tobago recruit their members differently from other gangs worldwide. The Los Angeles gangs are huge in numbers, and members come from different areas of the United States and settle in L.A. Therefore, these gangs have several initiation tasks that new prospects must perform to prove their future loyalty to the gang. When carried out, these initiation tasks prove to be a measure of trust that must be established. In Trinidad, gangs do not rely on the same initiation of trust, probably because the members already know of each other. In Trinidad, during the initiation phase gangs use the knowledge of members' backgrounds, affiliations, family histories, and areas of residence to determine recruitment and level of trust.

Gang Activities. McCree's 1998 Laventille study reveals that gangs were involved in four major activities. These included robbery and muggings (37 percent), drug trafficking (10 percent), assault (8 percent), and gun making (7 percent). McCree further notes that 18 percent of the people identified drug trafficking as one of the main problems in the community. Another prevalent activity of the gangs is described as tit-for-tat killings. For instance, the cohorts of a slain gang member will hunt down and execute persons from other gangs who are believed to be the killers of the slain member.

The younger teenage gangs tend to intimidate others by stealing their clothing, jewelry, money, and shoes. In Trinidad and Tobago, American brand-name sneakers are coveted items on the streets. The teenagers steal these items not only to make money but also to collect as personal trophies.

Kidnapping. A new focus in gang-related activities was the rise in kidnappings, which required national security involvement. This trend escalated in 2002. These recent "kidnapping gangs" are using kidnapping as a means of earning easy money. The gangs, which are targeting wealthy businessmen and their families, comprise professional kidnappers and small splinter groups (these groups have broken off from larger organized gangs) (Seetahal, 2002). The professional gangs are structured in such a way that the leader alone knows all the details of the kidnapping. Neither the ransom collector nor the "snatcher" knows where the victim will be hidden. The distribution of ransom money is not split equally among the abductors, which has led to financial dissatisfaction. These unsatisfied kidnappers "splinter" from their kidnap gang and form their own abduction groups. The splinter groups try to do everything themselves so as to keep all of the money; they take the victim; make arrangements for the detention of, guard, and see to the needs of the captive victim; and engage in negotiations (Seetahal, 2002). These kidnapping gangs often recruit young men and teenagers as "lookouts" and errand boys, and to take care of the needs of the captive.

Social Views. When conducting his gang study, McCree (1997, 1998) asked the members of the district who wielded the most power in the community: 34 percent cited drug lords, 26 percent cited criminals, and 8 percent cited a combination of both, while 26 percent cited the PNM (the political party currently in power), and 22 percent cited politicians. The data suggest that hard-core and semi-hard-core gangs are prevalent, and that the criminal element has assumed a powerful position in the lower-income communities of Trinidad and Tobago (McCree, 1998).

POLITICAL AND SOCIAL RESPONSES

Upon investigation of the problem of teen gangs in Trinidad and Tobago, it is apparent that the youth of the nation lack positive role models and heroes, a shortage that is evident in the basic institutions (government, religion, and family) where men have traditionally dominated and were expected to demonstrate positive leadership (Husbands, 1998). Youngsters witnessing politicians committing adultery, indulging in corruption, and accepting ill-gotten gains are bound to become disaffected. Absentee fathers and corruption in social institutions do not provide needed role models, especially for young males.

The Gang and the Community

In certain neighborhoods, gangs can be perceived as being somewhat beneficial. McCree (1998) observed community-gang relations to be either antagonistic, apathetic, or mutually supportive. Gangs can appear to help the community by providing basic financial assistance and protection from outsiders and other criminal elements that invade its surroundings. In return, the community can assist the gang by offering protection or refuge from law enforcement and by providing information on possible police action or rival gangs. In addition, the community also serves as a source of recruitment for new gang members. The gang-community relationship is kept alive because each group can identify with the other's struggle for survival. However, McCree (1998) noted that the relationship could be severed if either party did not live up to the "contracted rules." If the relationship were to be ended, the gang would lose its hold on the community. Hence, without the community's support the gang could not survive. When adults hold gangs in high esteem and cooperate with them, it is not surprising that teenagers want to become more involved.

Shabazz (1997) further revealed the functional importance of gangs and the community:

Most of the gangs are really no more than territorial groupings. In a place like Vegas [the name of one of the communities in Laventille], you have a leader who controls the area. Vegas is like a one way area. You might have another area like Never Dirty [another community in Laventille], which is also a one-way area where the fellows feel comfortable, but they are also protecting their turf. The turf might not be selling drugs or anything like that. They are just protecting it and trying to maintain a name for the area so that no one would come in and take advantage of the people.

Although you may regard the gang leader as a bad person, in the area he is seen as a good person. You go into the area and see a fellow who is known as a gang leader. While you are there, a little child might come to him and say, "Daddy, I don't have money to buy food." And he will say: "Well, go in the shop and tell them to give it to you. I will deal with it." Or he might take money from his own pocket; he will help the people in the area. The people in the area might even know that he is dealing roughly with their daughters, or that he beat up a woman the other day, but he is regarded as the man providing for the village. So the village will protect him; and that is the story of crime and gang life in Trinidad and Tobago. (pp. 97–98)

Community Policing

In Trinidad and Tobago, community policing is the initial response, uniting the police service, social agencies, community groups, and families together in concerted efforts to provide support to families in addressing problems like gang involvement. Community members, acting in support of one another, are more equipped to serve as positive role models for at-risk youth. For example, in the schools the police can assist in implementing gang assessment programs that examine factors such as graffiti, drugs, weapons, racial or social conflict, truancy, sexual abuse, theft, and vandalism (Husbands, 1998).

School principals should be able to determine the extent to which a gang or problems exist. The community needs to magnify the consequences of deviant behavior and negative models (gang involvement and gang apparel) to the youth. The community police can establish central gang control units to reduce turf wars. A database on at-risk youths would assist police in tracking and documenting gang involvement. In essence, effective gang prevention and alleviation requires collective action to obtain the lasting results for which Trinidad and Tobago is aiming.

POLITICAL INITIATIVES AND POLICIES TO ADDRESS THE TEEN GANG PROBLEM

The past and present governments of Trinidad and Tobago have made fighting crime and reducing gang involvement a number one priority. However, they have not organized funding for research to support this anticrime commitment (Deosaran and Chadee, 1997). The government has poured enormous resources into policing and prisons, which may seem like an obvious solution to the crime problem. Enlisting more experts, purchasing more police vehicles, increasing the number of law enforcers and patrols, buying more guns, and holding more seminars only marginally improves the crime and gang situation. In essence, responding to the growing crime rate by building bigger prisons is as hopeless as trying to "cap a flooding water pipe without turning off the valve" (Barlow, 1995, pp. 18–19).

To address the crime problem, the government and the scholars need to consider creative, imaginative responses that go beyond just lamenting racism, poverty, and other social factors. Many of the existing intervention strategies to deal with violence and crime have focused on youth gangs. These programs include youth training and apprenticeship programs, police youth groups, and sporting competitions. However, these groups have only begun to scratch the surface in preventing youth crimes.

Within the last ten years much time and many resources have been spent in trying to cope with violence and delinquency in schools and in the communities of Trinidad and Tobago. Such measures included adding more counselors and conflict resolution programs as well as formulating new rules and regulations. However, these steps to deal with the crime and gang problem have been not been based on any systematic or scientific studies. Such studies are critical for meaningful interventions to be developed.

FUTURE PLANS TO ADDRESS THE TEEN GANG PROBLEM

Ramesh Deosaran, director of the Center for Criminology and Criminal Justice at the University of the West Indies in Trinidad and Tobago, and his colleagues have pioneered the first study of its kind in these islands. This study uses a holistic and comprehensive approach to understanding youth deviance and provides the first data that is scientifically based on the correlates of youths' social backgrounds, attitudes and values, social capital, self-esteem, and potential or actual involvement in deviance (Deosaran, 2002). The action plan developed from this study is a thoroughly researched collaboration of ideas and solutions. Deosaran and his colleagues have begun to implement strategies for guidance, rehabilitation, and training in the secondary schools in Trinidad and Tobago. This study consists of three phases that will measure and assess youth deviance and civic attitudes.

Phase One (Completed)

Some preliminary research has already been done on the social background of delinquency (Deosaran, 2001; Deosaran and Chadee, 1997; Lall, 2001). Phase one of the study was successfully completed in 2001. A random national sample of young secondary school students of both sexes was taken: a total of 3,525 students were surveyed.

Phase Two (Diagnostic Phase)—In Progress

More detailed diagnosis and analysis of data is being undertaken in some critical areas such as youth values and attitudes; views on school, parents, and peers; and the impact of community and social background. In addition, the researchers are examining the propensity for and actual involvement in deviance and gangs. In-depth interviews with selected students have been conducted to enhance the already existing data and to provide researchers with a scientific basis for devising intervention strategies that will be undertaken in Phase Three.

Phase Three (Intervention Phase)—In Progress

An intervention module is being designed using the data collected from the in-depth diagnoses completed in Phase Two to incorporate guidance, rehabilitation, training, and school management strategies geared toward deviance reduction. Phase Three is scheduled for completion in June 2004.

Intended Outcomes of the Study

This landmark project will enable teachers and school administrators to detect early signs of deviance and gang involvement. It will provide them with a prevention framework for practical applications. This work will also promote further research and improve policies on preventing gang involvement and delinquency in Trinidad and Tobago. The Model for Healthy Schools will form the basis for implementation in schools throughout the Caribbean region through the continued work of the Center for Criminology and Criminal Justice and the partnership of the Trinidad Hilton, Caribbean Common Market, various heads of government, and the Association of Caribbean Commissioners of Police.

Research Programs for Youth

As part of the annual research schedule, the Center for Criminology will undertake several projects designed to alleviate gang involvement, school deviance, juvenile delinquency, and youth crime. These projects will include community empowerment programs, juvenile homes, and a focus on rehabilitation and restorative justice.

Community Transformation Programs

The Weed and Seed program will combine the aggressive weeding out of the criminal elements in neighborhoods with the seeding of new positive influences. For example, seeding means taking young leaders who have gone through the youth programs and integrating them into the district areas where criminal influences have been weeded out, thus giving the youth of the community a new role model to emulate.

A strengthened community policing program will stress the importance of improving the relationship between law enforcement and the public. Police, youths, and neighborhood clubs will work together to create an environment in which members of the police service join with young people to plan and participate in various sports, games, and community-related activities.

CONCLUSION

Trinidad and Tobago is undergoing a substantial change in its social, political, and psychological character (Deosaran, 1992). With the advent of modernization and industrialization, youths in society are confronted with the uncertainties and stress brought about by this rapid social change. Traditional cultural and family values now have to compete with the teenager's reliance on peers, video games, and the "glamor" of modernized values and outside "heroes." However, young people can be similarly influenced for the good by their family and home lives: positive role models, encouragement, family stability, and empowered communities are all essential elements in reducing gang involvement. Carter (2002) noted that when putting crime under the microscope, the medium in which deviance should be studied has often been avoided: that medium is the home.

Leaders in Trinidad and Tobago have recognized that a comprehensive study of youth psychology—along with the implementation of youth programs, parental involvement, and community policing—must accompany the modernization of society. The youth of Trinidad and Tobago are not merely passive reactors to social influence but also potential shapers of the social environment (Fisher, 1982).

REFERENCES

Barlow, H. D. ed. *Crime and public policy: Putting theory to work* (Boulder, Colorado: Westview Press, 1995).

Cain, M. *Crime and punishment in Trinidad and Tobago: A collection of papers* (Trinidad: University of the West Indies, 1995).

Carter, L. "Fighting crime from the home." *The Trinidad Guardian* (27 August 2002): 13.

Central Statistical Office. *Annual Statistical Digest* 41 (Port-of-Spain, Trinidad and Tobago: Author, 1997).

———. *Annual Statistical Digest* 45 (Port-of-Spain, Trinidad and Tobago: Author, 2001).

Deosaran, R. *Social psychology in the Caribbean: Directions for theory and research.* (Longman Trinidad Limited, 1992).

———. *Youth crime, psychological capital and relative deprivation in the Caribbean* (Trinidad: University of the West Indies, St. Augustine Campus, Center for Criminology and Criminal Justice, 2001).

———. *Youth deviance and civic attitudes in secondary schools, Trinidad and Tobago: Strategies for guidance, rehabilitation and training* (Trinidad: University of the West Indies, St. Augustine Campus, Center for Criminology and Criminal Justice, 2002).

Deosaran, R., and D. Chadee. "Juvenile delinquency in Trinidad and Tobago: Challenges for social policy and Caribbean criminology." *Caribbean Journal of Criminology and Social Psychology* 2 (1997): 36–83.

"Editorial: A Distressing Record." *Trinidad Express* (2 January 2002): 10.

Fisher, R. *Social psychology: An applied approach* (New York: St. Martin's Press, 1982).

"The Gambinos." *The Independent* (16 July 1998).

Hoge, R., and D. Andrews. *Assessing the youthful offender* (New York: Plenum Press, 1996).

Husbands, G. "Tainted heroes put youths at risk." *Caribbean Journal of Criminology and Social Psychology* 3(1/2) (1998): 194–200.

Jankowski, S. M. *Islands in the street: Gangs and American urban society* (Berkeley: University of California Press, 1991).

Jensen, G., and D. Rojek. *Delinquency and youth crime* (Prospect Heights, IL: Waveland Press, 1997).

Joseph, F. "End of a gangland boss: The rise and fall of Dole Chadee." *The Trinidad Guardian* (11 June 1999a): 5.

———. "Chadee did not have a chance . . . legally: The rise and fall of Dole Chadee." *The Trinidad Guardian* (13 June 1999b): 5.

Lall, V. "A social psychological analysis of deviance among male adolescents in Trinidad and Tobago" (Unpublished thesis, Trinidad: University of the West Indies, St. Augustine Campus, Center for the Criminology and Criminal Justice, 2001).

Laws of the Republic of Trinidad and Tobago. (1980a). *Young Offenders Detention Act* (Ch. 13:05).

———. (1980b). *Children Act* (Ch. 46:01).

McCree, R. D. "Security and solidarity in Laventille." In *Behind the bridge: Poverty, politics and patronage in Laventille, Trinidad*, edited by S. Ryan, R. McCree, and G. St. Bernard (Trinidad: University of the West Indies, The Institute of Social and Economic Research, 1997).

———. "Violence: A preliminary look at gangs in Trinidad and Tobago." *Caribbean Journal of Criminology and Social Psychology* 3(1/2) (1998): 155–173.

Seetahal, D. "Kidnappings—Real and imagined." *The Trinidad Express* (3 September 2002): 10.

Shabazz, M. "A voice from Laventille." In *Behind the bridge: Poverty, politics and patronage in Laventille, Trinidad*, edited by S. Ryan, R. McCree, and G. St. Bernard (Trinidad: University of the West Indies, The Institute of Social and Economic Research, 1997).

Wilson, F. "Clint Huggins did it." *The Trinidad Express* (6 September 1996): 4.

"Youth gang." *Trinidad Express* (5 August 1998).

14

THE UNITED STATES

Scott E. Gillig and Pamela A. Cingel

INTRODUCTION

Although there is little doubt that youth gangs have been, and continue to be, present in the United States, the question of how gangs have changed and evolved over the years requires a closer examination. In researching gangs, there are definitional problems about what constitutes a gang and gang activities. There are a number of questions of interest in examining youth gang activity in the United States. Are gangs a threat to contemporary society? What impact do gangs have on the country? How has the country responded politically and socially to gang activity? What is being done to address gang-related problems? How do gangs organize themselves socially? What are the trends toward addressing youth gang problems likely to be in the future?

The youth gang problem in the United States has been monumental and widespread. The number of vicinities reporting gang problems showed a considerable increase from the 1970s to the 1990s. By the late 1990s, 2,550 cities, towns, and villages and 1,150 counties had reported the existence of gang activities. These statistics indicate an almost tenfold rise in the number of cities and an elevenfold growth in the number of counties reporting gang activities during this time (Miller, 2001).

BASIC POLICIES AND LEGISLATION

Gang members have a very clear understanding of the activities that are required to maintain membership in the gang and to evolve through the ranks. However, a predominant difficulty legislators have in dealing with gangs has been the lack of a clear description of just what constitutes gang-related problems. One view is that such problems include several similar destructive episodes in a community that cause distress to the public (Bureau of Justice Assistance [BJA], 1997). Another author cites several useful definitions of a gang:

1. A group must be involved in a pattern of criminal acts to be considered a youth gang. These groups typically are composed of only juveniles, but may include young adults in their memberships.

2. A criminal street gang refers to three or more persons having a common identifying sign or symbol or an identifiable leadership who continuously or regularly associate in the commission of criminal activities.

3. A street gang is a cohesive group with most members between the ages of 11 and 21 that has a recognizable geographical territory (usually demarkated with graffiti), leadership, a purpose, and various levels of organized ongoing criminal activities. (Langston, 2003, p. 8)

Some of the current gang-related legislation reported by the Institute for Intergovernmental Research (2003b) deals with bias crimes, curfew, gang recruitment, graffiti, institutional vandalism, juvenile gatherings, loitering, parental responsibility, truancy, weapons, carjacking, drive-by shootings, and gang-related clothing styles. On a positive note, policy makers and legislatures currently stress a spirit of collaboration and teamwork in addressing gang activities. Such collaboration often focuses on containment, intervention, and prevention. In these collaborative efforts a management group made up of representatives from participating agencies can steer the agencies in their roles and responsibilities in addressing gang issues. The development of clear and measurable objectives will serve as markers that the interventions designed to reduce gang activities and membership have been effective (BJA, 1997).

DEMOGRAPHIC INFORMATION

There are about 4,800 gangs, with estimates of membership ranging from 250,000 to 650,000, in the United States. It has been predicted that the incidence of gangs will increase, partly because gang members are recruited at younger ages and preserve their gang standing into their late thirties. With this increase society can anticipate a swell in gang-related crime and violence, including robbery and drive-by shootings (Reiboldt, 2001).

From 1991 to 1996 the total number of gang homicides declined among the 408 U.S. cities in the survey by almost 15 percent, from 1,748 to 1,492 incidents. Although the homicide rates of Los Angeles, Calif., and Chicago, Ill., decreased dramatically from 1996 to 1998, both are among cities with the highest rates of gang homicide. In 1998 Los Angeles reported 173 gang homicides, and Chicago reported 180 (Curry, Maxson, and Howell, 2001). Vigil and Yun (1998) refer to Los Angeles as the "street gang capital of the United States and of the world as the number of US gangs dwarfs that of other industrialized nations" (p. 117).

Law enforcement agency surveys estimate that about 8 to 11 percent of all gang members are female, while the proportion of self-identified gang members who were female ranged from 8 to 38 percent. Age of respondent may have been a confounding variable in these surveys, however. It is also reported that females tend to drop out of gangs younger than males, often because of pregnancy (Moore and Hagedorn, 2001).

HISTORY OF THE YOUTH GANG PROBLEM

Across the country there appears to be no agreed-upon account of the beginnings of youth gangs (Hazlehurst and Hazlehurst, 1998). Reiboldt (2001) indicates that gangs have been studied nationwide since the 1920s. In examining the history of the youth gang problem in the country, it is important to realize that historical development differed depending on the ethnicity of gangs and their members. Hunt and Laidler (2001) credit Thrasher in the 1920s as having conducted the first major scientific study of youth gangs with his study of 1,313 Chicago gangs.

Adamson (2000) reports that while black youth gangs did not appear to be a social problem until the great migration of the 1910s, when many African Americans moved to the Northern cities, white youth gangs existed at the very establishment of the nation, perhaps as early as the 1780s. By the 1820s gangs of white youths in their teens and early twenties fought youths from other neighborhoods for command of street corners in Boston, New York, and Philadelphia. New York gangs such as the Smith Vly Boys fought rivals on what is today called Grand Street, while the Roach Guards battled with the Plug Uglies and the Dead Rabbits. The Dead Rabbits, wearing a red stripe on their pantaloons, carried a dead rabbit pierced on a spike at the head of their bats, while the Roach Guard wore blue stripes. Around the 1820s white gangs were often international, especially in neighborhoods that were not strictly separated by ethnicity. Dutch, English, Welsh, Scots, Irish, German, and other youth with diverse descent could be found in the same youth gang. Territory was often more important than ethnicity in forging the identities of white youth gangs.

By the 1920s, of the 880 gangs across the United States, nearly 90 percent were European American, and of these nearly half were of varied European-American ethnicity. Most of the remaining 10 percent of gangs were African American or mixed African American/European American. The gangs of Chicago in the 1920s through the latter part of the twentieth century primarily fought over territory. Political figures and organized crime members supported such gangs (Adamson, 2000).

African-American youth gangs had their origins in Chicago and accounted for over 7 percent of the total number of gangs in that city in the 1930s. That the participation of the African-American youth in gangs was greater than their proportion in the overall population of young people is logical given that they were banned from most factory jobs, office positions, and even unskilled part-time jobs (Adamson, 2000).

Mexican American youth gangs began to form in Southern California as early as the 1940s. These gangs, although small in number, were involved in violence and destruction on the streets in their neighborhoods. Factors such as racial discrimination and economic hardships fractured families and laid the foundation for youths to join gangs for protection and financial incentives. Currently, between 4 percent and 10 percent of Mexican American youth belong to gangs. While Mexican American youth gangs have typically engaged in conflict and violence, recently drugs and weapons have dramatically increased gang-related and bystander-related homicides (Adamson, 2000). While Mexican American gangs were once restricted to the many low-income barrios (neighborhoods) in the Southwestern United States, they currently exist in working-class and lower-middle-class suburban areas as well (Vigil, 1997).

By the mid-1900s the quickly growing inner-city black populace led to an increase in the number of African-American youth gangs. Along with the increase in black poverty, black youth gangs began to protect themselves and enter adjacent white territory. However, intense poverty eventually cut black youth off from white sections of the city, so that black youth gangs started to prey on each other. Their members still barred from legal jobs, black gangs battled violently with each other. By the 1970s family difficulties coupled with decreased policing procedures led to an increase in street violence and gang activity among black youths, who ran to street gangs for protection against rival gangs and acceptance by their peers (Adamson, 2000).

In general, by the 1980s gang investigators commenced to claim that youth gangs had evolved in a qualitatively different way from those in earlier eras. The new type of gang holds an identity no longer built on cultural factors but rather centered on the underlying fiscal principle of making money (Hunt and Laidler, 2001).

POLITICAL AND SOCIAL RESPONSES TO THE YOUTH GANG PROBLEM

With the introduction of drugs and automatic weapons, gangs have evolved from turf fighting to a much higher level of violence. The Bureau of Justice Assistance (1997) acknowledges that programs geared to fighting gang-related criminal activity must include both crime prevention and crime control schemes to be effective over the long haul. Several effective gang control methods have been developed throughout the United States.

The Comprehensive Gang Initiative model was developed as a process for overcoming the obstructions faced by communities in endeavoring to deal with gang-related problems. This model involves principles of adaptability, flexibility, comprehensiveness, a focus on harmful behaviors, continuous problem diagnosis, response coordination, continuous monitoring, and impact evaluation (BJA, 1997). The Dallas Police Department initiated an antigang program that was intended to curtail gang violence. It was found that while forceful curfew and truancy implementation led to significant decline in gang violence, simple dispersion patrol did not (Fritsch, Caeti, and Taylor, 1999).

Howell (1999) indicates that prevention and suppression of youth gang homicides should be a main concern in crime strategies in the United States. Youth gang homicides accounted for almost one-fourth of all homicides in Chicago and one-half of those in Los Angeles in 1995. Gang-related homicides have reached epidemic proportions in these and in other major cities. Some of the encouraging gang homicide interventions include using automated information systems to identify gang locations, long-term surveillance of gangs, banning guns, arresting and prosecuting dangerous gang members, collaboration in community policing of gangs, rehabilitation services, early interventions, prevention programs, and program evaluation.

Schools can fight gang activity by banning certain items of clothing, weapons, violence, illegal activities and other things related to gang membership. School personnel need to be clear about strictly enforcing discipline. Painting over graffiti and transferring disruptive students who are gang members can be helpful responses to gang action. Prevention and awareness are important to avoiding and curtailing gang activities in the schools. Schools can work together with the community including the local police to reduce and eliminate school related gang activity (Gaustad, 1990).

SOCIAL VIEWS, CUSTOMS, AND PRACTICES

Some of the activities that gangs engage in are a concern to the communities in which they reside. For example, wearing clothing that displays gang colors to school can give rise to conflicts among competing gangs. When gang members occupy certain public sites and make threatening statements, the public may fear being attacked and may thus avoid going out in public in their own communities. Leaders realize that to find solutions to gang related problems, patterns of harmful behaviors must be identified first (BJA, 1997).

In Chicago between 1987 and 1990, the city's four largest and most criminally active street gangs—the Black Gangster Disciples Nation (BGDN), the Latin Disciples, the Latin Kings, and the Vice Lords—accounted for 69 percent of all street-gang-motivated crimes and for 56 percent of all street-gang-motivated homicides. This was the case even though these gangs represented only about 10 percent of the major Chicago youth gangs and 51 percent of the estimated number of street gang members. Peaks in homicide rates are generally related to a cycle of increasing conflicts, usually over control of either conventional street gang turf or a capitalist drug market (Howell, 1999).

Howell (1999) notes that gangs in Chicago circa 1993 differed in the types of criminal activities in which they engaged. For example, Latino gangs focused on turf-related violence, while African-American gangs concentrated on drug offenses. Most gang violence is largely related to emotional protection of one's character as a gang member, defense of the gang itself, defense and veneration of the standing of the gang, gang member recruitment, and territorial growth.

According to Hazlehurst and Hazlehurst (1998), "Adolescent male membership is incontestably, almost tautologically, a defining element of the juvenile or youth gang" (p. 5). While most youth gangs are made up of males, female gangs do exist. Female youth gangs are predominantly Latina or African American, with growing numbers of Asian and Caucasian counterparts. Ethnicities tend to differ in gender expectations about autonomy and male dominance. In general, African American and Caucasian female gang members tend be more autonomous and Latinas more subordinate to males (Moore and Hagedorn, 2001).

Gaustad (1990) indicates that most gang members publicize their gang connection by idiosyncratic dress and behaviors, including bandanas and shoelaces of certain colors, jewelry, tattoos, idiosyncratic language styles, and hand signals. They mark their terrain and deter other gangs with spray-painted graffiti or gang signs. Gangs tend to form in both poor and affluent communities, as alienated youth try to gain self-esteem, financial gain, and power. Hixon (1999) reports on warning signs of gang involvement such as the presence of tattoos or clothing with gang symbols, keeping of late hours, wearing specific colors and style of clothes, truancy and poor school performance, a new group of friends, and a new lack of interest in family activities.

Reiboldt (2001) indicates that potential gang members are typically recruited as they reach the teen years, when they are involved in identity development. Gang membership can contribute to identity and a sense of belonging for some teens, particularly males. From research it appears that Latino gang members are most interested in being "macho," while African American gang members are more interested in being "cool" (Hunt and Laidler, 2001).

Vigil and Yun (1998) report that in some cities such as Detroit, African-American gangs have changed their primary attention from fighting with other gangs to dealing drugs. In other cities like Los Angeles, African-American gangs remain loosely structured and geared more toward conflict than organized crime. On the other hand, Chicano youth gang members in Los Angeles tend to focus on defending their neighborhoods and acting aggressively as a means to resolve inner conflict. It appears that Vietnamese youth in Los Angeles tend to be materialistic and seek to own new clothes and cars and to spend their evenings in prestigious establishments such as nightclubs and restaurants. They want to obtain money, and are often involved in thefts and robberies.

When not involved in illegal drug activities and violence, how do gang members spend their time? Gang members spend the majority of their day "hanging around" or "doing nothing," but not in the ways that adults define these phrases. While doing nothing, gang members can be incredibly occupied with activities such as talking about business, keeping one's respect, telling jokes, avoiding police, cruising in cars, defending turf, drinking, drugging, and partying (Hunt and Laidler, 2001). Esbensen, Winfree Jr., He, and Taylor (2001) found that in general, gang members are more impetuous, engage in more risky behavior, have more criminal friends, have fewer pro-social friends, report less felt guilt, are more violent, are more committed to delinquent friends, and are less committed to positive friends.

THE FUTURE OF THE YOUTH GANG PROBLEM

Collaboration, networking, technology, training, and prevention appear to be future-oriented methods of dealing with gang activity. For example, the Institute for Intergovernmental Research (2003a) maintains databases on a multitude of gang-related publications that relate to schools and communities, a listserv, links to joining professional organizations that collaborate on solving gang-related problems, training links, and funding links.

The Shop Light investigation is a method that law enforcement jurisdictions can use in the fight against drug distribution in gangs. Using the Shop Light investigation, police can survey paraphernalia that store customers buy. During surveillance of customers investigators can decide to follow anyone carrying a box from the store that seems inconsistent with the purchase made. Typically, members take the package of paraphernalia to the safe house of the gang, where they maintain considerable quantities of drugs, money, weapons, and records. A primary benefit of using this technique is that it provides instant detection of the upper echelon of those who traffic in such illegal drugs. Surveillance of that setting will identify the pecking order of that particular gang (Sheehy and Rosario, 2003). It may be that "Big Brother" and advanced technology is in the future arsenal of gang suppression activities.

CONCLUSION

While female membership in youth gangs is in the minority, it cannot be ignored. Youth gang membership can contribute to the identity and sense of belonging for some teens, particularly males. It appears that youth gang motives have evolved from primarily defending turf to drug dealing and other criminal behavior. When not involved in crimes, youth gang members tend to "hang out," which can include activities such as defending turf, drinking, drugging, and partying. Effectively confronting problematic gang behaviors—whether now or in the future—involves the cooperation and coordination of several agencies, focusing on containment, intervention, and prevention.

REFERENCES

Adamson, C. "Defensive localism in white and black: A comparative history of European-American and African-American youth gangs." *Ethnic and Racial Studies* 23(2) (2000): 272–298.

Bureau of Justice Assistance. *Addressing community gang problems: A model for problem solving* (Washington, DC: U.S. Government Printing Office, 1997).

Curry, G., C. Maxson, and J. Howell. *Youth gang homicides in the 1990s* (2001) (Washington, DC: U.S. Department of Justice, Office of Justice Programs, Office of Juvenile Justice and Delinquency Prevention). Retrieved March 15, 2003, from http://ericcass.uncg.edu/virtuallib/gangs/1008.html.

Esbensen. F., L. Winfree Jr., N. He, and T. Taylor. "Youth gangs and definitional issues: When is a gang a gang, and why does it matter?" *Crime & Delinquency* 47(1) (2001): 105–130.

Fritsch, E., T. Caeti, and R. Taylor. "Gang suppression through saturation patrol, aggressive curfew, and truancy enforcement: A quasi-experimental test of the Dallas Anti-Gang Initiative." *Crime & Delinquency* 45(1) (1999): 122–139.

Gaustad, J. *Gangs.* (ERIC Document Reproduction Service No. ED321419, 1990).

Hazlehurst, K., and C. Hazlehurst. *Gangs and youth subcultures: International explorations* (New Brunswick, NJ: Transaction Publishers, 1998).

Hixon, A. "Preventing street gang violence." *American Family Physician* 59(8) (1999): 2121–2132.

Howell, J. "Youth gang homicides: A literature review." *Crime & Delinquency* 45(2) (1999): 208–241.

Hunt, G., and K. Laidler. "Alcohol and violence in the lives of gang members." *Alcohol, Research & Health* 25(1) (2001): 66–71.

Institute for Intergovernmental Research. (2003a). Retrieved February 12, 2003, from http://www.iir.com/nygc/.

———. (2003b). *Compilation of gang-related legislation.* Retrieved February 12, 2003, from http://www.iir.com/nygc/gang-legis/Default.htm#Municipal.

Langston, M. "Addressing the need for a uniform definition of gang-involved crime." *FBI Law Enforcement Bulletin* 72(2) (2003): 8–12.

Miller, W. *The growth of youth gang problems in the United States: 1970–98.* (2001) (Washington, DC: U.S. Department of Justice, Office of Justice Programs, Office of Juvenile Justice and Delinquency Prevention). Retrieved March 15, 2003, from http://www.ncjrs.org/html/ojjdp/ojjdprpt_yth_gng_prob_2001/index.html.

Moore J., and J. Hagedorn. (2001). *Female gangs: A focus on research.* Juvenile Justice Bulletin (Washington, DC: U.S. Department of Justice, Office of Justice Programs, Office of Juvenile Justice and Delinquency Prevention). Retrieved March 18, 2003, from http://www.ncjrs.org/html/ojjdp/jjbul2001_3_3/contents.html#acknowledge.

Reiboldt, W. "Adolescent interactions with gangs, family, and neighborhoods: An ethnographic investigation." *Journal of Family Issues* 22(2) (2001): 211–242.

Sheehy, R., and E. Rosario. "Connecting drug paraphernalia to drug gangs." *FBI Law Enforcement Bulletin* 72(2) (2003): 2–7.

Vigil, J. (1997). *Learning from gangs: The Mexican American experience* (ERIC Document Reproduction Service No. ED405157).

Vigil, J., and S. Yun. "Vietnamese youth gangs in the context of multiple marginality and the Los Angeles youth gang phenomenon." In *Gangs and youth subcultures: International exploration,* edited by K. Hazelehurst and C. Hazelehurst (New Brunswick: NJ: Transaction Publishers, 1998), pp. 117–139.

INDEX

ABOUT THE EDITORS
AND CONTRIBUTORS

LORNA BLACK is a doctoral candidate at Barry University in Miami Shores, Florida. She is a licensed mental health counselor and a National Certified Counselor. She is an adjunct instructor of psychology and communications at Miami-Dade Community College and her research interests include the experiences of families with a Rastafarian member and adolescent development within a multicultural context.

ANTHONY BORROW is a Jesuit who spent a summer in Honduras working with a rehabilitative program for gang members and recently returned to follow up on the evolving gang situation.

PAMELA A. CINGEL is the interim undergraduate dean of the Social Sciences and Counseling Department, and associate professor of counseling and psychology at St. Thomas University in Miami, Florida.

SINCLAIR DINNEN is a fellow in the Department of Political and Social Change at the Research School of Pacifica and Asian Studies, the Australian National University. His current research examines the relationship between traditional and modern justice systems in the Pacific Islands, as well as examining the dynamics of conflict and peacemaking in the Melanesian states.

JILL D. DUBA is a doctoral candidate in counseling and human development services at Kent State University in Ohio.

MAUREEN DUFFY is an associate professor and chair of the Counseling Department at Barry University in Miami Shores, Florida.

M. SYLVIA FERNANDEZ is an associate professor of counseling at Barry University in Miami Shores, Florida.

SCOTT E. GILLIG is a professor and coordinator of the mental health counseling specialization at Barry University in Miami Shores, Florida. His research interests include counseling outcomes, depression, chemical dependency, treatment planning, and student mentoring.

JOANNA E. HEADLEY is a licensed mental health counselor in Miami, Florida. She is also a doctoral candidate in counseling at Barry University.

MARTY JENCIUS is an assistant professor in the counseling and human development program at Kent State University in Ohio. His main research areas are global views of mental health and counseling, multicultural counseling pedagogy, and technology and its application to counseling.

BETTINA LOZZI-TOSCANO is a licensed mental health counselor in Miami, Florida.

LOAN T. PHAN is an assistant professor at the University of New Mexico.

EDIL TORRES RIVERA is an associate professor at the University at Buffalo–SUNY.

RICHARD A. VAN DORN is a postdoctoral research fellow at Duke University in the Department of Psychiatry and Behavioral Sciences.

SLOANE VESHINSKI is the director of the Barry Family Enrichment Center at Barry University in Miami Shores, Florida.

JENNIFER WALKER is an assistant professor in the Department of Counseling and Family Therapy at Saint Louis University in Missouri.

ROB WHITE teaches Sociology and Law at the University of Tasmania.

JULIA YANG is a professor of counseling at Governors State University in Illinois.